CHAPTER 1

I don't remember much of the accident and from what I've been told that is for the best. I guess they say a lot of things; my days here have been long and drawn out. Lying flat on your back staring at the ceiling had started to become a daily ritual for me. I've never been too interested in television the blank flat screen stares back at me, I can see my reflection in it. I knew I hated the tube for a reason. The one eye that I could see out of gave me all I needed to see. I was a barely alive- I'm a living nightmare.

"Mr. Hart are you awake?" This was the evening nurse. I had started to know the time of day by which nurse came in. I think her name was Cassie or Candy or something like that. I don't know if she is tall or not. Everyone looked towering when you were lying down. Her hair was the color of a field mouse; she was cute in the face. Not my type by any standards. I liked them thick, a little cushion for the pushing I always say. They had to be blonde too. With wavy hair, high cheek bones and blue eyes.

My throat was dry so I nodded that I was awake. She took my blood pressure, checked my vitals or whatever. She gave me a nervous smile. I wondered did she go out with her friends and talk about the monster that she had to check on. Did she tell them stories about me? How she had to clean me up when my bowels didn't want to work, or how I couldn't wipe my tears when she had to turn me to wipe shit off my back?

I kept telling myself that it was her job to do those things, that's what she got paid to do. It still hurts, but thinking about it I wanted to feel the pain maybe know that I was still on this side of the grass. I was completely numb from the neck down. The first day that I was fully conscious I got scared, thinking that I would never walk again. My doctor, something like Mohammad or something. Informed me with a stern look that I had a ton of bruising and swelling, but there was no permeate damage to my spinal cord. He and I both thanked God that I picked the profession that I was in. It saved my life or what was left of it.

I watched as my evening nurse tried her damnedest not to look me in the eye. Just tossing my limbs around, treating me like a store mannequin propping me up in a window. She didn't even say goodbye after she borderline assaulted me. I just watched with my good eye as she walked to the door. I forgot to ask Cassie how many days I've been here. I'll just ask her when she comes back to see if I'm up and poke me in the arm.

My left eye gets tired from staying open so long, I have to close it. More times than not the nurses' talk over me. I heard them say if my bed sores don't kill me the staph or the lying flat on my back will. I'm a big man and I could feel every day that I spent in the gym become a useless waste of time.

"Um...Mr. Hart." Carrie or whatever her name poked her head back in my room. My tired eye sprang open. She looked behind herself making sure that no one was listening. She closed the door behind herself. Here it comes I thought. "Mr. Hart, um. Are you Devon Hart?" She could look at my chart and tell that I was in fact Devon Hart, but she wanted reassurance.

I was in no mood to confirm, but I just nodded. God my eye was getting tired. She clapped both of her hands and jumped up and down. Her brown hair bounced on her shoulders and for whatever reason I wanted to touch it. It seemed like forever since I touched a woman, even though she wasn't my type she would do. "My goodness!" She screamed quickly putting her hand over her mouth. "I thought it was you. I was talking to my boyfriend about you. About your injuries and he told me that you had to be Devon Hart. So you are really him, then?" I nodded. "Wow." That's all she could say as she looked me from my bandaged head to my broken arms, neck brace and cast on my right leg. Yeah, wow.

"Yeah, I'm him." My voice sounded heavier than I remembered. It was so strained like I was screaming through water.

"When you get up and ready to go, could you please sign an autograph for my boyfriend? He is such a big fan of yours." Then she began to retell me every single match that I've ever been in. I'm sure her boyfriend coached her on what to say. I smiled up at her and nodded. I closed my one eye and tried to block out her chirper voice. Just to have someone standing there talking to me made the loneness runaway.

"How long have I've been here?" I whispered and interrupted her from the blow by blow of my match against Franklin Miles.

Her eyes widened maybe because she thought I was totally wrapped in her story, like I wasn't there or anything. Or because she was a little peeved that I interrupted. "You've been here for almost three weeks."

Three weeks, I thought it was three days. Damn. She didn't let the minor setback stop her from continuing her story. Her boyfriend and a ton of his friends were over to watch the fight, then blah blah blah happened and they cheered and some more crap. Cassie, Candy or whoever she did one good thing. She put my ass straight to sleep.

It could have been an hour, day or another week that passed when I was able to open my eye again. The evening nurse what's-her-name was no longer babbling about things I was already knew. With more effort than I wanted to admit it was a struggle to open my good eye and with remaining strength to try to focus.

The curtains were open and it was night or early morning, all I knew it was dark with the sun either going away or making its daily appearance I wasn't sure. What I was sure of was that I wasn't lying flat, but propped up like broken doll that you see in old gift shops. Were the porcelain face was cracked or chipped. Its life like hair was either matted or missing strands. I hadn't noticed until now of the annoying pressure on my shoulder, the neck brace thing around my neck was pushing my chin up and I could only guess that my head was swollen too by the weight that was pressing down on my shoulders.

This was the first time that I could remember that I could almost open my other eye. Assessment time, I thought. I ran my dry tongue over my teeth; okay they were all there nothing missing. I thanked God. Without any movement from my head, I leaned back into the stack of pillows and took a look at my arms. My right was in a cast up to the middle of my bicep with a wicked looking pin sticking out of my forearm. Great. The left was casted to my elbow. Both sets of fingers were bruised and swollen sticking out of the cast like fat breadstick jammed inside a block of play doe. I wiggled them, they were slow moving but they moved. I thanked God again.

I pinched at the thin covers that lay over me and began to pull up. It took me longer than I wanted to admit to see my feet. Both of my legs were wrapped in what resembled inflated leg warmers that went from my heels to just below my knees. My toes looked like my fingers, beat up and twice their normal size. I sent up another prayer and they wiggled with a ton of sweating and heavy breathing. By this time I was exhausted. I heard the soft ding of my medication being pumped through my veins. I blame the fighter in me wanting to push myself, maybe move my legs. Unfortunately, the drugs that they gave me stung a bit when it ran through my body it was tougher than any other opponent that I've ever faced. It knocked me out.

"Devon." The soft whisper of my name gave me comfort you wouldn't believe. The hospital, insisted on calling me Mr. Hart or Sir. I'm only 26 years old and the thought of older people addressing me as such made me fear that I was worse off than I thought. "Devon, honey can you open your eyes for me?"

As if someone finally turned the channel off static to ESPN, both my eyes opened to look up at my mom. All the reasons that I was mad at her, every horrible thing that I thought or said about her went away. "Mom." I croaked out. "You're here."

Her dark brown hair barely touched her shoulders. It fell over on my cheek when she kissed the top of my head. "The police came to the house Devon a few weeks ago. They said it was an accident I been here since they came."

The woman that I hated more than anything in this world was standing at my side holding me hand, like she used to when I was a kid. "You're here." Is the only thing that I could say to her. She pulled up a chair next to my bed. Putting her designer purse on the edge of my bed she smiled.

"Devon, why wouldn't I be here? You're my son and despite what you think I do love you." It had to be five years or was it six since the last time I saw her. Her screams, seemed a thousand miles away now. My rage at her was as far as East was from the West. "Devon, honey. After you get out of here I would like for you to come and stay with me and Anthony in Atlanta." Before I could open my mouth to tell her that there was no way in Hell that I was leaving Tennessee. She put her hand up to silence me. "Honey, I've spoken to the doctors." My mother's face twisted in pain. "It doesn't look good for you and you will need around the clock care. Anthony says that it won't be a problem. You can stay with us as long as you like." Every time she said her new husband's name her voice got a little higher with excitement.

As a kid me and my buddies would play a game what-would-you-rather on the way home on the school bus. The game consisted of hellish tortures of pick your poison. Would you rather kiss Jessica Gregory, the girl with the worst hygiene in our school or never kiss a girl until your senior year. With this heinous dilemma that I was currently in, would I rather live in Atlanta with my mom and her new husband and get better or go back to my apartment all alone. Neither option was anything that I wanted. "Mom, I think I want to stay here. My gym is here and friends. I want to stay here in Nashville." Without the movement of my head my eyes strained to gauge my mom's reaction.

Crossing her legs, she stiffened in her chair. "I know that this-" "Waving her hand back and forth between the both of us. "This relationship between us has been…well strained. I want you and me to be a family again. Like how it used to be." Giving me that beautiful smile, the kid in me loved to see her smile in approval and hear her laugh with amusement. As an adult neither did anything for me.

"You said that you talked to the doctors what all did they say?" She smirked at me letting me know that she caught me in my rapid subject change.

She laced her fingers on her lap, cocking her head to one side. "Devon, you shouldn't worry about things like that."

"I want to know."

The face that she was giving me was all too familiar. It was a mix of a tad endearment and a splash frustration

"I wouldn't want it any other way, mom. Just tell me." I closed my eyes and waited for it. Like a ton of brick were dangling over my head and my mom was holding the rope.

She cleared her thought. "Devon-"

"Today mom."

With an exaggerated sigh. "Massive concussion. You broke both of your arms; the right was broken in three places. Two broken ribs, one cracked. Your hip is broken. Your right femur was crushed; your femur and tibia on your left leg were sticking out of your body. Also, the ankle bone on your right leg was pretty much shoved out of your heel. Are you happy now?" I opened my eyes and saw the tears streaming down her face. "What will you do with that information, Devon? What did it help?" She stood so fast the back of her knees kicked the chair back, making the legs on it screech across the floor. "I know how you feel about me but I'm still your mother and I hate to see you like this. You could have been killed that morning."

The tears still fell and plopped on my covers. "Didn't want to upset you. I wanted to know, so I can beat it mom."

"Beat it? You should be dead. Be happy that you still are breathing Devon, please." She put her hand over her face and sighed. "Don't do this to me."

"To you? Last I checked I was the one laying in this bed for weeks." A surge of pain ran up my spine to the base of my skull. My brain began to throb inside my head as if the drummer from Creed was practicing right behind my eyes. "Mom, I'm going to get better." I closed my eyes and gritted my teeth. Times of stress like this I would of pinched the bridge of my nose, but the cast wouldn't let me.

"Eventually, yes you will. But I need you to understand." She paused and stared at me dead on, just like she used to when I did something-anything that she didn't agree with. "Devon, you may not ever walk again."

If I were able to shake my head back and forth I would, but this damn brace was preventing me from doing what came natural. "I spoke to the doctor, he said that there was a lot of swelling on my spinal cord and once that had gone down I could walk." I hadn't realized that I was talking so loud, on the cusp of shouting."

"It's not your spine-it's your hip. Devon when they found you-"My mom stopped as if to gather words that were stuck in her brain willing them to form and come out her mouth. "You were in a bad way. Your hip is-well was twisted and fragmented. Currently, there is a bracket that is allowing you to bend at the waist." Her long manicured nails touched my thigh. "Just the pain of standing would knock you literally off your feet, not my words but the doctors. If there was any other way-"

"Get out." Tiny rivers of sweat started to drown my neck in the brace. My mom's voice became the irritating white noise that was slowly driving me crazy. "I want you to leave now."

There was no argument; there was no drama from me. No rolling over and throwing the covers over my head to push my point of wanting her to leave. She didn't yell or demand that I finally grow up and take some sort of responsibility in this. No begging to be the mom or love one that I needed. She took her bag off the corner of the bed and threw it over her shoulder and walked to the door. The click of her heels going to the door was like the sound of nails slowly being driven into my coffin. I welcomed the sound.

"Mr. Hart, it's time to shift you." It was morning I could tell by the small voice of my nurse. She was tiny Asian woman, maybe in her early to mid-thirties. At least this time she asked me, up until a few days ago she would shake the hell out of me, pull and yank at my sheets and basically toss me to the other side of the tiny bed. "I just need for you to relax." I couldn't help but do the opposite; I tensed every muscle in my body. One wrong move on her part she was going to have 215 pounds of dead weight on her. "Mr. Hart, I've been doing this a long time. If you don't relax and let me move you and change your bedding you are going to hurt yourself not me."

I couldn't help but smile. "I'm at least four times your size."

"Well, if you keep stiffing up it feels like I'm moving lumber. You and I are going to have to work together. Now please relax. Close your eyes. I heard it helps when you just ignore what I'm doing and think of a pleasant memory."

I felt her small warm hands on right shoulder and on my lower back. "I don't want to hurt you."

"And you won't if you relax." I simply gave up the fight and went limp. The only pleasant thought that I had wasn't a memory but what was coming. Me fighting again.

"Ya see you and I make a great team." My nurse smiled down at me. "I like it better when the patient is up and conscious before I go moving them around and stuff."

The old Devon wanted to say something extremely sexist something on the line of since we make a great team what about you and I start our own moving around and stuff in this bed. I wasn't in the mood, so I simply smiled back and wished that her day would get better from moving a small giant around. Her little hand went to her forehead and gave me a mock salute with a promise that she would be back in about an hour to check on me. I would have returned the salute but my arm wouldn't bend and it would of look as if I was hailing Hitler so I just smiled.

I was having the best dream of my life. I was in the gym and my sparring partner Henry was giving me pure hell on the mat. Then the overwhelming smell of fried chicken, green beans and mashed potatoes engulfed the gym. Everyone stopped working out, stopped throwing jabs, and ceased kicking. The smell flooded everyone one of senses.

"I knew that's all you needed was a home cooked meal." Both of my eyes opened, it was real. There sitting on my lap was a plate with everything that I desired. Fried chicken drowning in gravy, just the way that I like it. My mouth watered. "There he is bout time you woke up thought you were going to sleep your life away." Jerry my trainer stood smirking. No one that currently walked the earth knew Jerry's age, it was gauged in between late 50s to a 100. I've personally seen him knock a kid out for mouthing off in his gym. The kid God bless him last I heard was eating and crapping out of a tube. The old guy had forgotten more moves and submissions hold than I currently knew. He's smart in and out of the ring and that's what made him dangerous.

"Thought I wouldn't see your ugly mug." I tried to sit up but lack of movement in my arms I just had to lay there like a slug.

His barrel laugh cracked the small hospital room in half. "Been here every Wednesday with a plate from Maggie and every Wednesday I go back home and eat it myself. Now let me help you." Jerry put the drumstick to my mouth and I damn near took off his finger. "Slow down kid before you choke." Looking back at my closed hospital door. "Nurse finds out I brought this in here I'll be in a bed next to ya."

With a mouth full of food. "I don't care. I need the company." I barely chewed just swallowed. "Please tell Maggie that I am forever in her debt."

"She sends her love. You know that she wanted to come but-"

He didn't have to explain. Maggie his wife of I guess a million years, never once stepped foot in the gym. Never came to a match. Jerry said that her heart couldn't take seeing one of her boys hurt. "No worries. Once I get out of here I'll thank her myself."

He stopped forking mashed potatoes in my mouth. "Son, you just need to get better okay? There's no rush."

I knew I had been here for almost a mouth and time seemed to be slipping past me. While I lay here, there was a guy training getting better and faster. There was no use in arguing about it, I allowed my friend to keep feeding me. "So what you know good?"

"Well, Frank is still an ass. Marcus is getting better still getting winded, needs to work on his finishing game. All in all same ol same." Jerry handing me a napkin and I struggled with it to wipe my mouth.

"Where's Harris standing right now?" It was the question that started to plague me. Michael Harris was mediocre at best but the kid was steady at my heels waiting in the wings.

Jerry shrugged and put the fork back to my mouth. "After what happened to you, Harris has turned into a beast." My stomach twisted. "Hell, he's there just as much as I am. Working, training. His determination reminds me of you." My eyebrow hitched. "Don't look so surprised. Stevie Wonder can see that you don't like the kid. Have you ever thought the reason why you don't like him?"

"He's cocky for no reason. He's sloppy and he tends to cut corners. And he-"

"He's just like how you were. Natural talent can only get you so far in this game and you know that. Harris is young just like you but since he doesn't have you there to push himself he fighting our own greatest enemy."

"Ourselves." Jerry nodded.

He and I talked for another hour or so about this and that. About he's beautiful curses. Jerry and Maggie have five daughters. They all looked like fashion models, their beautiful faces splashed on every grocery store magazine or something. All of them banned from the gym or any type of match. I guess that's why he put his heart and soul in the boys and men that he trained.

After nearly consuming the tiny flowers on the plate. Jerry prayed that I would return to the gym and that it wasn't the same without me there. It felt great to be missed. The look in his eyes and the not so subtle hints he dropped gave me the impression that he knew that my fighting days were all over.

Offering me a job as an assistant trainer, someone to help out around the gym. I couldn't see myself picking up towels off the floor and sweeping up after the lights went out. My best friend a man that had become my father after my own had died was telling me that I was useless. Hinting that I had nothing left to offer to the sport. Jerry had given up on me. I just added him like my mother another log to the fire inside me.

CHAPTER 2

"So Mr. Hart how are we feeling today?"

I have been here for 44 days-a few days over six weeks and my doctor was asking how *we* were feeling? I feel like hammered shit, that had been tossed into a blender then left out in the sun to dry out and this process was repeated for the last 44 days. I muttered. "Fine."

"Well, the day has finally come-"

"I'm getting out of here?" Both the cast on my arms were gone and the brace on my neck. My left leg was still stabilized with an air cast; my right was in a brace. I was on the mend.

My doctor who looked about my age twisted his stethoscope. "Kind of. " His features softened. "You went through a very traumatic ordeal, Mr. Hart. Your recovery most likely is going to be ongoing. Your next step in your treatment will be physical therapy." I gave him a blank stare. "Your muscles have been inactive for quite some time now. I will not lie to you and I will not sugar coat. The therapy will give you about up to 65 percent of your mobility."

"So you are saying that walking will be out of the question then?" I barked at him.

He took in a slow breath. "No, I'm not saying that. Mr. Hart, I knew of your profession before your accident. I know that's what you want to go back to. If anyone told me that I was unable to practice medicine again I would be devastated. So I can only imagine what you are feeling right now. Mr. Hart you have your life, not being able to walk or run without pain is a small price you have to pay for what you went through."

"So when do I start?"

"At the end of this week."

"Who will be my therapist?" My fighting nature never seemed to turn off; I always wanted to know what I was up against.

"With your insurance you have a few options."

"I want you to give me the hardest, meanest son of a bitch you can find."

Since I've been here I hadn't seen my doctor smile until now. "I know just the therapist."

My tiny Asian nurse would come in and run me through a few exercises you could say. She got more of a work out than I did. She'd take my covers and pull them up to my knees, rotating my ankles then up to my knee slowly bending it until I thought I was going to pass out or tap out. "Your mobility is getting better Mr. Hart. You should be very proud of yourself."

"You have been in my life longer than most of my girlfriends can you please call me Devon."

Her face lite up. "Sure, and you can call me Annie."

"Ok, Annie you and I can speak candidly since you seem to be my only friend. What are my chances of walking out of here on both feet?"

Putting the cover back over my legs, Annie walked over to my side. "I'm not a doctor so I won't pretend to be. Mr.-Devon, I have seen a lot of things in this place. I saw a guy in perfect health, he was a runner."

"Was?"

She put her head down. "Yeah, came in here with a cough that never seemed to go way. He had stage four lung cancer, never smoked a day in life. He died two weeks later." Clearing her throat and forcing a smile. "Then it was a girl that was skiing up in the mountains took a bad fall, real bad. Slipped into a coma, parents were seconds away from pulling the plug she snapped right out of it." Snapping her petite fingers together. "That was a few years ago, now she's like some professional cross country skier or some jazz like that. Look, Devon I don't know what you believe in or where your faith lies, but if God wants you to stay in a wheelchair or run marathons it's all in His hands, you know?"

I nodded. "I can't see myself living or existing in constant pain not able to get up and change the channel if I want to you."

"That's why God gave man the know how to make remote controls." She smiled and patted my shoulder. "Think of it like this. Nothing in this world can stop your destiny. We are never denied just maybe delayed. Whether you crawl, walk or wheel yourself out of here it's only because it's in God's will. Just stay encouraged as long as you have breath in your body, it's just another day for you to seek what God has for you in your life." Touching my hand. "I'll check up on you in a few hours gotta go to lunch and make my rounds. We'll talk later, Devon."

You know that feeling of the first day of school? Knowing that all your buddies are going to be there, you've already discussed what classes you all would be in. Yet there was this sense of fear but excitement all in the same time. That's how it felt when the day finally came for my physical therapy.

I wanted someone tough, someone that wouldn't slack off and who would push me. Get me back to where I needed to be. Walking and fighting again.

"So are you ready?" Annie asked me locking the wheelchair in place.

"I guess as ready as I will be." With as much effort as picking up and putting down a child, Annie put me the chair. I thought I was going to pass out from sensory overload; there were so many people in the hallway walking around. Going on about their lives without a care in the world. I guess from being only around a hand full of people will do that to you. She wheeled me through long corridors and an elevator. "Am I going to need bread crumbs to find my way back to my room?" A twitch of anxiety washed over me. I've been stuck here for over a month and I had no idea where the hell I was at.

She laughed. "Your session is going to be an hour and when you are finished I'll be right out here to wheel you back. No need to call a search party." She took me to a separate part of the hospital through a breeze way into another building.

Before she could open the door. "Um...do you have any advice? Any words of wisdom before I venture off into another step to my road to recovery?"

"Yeah, don't make eye contact and let her talk." Her? Before I could ask her what in the world she got me into the front door opened so fast, if I wasn't already sitting down I would have fallen over.

"You're late." Whatever I was doing five seconds ago was completely sunk in my mental ship. She's beautiful. Tall, blonde thick like I like them. Her features were soft big blue eyes that I could see myself waking up to every morning. "What the hell are you staring at?"

Ok. "Um...I'm sorry. I was just um...-"

"Annie is this the new guy?" I guess she was referring to me.

"Yeah, I have him scheduled for his first session with you today at noon." Annie smiled which wasn't returned.

"I told administration that I wasn't taking on any more patients until the end of the year. I swear." She threw her toned arms in the air and huffed. "Well you're already here might as well, come on."

I couldn't help but watch the cutest behind I've ever seen switch back and forth in front of me. If I could kick myself I would for that amount of lust that was probably oozing out of my pores. She had on a pair of jet black scrubs that didn't fit like the other nurses or staff that I'd just seen. Hers fit her perfectly. She stopped suddenly making Annie jerk the chair that almost had me face down on the floor. She turned to me and bent down at the waist. "Now since I'm sure you enjoyed the view, I'm going to work you." I'm all man and her last statement made me think of every little naughty thing that I've done in the past. I bit my lip to hide my smile.

"This is where I leave you. Remember no eye contact. Keep your hands to yourself and speak when spoken to." Annie whispered into my ear.

I tried to smile not giving anyone the chance to sense my fear. "You act like you are leaving me with wolves." I chuckled.

"I wouldn't feed you over to wolves, just offering you up to the alpha female. Good luck." She waved me off.

The large room had a ton of free weights, a couple of tread mills and half dozen medicine balls. This wasn't the type of gym that I was used to. It resembled a Curves workout room for women, but in my position this was going to do. "Everybody we have a new guy. I'm going to need all of you to welcome him in." She said not looking back at me but at a clipboard.

"I know who you are. You're Devon Hart aren't you?" Some kid asked limping horribly towards me. He stuck out his hand to me.

I shook it. "Yeah, that's me." I looked down at my chair.

"Dude, I saw your fight a few years ago in Chattanooga you totally killed that guy. You put that dude in a hammer lock and it was a wrap. Man, you have to show me how to do that."

"I'll see what I can do. But um, what's that chick's problem?" I leaned closer to the kid and whispered.

The kid who couldn't have been over 20 years old grinned. "Tia? I would love to say that she is the type of woman that has that tough exterior but has the stuffing of a teddy bear, but I can't- no one's ever seen it. Just do what she says, believe me the woman gets results." He smiled.

I gave this Tia another once over. What felt like a life time ago I would tame her and have her in my bed. "Results, huh?"

"Yeah, I came to her about 3 years ago. Started working for her about six months ago." Taking a quick peek over his shoulder. "She's really not that bad."

"Right she damn near bit my head off before I could get in the door." Trying to keep my voice down so the she-devil wouldn't hear me.

"When she doesn't talk to you that's when you should worry. Look, some of the guys give her a rough time, you know because she's not hard on the eyes and all. She's got to be tough. She can handle herself if you know what I mean. She broke one guy's nose for trying to sneak a touch."

I took a quick survey of the other members that occupied my second realm of hell. "So what you in for?" I asked.

The kid rolled his eyes. "This isn't prison its physical therapy." He seemed to put all his weight on his left leg and pulled his pants leg up on his right. There sticking out of his shoe was a plastic calf. "Afghanistan was there for only two and half months. Driving a truck with supplies then boom. We caught fire." Forcing a smile. "I'm the only one that made it out."

Was that shame that I felt? Or guilt? This kid was walking/limping around happy as a lark with one leg. And I was constantly bitching about fighting. God help me.

"The guys in here are all military. They needed a therapist that's tough; it kind of helps them adjust back into civilian life. You know us grunts we ain't happy till someone is shouting and barking orders to us." I couldn't help but find myself envious of the guy. Despite his disabilities he had found his grove. "She likes her classes' small it's best so she could give all of them a lot of attention. Don't take it personal. Oh, by the way name is Mac, short for Makenzie. Just relax and listen."

"Hey hot wheels come here." Tia motioned me from the far corner of the room. I'd never used a wheel chair before and it took me a second to get the hang of it.

My shoulders down to my fingertips were on fire by the time I reached her. She stood unimpressed by my sweat drenched hair. She tossed a pair of fingerless gloves into my lap. "You're going to need these, put 'em on." She walked right past me to the other corner of the room and called back to me. "Hot wheels come on."

I gritted my teeth and wheeled over to her. For the next 50 minutes, she'd call and I would come like a trained dog. I hit every corner of this gym; everything from my waist up was killing me. By the time that Annie came to get me I felt I had done the Boston Marathon.

"You did good today hot wheels, day after tomorrow we'll do it all again."

"Hey!" Tia turned and gave me a look of displeasure. "My name isn't hot wheels, its Devon. When are you going to teach me to walk?"

"That's something that your mommy teaches not me." She said.

"I'm not going to be in this chair long. I'm going to get out of it."

She folded her arms over her chest and smirked. "Annie lock the chair in place for me please." Annie did like she was told. "Now stand up for me." Tia walked over slowly to me. "Stand up."

She might as well have asked me to do a double hand spring. I used what little strength I had in my arms to push myself up and off the chair. Internally, I thanked God that I still had the brace on my leg to support me. I looked like a newborn giraffe, knees wobbling, and my back still a bit hunched over. I felt like was standing on a tight rope feet above the ground.

Standing in front of me Tia put her pointer finger in the air. "I have one rule and that's for you to listen." Tia took her finger and gently pushed at my right shoulder, all strength in me left and I flopped back into the wheelchair. She squatted down in front of me and her blue eyes shined back up at me. "Please leave your ego somewhere else, I already have one. Thank you. I have to get you in a place where you are able to get up before you can walk. So let me do my job." She stood and walked back to her desk on the opposite side of the room.

"I could have sworn that I told you to keep your mouth shut." Annie whispered

"I thought you knew by now that I have a hard time following the rules."

I wanted to push myself back to my room. Crawl back into bed and die, I couldn't remember a time that I was this sore. At a young age my father trained me to be fighter, so there was never a day that I wasn't lifting weights, running miles at a time or in the ring or cage. Annie put me back in bed and put the covers back over my legs. "Okay please promise me that you won't piss Tia off anymore."

"Me? That woman is a psychopath. She's mean and rude-"

"She's doing her job." Annie sat on the edge of the bed and closed her eyes. "Look Devon she has to be in control of her class, if not guys like you would take over and you won't get anything done."

My mouth fell open. "Guys like me? What's that supposed to mean? Annie I thought you and I were friends you're supposed to be on my side." At that moment I felt more alone since the accident.

"I am on your side and don't ever say that again. I am your friend. For once in your life stop fighting."

She let the words hang there in my hospital room. "I don't know how." I balled my fist up at my side. Tension rose up in every one of my joints.

"Stop that! You are going to wear yourself out. Get some rest I'll be back."

For the first time Annie walked out of my room without smiling or giving a time when she'll be back.

There was never a time in my life on this earth that I wanted to physical hurt a girl. I take that back, once in the fourth grade it was this girl name Sarah. She had braces, glasses and skinny as a rail. Her glasses were so thick that I was sure she could see the future. Me and my boys were throwing a football around on recess. It still baffles me that with those glasses she didn't see the football volley out of my hand and in her direction. The football hit her temple with a crash she went one way and her glasses went another. Being fourth graders we busted up laughing.

Sarah wiped the tears off her cheeks, fumbled around for her glasses made her way to me and kicked me square in the balls. Lying in the school nurse's office with an ice pack on my junk all I thought was getting revenge on the four eyed geek.

History repeating itself, I lay here not with bruised junk but battered ego. I had the rest of today and all day tomorrow to think of what I could do to get this Tia chick in check. The more and more I thought about her the more and more I wanted to ring her neck or kiss it. Focusing more on the latter. I shifted around in my bed thinking if she would be that big an ass if she and I met under different circumstances.

I never had any trouble with the ladies. Once a chick heard I was a fighter I couldn't get rid of them. I put the big brown eyes on them they were nothing but victims. Now I would have to try a bit harder, without full movement of my legs this task that I took upon myself was going to get harder but I knew that I could do it.

I ran over my mental check list. One-get to walking again. Second, contact Jerry see if he could get me back into fighting shape, I'm going to give myself at least six months for that. Third, find out how Tia screams out Devon instead of yelling hot wheels.

Annie and I barely spoke my first day of physical therapy and I barely saw her all day yesterday. She came in my room 15 minutes before my session with Tia started. Pushing the chair in front of her. "Ready?"

That pretty smile that graced her round faced was replaced by a thin line. "Annie, are you mad at me? I mean you and I haven't really talked since the other day, did I do something?" My heart was thumping around in my chest. She'd been the only constant thing in my life since I've been admitted to hospital hell.

She shrugged her shoulders took my hand and guided me to the chair. "Nothing." She whispered.

"The hell it is. What's wrong? Why are you mad at me?" I struggled getting the gloves on and before she pushed me out of the room I spread my arms out and dug in on either side of the door so she couldn't push me out. "Annie stop!" She continued to push I thought my arms would yank out of socket.

"You want to know what's wrong." She spun me around. "I googled you." Her little round cheeks were the color of fire and the small voice that was my reassurance was throaty and deep. "You want to get back on your feet for that?"

I was almost confused by her statement. "So and?"

She stomped her size five shoe on the floor. "So! I saw you fight on YouTube." She covered her face and walked back into the room. I pushed backwards on my already sore arms to face her. She sat on my bed feet dangling what seemed like feet off the ground. "My son is a fan of yours."

"You make it sound like a bad thing." I wheeled myself over to her.

"Mr. Hart-

I put both my hands out. "So we're back to that? Annie, I'm sure if you tell me what has you so upset we can talk it out." I have broken several jaws in my life and a few hearts, but putting together why Annie was so pisst off about I was ill-equipped.

"I know that you want to walk I get it. Who wouldn't want to? I saw you. I saw you fight." Her bottom lip quivered. She covered her face with her hands; her tiny shoulders began to shake up and down. "I saw what you did to him." She cried harder. "It was horrible."

I had no idea what to do with my hands. I wanted to touch her and tell her that everything was going to be okay. "Annie, it's a sport my sport that I rock at."

Annie bounced off the bed, faster than I thought she could. "He surrendered and you kept going." She sniffed snot.

I had a couple dozen YouTube videos that my sparring partner Henry put up for me and the one that she saw had to be the *one*. I reached out to her. "Annie. Look I was going through a ton of stuff at the time. I didn't-"

"The bone was sticking out of his arm. He was telling you stop his hand was hitting the floor." She scooted away from me.

"He was tapping out. That's what it's called."

"If you knew the name for it why did you keep going? My God, he was screaming for you to stop." Her hands went to her ears as if trying to block the screams in her head.

Lenny Morgan was a great fighter. I'm pressing the word *was*. I was a different person then, hungry to win. Jerry stayed in my behind about what goes on in the cage stays there and what's out is just that-out. My life outside of the cage was more chaotic then inside; my family life had all but crumbled. Not wanting to admit it at the time I was hurting and I wanted everyone around me to feel all that pain. Lenny Morgan had talked enough junk to fill a city dumpster. He called me out right then and there. The emotional junk I was going through I missed meals and sleep wasn't happening. I lost weight and I slipped down to his weight class he wasn't prepared and I exploited his weakness.

Morgan came straight at me that night and I got tired of his game and took him to the ground. Instead of playing I put him in an arm bar, my specialty. I'll give it to Morgan he was strong, but no one gets out of my arm bar. The second I arched I knew the kid was a goner. The crowd was hungry and I feed them the kid's detached and bloody arm.

Jerry cashed in every favor that he could not to get me barred. It was more than evident that the kid was tapping out. I didn't care then but I cared now. The way that Annie was looking at me, like I was some sort of monster.

Pressing her scrubs down. "I think that you and I should just keep our relationship profession." She walked behind me, turned the chair and proceeded to wheel me to therapy.

Unlike the other day were I wanted to look at the people in the hallways and breezeway I kept my head down trying the best I could to shield myself from all unwanted glares. She opened the heavy steel door and wheeled me in. All thoughts of revenge and getting back at Tia vanished.

There she stood with clipboard in hand in a pair of dark navy blue scrubs. No makeup, just a soft tint of pink lip gloss all desire of having the lip gloss staining my shirt was gone. "Goodbye, Devon." Annie locked my chair in place and walked out. In a room full of people I felt all alone.

"For a man that can't walk you sure have a talent for making people run away." Tia's long legs made their way in front of me.

"Do you want me to show you how I can pull a rabbit out of my ass next?" I stared up at her. The way that she looked down at me was doing something to me. I'm sure she put more regard in staring at a bar of soap than how she looked at me now.

With a smooth pivot she turned away. "Ok, fellas it's Sunday and you know what that means." Her voice was light but with dose of sarcasm.

"Come on, you said that we only had to do this once a month not every freaking Sunday." The guy that spoke I think his name is Andrew. Barrel chested dude missing his left hand and half of his right arm.

Ignoring his whining. "Come on everybody let's make a circle." She began to corral the seven of us in the center of the room.

I pushed at the wheels of the chair but didn't move. "You gotta unlock them first." Mac said unlocking the chair and pushing me to the circle.

"Tia, I mean we've been through this a thousand times. There is really nothing new to tell." Aaron grumbled. He'd suffered 3rd degree burns on his whole left side of his body. Aaron looked like your stereotypical jarhead. Thick necked with a dark blonde crew cut. The comic book fanatic in me compared him to Two-Face, the Batman villain. The left side of his face was puckered and stretched together. Freddy Kruger had nothing on this guy.

Tia turned and gave him a hard look. "This isn't for my benefit it's for yours, now stop your belly aching and come with it. Matter fact what about you start."

I had no idea what the hell was about to happen or what I had gotten myself into. My whole body began to ache. I felt Mac's heavy hand on my shoulder. "Relax; we aren't going to make you sing a solo." He winked. It still didn't make my nerves settle.

Aaron cleared his throat. "Well, as you all know I'll be getting out of this hell hole in a few days. I won't say that I'm gonna miss being here but I'll miss you all…well most of you." The group of men snickered. Aaron wore a short sleeve shirt that read. Yeah-I Woke Up Like This. As he picked at his leathery skin on his elbow. "Seriously, once I was discharged I thought I lost my brothers in the Marines but I found brothers and a sister here." Looking over at Tia who was actually smiling. She had a dimple that I hadn't noticed and the longing for her came back. Aaron continued. "Thank you." Aaron struggled to sit back down and the room fell back silent.

"Anybody want to go next?" Tia scanned the room.

Mac stood. "Um since most of you have heard this before, I'll keep it brief. It was four of us in the truck. I remember Chuck my sergeant was talking about how he missed the show American Idol and that he never liked watching the winner but would watch it for the try outs. How those people would get on national television and couldn't carry a tune in a bucket." Mac laughed. "We all did that, you know? Talked about the stuff that we missed the most. Being stuck in the desert all you have our memories of the world outside." All the men grunted in agreement. "I was driving and I remember looking at Chuck's face and before I could turn back to look at the road Chuck's face was gone."

The uncomfortable silence was unbearable in the room. Mac cleared his throat and rubbed the heel of his hand over his eyes. "Chuck, Paul and Ryan." Mac pulled his dog tags that hung around his neck and kissed it. Tears rimmed his eyes. "I continue to live because they would want me to. There isn't a day that goes by that I ask God why? They had families, children. Ryan's wife was on expecting their third. I had no one to come back home to, but I still came home." He looked down at his self. "I came home in pieces but I still came home." Then something that I couldn't imagine happened. Mac smiled a smile that brightened the entire room. "I didn't have to be here, so here I am. My work isn't done."

Then he sat down. Every man stood or tried to and told a similar story of lost and then redemption from demons that were half buried in the desert.

"Hot wheels what you got?" Tia sat back in her chair and looked me over.

"There's really nothing to tell. I got in a car wreck that's it." I rubbed my sweaty palms on my thin baby puke green scrubs and hunched my shoulders.

Tia narrowed her eyes. "Okay, not today but one day you're going to tell us."

"What that's not fair!" Jason shouted, who lost both of his legs defusing a bomb in Iraq. "How does the new kid get a pass and we don't?"

"My class my rules. Don't like it crawl out of here." She glanced at the wall clock. "You all have about 20 minutes left. Run through your exercise for the time being." She stood and everyone else rolled, limped or scooted away on walkers.

I pushed up behind her. "Thanks." Brushing my overgrown hair off my forehead.

"Don't thank me yet, hot wheels. It's the Sabbath and I try not to push my limits." She smiled at me which I took as a good sign.

"I was thinking are there any other exercises that I could be doing to help me speed up the process, you know. Get me back in shape."

"Now here you go pushing the limits. Hot wheels, you seem like a pretty okay person. Time heals all wounds. Take your time." I clenched my jaw in frustration. "I know what you are thinking."

"You have no idea what I'm thinking." I growled.

She took a step back not out of fear but in exaggerated shock. "Your first thought was how in the heck am I going to get this girl in bed.

Your second thought was how you were going to run after you did." She folded her arms and looked her nose down at me.

"Sorry, you're wrong." I lied through my teeth.

"Well, it wouldn't be the first or the last time I was wrong, but I know guys like you. I see them recycled in my class day in and out."

"You know nothing about me." I turned and looked at the door willing it to come closer to me so I could make an escape.

"I know enough. I know what really happened that day of your wreck." I couldn't help but ball my fist up in my lap. "Do you know a State Trooper by the name of Nathan Brown?" I drew a blank. "Of course you don't you were totally out of it when he found you. Nathan is a good friend of mine; I do research on everyone in my classes. Had to make sure that you weren't some crazy lunatic suffering for PTSD."

"Only lunatic I see is the one stand in front of me." Building blocks of rage were forming the Egyptian pyramids inside me.

"Well, you got that right. You haven't seen crazy yet, you'll get to meet her and soon." Without turning away from me she shouted. "Class is over."

Annie was nowhere to be found so I had to wheel myself back to my room. After getting lost twice I finally stopped and asked a group of nurses where I was and how to get back. My arms didn't hurt as much as they had before and I took that as a blessing. Until I saw my bed. You might as well have asked me to climb Fiji. I locked the chair in place and took a deep breath. I pulled on the railing of the bed to hoist myself up. My feet felt foreign to me, the hospital socks with the grips on them felt like they belonged to someone else. This was the longest I've stood on my own two feet in over a month. I was thinking how I was going to swing my leg over to get in the bed. "Annie where are you?"

Reluctantly, I let go of the rail and put both hands on the bed. The support brace on my leg was a God sent without it I would of face planted. I lifted my right leg, remembering to breathe as pain crawled up the back of my knee up my butt cheek. Then everything went black.

When my eyes opened by my surprises I was standing. Out of pure shock and terror my arms shoot out, gripping for something anything to keep me upright. But I was surrounded by nothing but wide open space. I looked down at myself and I had on my favorite pair of buckle jeans, and a black and white Tap-Out shirt. I was barefoot and I stared at them in amazement. The sensation of my feet being tickled by the blades of grass almost made me laugh out loud.

The confusion of me standing began to wear and the familiarity of my surroundings became clear. I was standing in my parent's farm house. Out in the field was Randle my father's only farmhand. The old man took off his Alabama Crimson Tide hat and wiped his sweaty brow.

He took one look at me and waved. Lifting my arm with ease and no pain I waved back. My forearm no longer had the patch work that it had this morning. My VW Beetle was still in front of the barn with the hood up like always.

Johnny Cash was going into his second verse of Ring of Fire, when I heard. "D, you coming in or what?" My insides flipped around inside me.

There was no fear when I ran up the five steps up the wooden porch, through the family room. My bare feet banging on the hardwood floor hugging the wall coming around the corner to the kitchen. "No." I wasn't sure if I said the word out loud or was I screaming it in my head.

My father Daniel McCall Hart, all six-two of him. Round belly with his large hand wrapped around a cold beer. Looking into a boiling pot of brats, the smell of the beer bubbling made my eyes close and remember the last time I was standing right here. It had to be six years ago, right? "You staying to eat or you running off tonight?" He said with a chuckle still looking at the boiling beer. The way that my father spoke it always had a humor it in, like every sentence was laced with a punch line on the end. He laughed and looked over at me. "Come here let me look at you." The hardwood floor was cool on the soles of my feet and if felt like Saturday mornings at our house in the summer. Screen door the front and the back always open and the floor was always cool.

I came forward and looked at my father that had been dead for just about six years, looked at me and smiled. "What you too big to hug your old man?" His large hand grabbed the back of my neck and he kissed me on the forehead like he always had. "Now go sit down. I need to talk to you." He stirred the pot of boiling beer before dropping a few brats in.

"Dad." I coughed out.

He raised a finger to me and smirked. "Don't you start." He warned with a smile. "No son of mine will weep for his dead dad, you hear me?" I bit down on the inside of my jaw to make the tears go away. "Son, I'm so proud of you." His statement shocked me. "What? You think a man can't be proud of his boy? What you did that night, that's what makes heroes I could of never, shown you that." He took a sip of the beer and placed back on the table. Wiping the sweat of the beer on his favorite sweat pants. He looked me over. "My son D. Look at you."

"Dad-"I started.

He shook his head at me. "D, I've taught you a lot because my father taught me a lot and his father before him. But there was one thing I didn't teach you and that was how to lose."

"Why would you want to teach me that? You showed me how to size up my opponent, find their weaknesses go in for the attack." My head was swirling.

"I know what I taught you, I was there when I said it." He winked at me. "I raised you to be a taker and not a giver."

"Dad, I'm a good person. You didn't have to tell me how to be you showed me how to be a man. Nights that I knew you were tired you still helped me train." I couldn't help but look out the kitchen window, right next to the barn at the make shift gym he built for me when I was thirteen. "I'm a good man."

My father just shook his head and grinned. "Devon I know that you are good. Son, it's nice to be important but what's important is to be nice." He leaned back in the wooden chair and the soft creak of it made my speeding pulse slow, I was at home. "What you did to that Morgan boy wasn't in your character I know."

I put my head down and stared at my hands that were no longer bruised and swollen. "You were dying and I couldn't do anything about it." Every muscle in my body flexed, cool sweat traced its way down my spine.

"What did it prove? You ripped that boy apart because of words and how you were feeling. Subtract one of the variables and the outcome would have been so different." My father sighed, leaned over with a grunt and tossed my hair out of my face. "I still died and there was nothing that you could have done…nothing. That night in my opinion you lost that fight you lost a lot." He was right and I had to live with the feeling every day since I felt the kid's arm snap in my hands.

"I'll make you proud of me I swear."

"I'm already proud of you." He glanced at the stove. "Brats almost ready." He slapped my knee. "So what are you going to do about Annie? Good friends are hard to find, especially in your condition."

"She up and left. Didn't give me a chance to explain." I felt like an ass sitting in that dumb chair waiting for her to come and get me.

"I taught you how to give things up and never look back. I was wrong for that, for the first time I wished you didn't listen to me. Annie is a good girl. Smart and funny, hell she'd be a good corner guy for ya."

"I don't know what to say."

"Try I'm sorry. I wish I would have said it a million times and when the words finally formed to say it. It was too late." He licked the beer foam from the corner of his mouth. "Me and your mom would have been in a better place if I had."

"That wasn't your fault. She was the one that cheated; she was the one that lied to you and to me." I felt my upper lip hike up in a snarl. Just thinking about my mom made me want to scream.

My father smiled. "Did I ever tell you how I met your mom?" Before I could say no, he started. "I was working security at some honky tonk out in Memphis. Some hole in the wall crap club. It was nearing closing, I'm pulling drunk skunks out by their ears and such and then I see this girl. Man, your mother back in the day damn she was hot-"

"Really, dad come on- its mom you're talking about." Gross.

My father laughed so loud it rattled the plates in the cabinet. "I'll spare you my mental dialogue son. Anyway she's there fumbling out of the club and there was something inside of me that kept telling me to keep an eye on her." He put his beer down. "I saw her walking across the street in these cute little cowboy boots clicking on the pavement. Some hick starts to chat her up and your mom, you know how she is. Can cut a man down to size with that razor blade for a tongue she has. So I muscle up on the guy, tell him to take a walk. The hillbilly makes a move and put him out." My father makes a fist. "From that day on I thought that one gesture would keep her happy." He shook his head and began to play with the lip of the empty beer bottle. "I was a great father but a shitty husband." He pointed a long finger at me. "That's one of the few regrets I have. I could have been better to her. I drove her away."

"You made a mistake dad you can't beat yourself up about it."

"Your mother made one mistake and you beat her up about it." Damn.

My father looked past me towards the front of the house as he stood. "Son, if you don't leave me brats are going to burn.

A sense of panic coursed through. "Dad, no. Let me stay. Please."

He laughed his laugh that made his belly shake. "D, you have to go. Son, you fight not because you are man. You're a man so you fight. Pick those fights wisely."

He turned and stirred the boiling beer. A bouncing noise drew my attention to the entrance of the kitchen; bouncing towards me was a red and blue ball. My heart seized in my chest. "Dad." I spun and he was gone just the steam rising from the pot on the stove was what remained.

"Devon! You have to help me get you up. Devon."

Annie's small voice was raised to an almost unbearable level of panic. My eyes opened and I was in a crumbled heap in my room on the hospital floor. The smell of the farm, the freshly cut grass, the oil that my father made me shine the hardwood floors was still under my nose. "Annie." I said out of breath.

Her soft brown eyes were wide with surprise. "Did you wheel yourself back here?"

Unwillingly, I pulled myself out of my parent's farm house in my mind and stepped back into my hellish reality. Slowly, taking everything to release the death grip I had on Annie's scrubs. My battered hands and my white knuckles must have scared her more than my own fear. "You were gone-you didn't show up after class so I tried to get back in the bed. I guess I didn't make it." I looked at my stupid chair to my left-just sitting there unwilling to help me. "I guess I blacked out."

Shaking her head and with brute like strength she lifted me up in the sitting position. "I had to get my son from the sitter's house. I told Cassie to come and check on you." She mumbled a few curse words under her breath and I had to smile. "Now come on you goof ball and help me help you back in the bed."

I was pretty much useless, just an oversized ragdoll being flopped around by my tiny friend; well at least I hoped we were still friends. "Annie."

"No." She said as my butt hit the mattress. It hurt like hell but it was better than taking a nap on the floor. "I should have never talked to you like that." Putting her head down. "Who am I to judge you?"

"You don't have to say that." I huffed. My brown hair felt like weeds sprouting out of my head and I probably stunk to high heaven. "Pull up a chair, let me explain."

"Devon, you don't have to do that. I was wrong I'm your nurse and I shouldn't have gotten so wrapped up or involved with my patience's life like that." Lifting my legs by the back of my knees and putting them in the bed. Taking the covers and putting them up to my waist. "I'm sorry."

"You are my friend. Regardless if you are paid to be here or not.

You have been good to me and I owe you an explanation, so please humor the crippled guy, please." I looked over to the single chair in the room. Annie pulled the worn chair to my side and smiled. Her short legs barely touching the ground. "My father was a golden gloves champ in Knoxville." I closed my eyes and remember the pictures that hung on the wall in my father's study as a kid. "When I was a kid my father trained me to be a champion. I grew up fighting, you know. Every day for as long as I could remember I was training. It use to drive my mother crazy, me lifting everything heavy that wasn't bolted down. Running instead of walking." I smiled. "I wanted him to be proud of me."

"I'm sure he is." Annie touched my hand.

"He was." I could smell the brats boiling again on the stove. "My father was diagnosed with leukemia when I turned 20 years old. It moved fast and it was aggressive. The doctors said that he need bone marrow and with me and my mother being his only living relatives we all assumed that I would be a match for him, but I wasn't."

"Oh Devon, I'm sorry." I saw tears form in Annie's eyes that she quickly tried to push away.

"So I go in to get my blood work done and I remember my mom pulling me to the side." I had thought of this day over and over again for the last six years, but saying them was turning and tearing away at my insides. "She pulled me by my arm before I could reach the lab to get my blood work done. Then she drops the bomb on me."

"What?" Annie scooting to the edge of the chair.

"My dad wasn't my dad." I could remember my mother's face as she told me. Tears fell, her eyes almost drowning. "Her and my dad had got into this big blow out one night, she took off went to some bar- some guy knocks her up and she pretended all these years that I was my father's son, but I wasn't. So with no time left to find a donor I watched the cancer eat away my dad. During that time, I started slacking off at the gym shit was taken its toll. I know that you don't know a ton about the sport but it's competitive."

With a smile. "I got that part."

"Yeah, so I wasn't training like I was supposed to and not eating right so this guy thought he could take advantage of my situation. So I took his arm." Annie nodded and I wasn't sure if she truly understood.

She stood and pushed the hair out of my face. "Everyone handles grief and sorrow in their own way. It was wrong for me to judge you and I apologize. You are a good guy and I think you will walk out of here with a better understanding of things."

"How so?"

"When you are flat on your back all you can do is look up right?

"You know that you would make an excellent corner guy you know that?"

"I don't know what that is, but if you say so." She looked down at her watch. "Look, I will see you tomorrow my kid is here so I got to run."

I've never been too fond of children, maybe because I never had brothers or sisters or cousins around, but the thought of Annie's son being here did something to me. "He's here? Can I meet him?"

Annie rocked back on her heels. "I guess, I mean if you are really up to it."

"I want to."

"He can be a hurricane so thank God you are sitting down. He's at the nurse's station, I'll be back."

I rubbed my hands together finally another person that I would get to meet. Annie had said that the kid was a fan. The door opened and there stood a little boy with eyes like Annie's soft and bright. Only difference his left eye was nearly swollen shut and black. My heart stopped. The kid couldn't have been over ten year's old standing shoulder to shoulder to his mom. "Hi, I'm Devon what's your name?"

The kid smiled an adolescent tooth grin. "Luke. My name is Luke. Wow, you are really Devon Hart, huh?"

Luke took a few rapid steps closer to my bed. "Yup, that's me. I hope the other guy looks worse than you do."

Luke put his head down. "I lost."

"There's always tomorrow." I said with a wink and the boy gave me the same silly grin.

"Devon, I don't want him out fighting at school. He is there to get an education not be Hulk Hogan." Her reference to the aged fighter made me laugh.

I looked at the boy. "Hey Luke can you do me a favor and wait right outside for your mom, her and I have to talk." The boys head bobbed up and down and ran to the door.

Before the door was shut all the way I started. "Annie, the kid has to learn how to fight or one of two things are going to happen. The first-" Pointing one finger up and Annie putting her hands on her hips. "He's going to get picked on for the rest of his life. What I'm guessing he's in elementary school right?" She nodded. "He will be an easy target through middle school and high school."

Unimpressed with me. "So what's the second thing?"

"I know you heard of Columbine High School."

"Jesus, Devon. My kid isn't a killer." She put her hand over her mouth.

I was only half serious. "Annie, you've never been a boy and there is a food chain and you don't want Luke to be a bottom feeder do you? We're friends and what you love I love too. Let me teach the kid to fight and I promise you next time you get a call from the school it won't be from him getting his ass kicked."

I saw the wheels turning in her head. "Just show him how to defend himself. I don't want him to break a kids arm or something I can't afford the lawsuit." Shaking her head. "It's this little snot nosed kid at his school. Big kid, it just started this year. Luke used to run home and tell me all about his day, now he goes straight to his room and closes the door. I just want my son back, you know."

By the look in her eyes she gave me the approval that I needed.

"Bring him here on the days that I don't have therapy." I looked up to the celling and thought for a second. "So tomorrow bring him here and we can get some lessons in. I promise you I will teach him the basics in the arts, nothing lethal." I put my hand over my heart. "I swear."

She pointed to me. "Devon."

"I swear. Just to defend himself, I promise. Once he gets one kid off his back I guarantee if there are any others they will back off and quick. You just need to whip one kid's ass and the others will fall in line. I promise."

"I'll see you tomorrow got to get Rocky something to eat." She had her hand on the knob.

It was a horrible habit that I had that I knew would one day get me in trouble, I always reacted before I thought. "Annie." She turned. "I'm sorry-I don't want to step on anyone's toes. Maybe this is a job for Luke's father."

All the air seemed to leave my friend's body. "Devon don't worry about stepping on Luke's father's toes. He passed away a few years ago."

Chapter 3

That night I dreamt that Luke and I were fighting off bandits on my parent's farm. The kid had great form and he was quick. In the dream he saved my bacon from being hit in the back of the head with a shovel. After he and I kicked numerous butts we sat in my kitchen and drank a cold one for the victory.

I was still smiling when I heard the knock on the door. Annie walked in with a weak smile. "What's up buddy?"

"I'm here to take you to Tia's class." Speaking without looking at me.

"There's no class today."

"I know but you should go." Without saying another word she lifted me up and put me in a chair and slow walked me to therapy.

"Is it someone's birthday?" I said to her when we got to the door.

"I wish." She pushed me in. "I'll be right outside when you are done." Closing the door behind me.

I wheeled myself to the center of the room where everyone was already gathered together. I positioned myself next to Mac who had his head in his hands. "Mac, what's going on?" I whispered to him. I scanned the room and Tia was in the far corner at her desk talking to some guy in a suit. I couldn't make out all what they were saying, but by the looks of things it wasn't good.

"It's a sad day bro a very sad day." Mac said with tears running down his cheeks. Everyone in the class was either crying softly or staring off into space. I looked over to Tia to see that the suit had given her a cardboard box. He put his hand on her shoulder and walked pass the group without a word.

Tia balanced the box on her hip and carried it to her unoccupied chair towards the group. "Most of you know this, but for the ones that don't" She looked square at me. "Aaron took his life this morning at his home." The big guy I thought the one with the burns. "There will be a service for him this weekend. If you want to go, please let me know and I will make arrangements with the hospital to get you all there." Her eyes were puffy, cheeks red. Placing the box on the floor. "Aaron didn't have any family but us, so here are a few of his valuables that he wanted us to have.

Jason looked at the box and snarled. "Weak bastard."

"Come on." I said not knowing why I was defending a dead guy that I didn't even know.

"We all had our days-all of us." Jason shouted looking in the faces of everyone in the group. "There were days that I wanted to put a gun between my teeth but I didn't. I didn't want you all to be rummaging through my old shit." He turned to Tia. "Aaron was weak and selfish. No way am I going to shed a tear for him-ever." Both of Jason's leg were gone and I could understand where he was coming from. At least one day I will walk again, but this guy had no chance, no hope of regaining what he once had.

I waited for her to rip this guy a new one, but Tia stood there looking in the box. I couldn't grasp on what she was thinking.

"Look, let the ones that want to grieve-grieve. If you want to rant and rave do it elsewhere." I said daring him to come closer.

Jason just wheeled himself out of the room and the tension slowly began to disappear. "Have you thought about it?" There were five other people in the room and I had no idea if she was asking me a direct question. "Have you thought about killing yourself?" Tia said still looking down at the box in the center of the circle.

Andrew spoke first. "I always chicken out at the last second. But like Jason said I know that I have had my days? Then there are the days when you look outside and the sun is out and I think if I offed myself I would never see it again."

Clearing my throat I looked up and thought, if I say yes, would it make me weak? And if I said no I would be a liar. Most of the guys had started to tell their favorite Aaron stories. And on a strange level I missed the guy, wished I could have known him, but I knew that I'd never will.

The room fell silent. "So you thought about it too hot wheels, you thinking about ending it all?" Tia finally stop looking at the contents of the box and looked right at me.

Everyone stopped talking and looked dead at me. "The first few days when I wasn't getting answers." My hands began to sweat and I could hear my heart beat in my ears banging. "The medication that I was on I felt was making me feel worse, I couldn't feel my legs and I thought that my life that I knew was over. I wanted it to be over." I felt Mac's hand on my shoulder. As if pushing me to go on. "Before the wreck I thought...I thought."

"You were indestructible. Right?" Andrew said.

I nodded. "I thought things like this happened to other people not me. I had too much going for me."

"We all did." Quincy said who had most of his right arm missing. "The things that we felt were important aren't anymore." He wiped his face.

"Yeah, all I wanted to do was fight and get laid. Now it's a struggle to try not to crap myself." I paused and thought. "Aaron, I didn't know the guy. Maybe he had the courage to end it or the cowardice not to go on, I don't know. I hope that he has peace where ever he is." Glancing back to the group. "We are going to get out of here, all of us. Together."

For the first time ever, Tia smiled down at me. Not a smile of hey let's hop in bed but of appreciation. "Guys there will be grief counselors here later on today and the remainder of the week if you would like to use their service. You are more than welcome to stay here or go back to yours rooms." She turned and made her way back to her small desk.

Mac volunteered to stay and wait for the counselor, Quincy and Phil thought it would be best to go back into their rooms. Andrew thought he would just hang out and talk it out. I had no idea what to do, but leave.

"Hot wheels, you're not going to stay for the crap tasting coffee and three day old cookies." Tia yelled from the other side of the room.

Instead of yelling back I pushed myself to her far corner. She waited patiently until I finally arrived in front of her. "Um...I really didn't know Aaron. I think I should just go back to my room." I didn't know what to say. "If it means anything to you I'm sorry for your loss, I'm sure that you get close to these guys and for you to lose one must hurt a lot." I ran my hand through my wild hair.

The side of her mouth hitched up in a smile. "Yeah, they are a part of my family. We got to stick together in the good and the worst of times." She looked back to the broken circle of wheelchairs and walkers.

"So do you have family here in Tennessee?" She gave me a side look. I put my hands up in surrender. "I'm not trying to get all in your business just asking a question."

"My parents live up in Michigan, I have a sister in Ohio who's a doctor. So it's just me here." Tia folded her hands in front of her. I just noticed that she wasn't wearing her usually scrubs but a pair of relax fit jeans and graphic t shirt. I couldn't help but smile. "What are smiling at?" She barked down at me

"You have a Batman shirt on. He's probably my favorite comic book hero." Which was the truth.

She looked down at herself. "Yeah, I got the call this morning about Aaron and I just threw it on." The shirt was kind of big; I wondered was it her boyfriend's shirt. Last week I noticed she wasn't wearing a ring. She pulled at the hem of the shirt and twisted it. I could see her standing there but her mind was somewhere else probably thinking about Aaron.

"Well, if class is still on tomorrow I will see you then." I waited for her to say something but she was staring off at something that I couldn't see. I started to wheel away and heard her say something that I couldn't hear. "Tia, are you okay."

She put her hand on her forehead and closed her eyes. "This shouldn't have happened."

"It's not your fault."

"Flipping military. When he couldn't fight anymore they just threw him out like trash. He put years in the service and he couldn't get the care that he needed." She put her head down and drops of tears hit her Batman shirt. "It's not fair." She whispered. Her blonde hair fell over her shoulders. "The men here, I have to be everything for them-sister-therapist-friend-counselor and mom." She looked over to Mac balancing on his good leg. "Mac is just a kid. Leg blown clean off and the VA gives him some recycled leg that doesn't fit him right. It's messing up his back by the time he hits thirty his spine will be completely out of line." She shook her head.

"What do you need me to do?" The words came out of my mouth before I realized what I had said.

Tia looked up at me, her long eyelashes all spiky from tears. "Hot wheels there's nothing that you can do. If you were a millionaire I would ask you for a donation, but we're all in the same boat." She smiled. "I'm working with hand me down equipment. The men in here gave their best to their countries and they are now receiving the worst I can offer."

"Again-none of this is your fault. You come here every day and put up with me and for that only you should get a medal."

She laughed and put her hand over her mouth. Could that be the laugh that I could hear every morning when I woke up? The laugh that I would hear in the shower when I went out to train. Her laugh was pure music. "You are an ass but I can fix that." I reached out to touch her hand; she pulled away from me as if I were on fire. "Don't"

I exhaled. "I wasn't trying to-"

There was the iron lady again, her back grew stiff and her blue eyes bore down on me. "Don't press your luck, hot wheels. You said you wanted to go back to your room now go." I didn't have to leave she walked away first leaving me sitting in front of her desk. Then I saw it, I'm more than positive she didn't want me to see, but she was favoring her left leg. I found Tia's weakness.

Annie helped me back into my bed and she sat down on the corner. "I'm sorry to hear about Aaron, I know that you didn't know him well but just the thought of someone that you were just speaking to passing does something to you."

"Yeah. It's crazy."

The room was unusually warm and I felt my scrubs sticking to me. "You promise me whenever it gets rough you talk to me, okay? No matter how hard it gets in here you talk to me first."

"I'm not going to kill myself." What I had said to the group was completely true. When the nurses would walk in and they would talk around me; I would pretend to be sleep. They say how there were worse things than death and it was lying right in front of them. How easy it would be for me to take out my IV and blow air in it and wait to the air bubble reaches my heart. My dad was gone; my mom was in Atlanta living a life completely without me. The friends that I thought I had hadn't even thought about seeing me. I was alone and 90% of every waking moment I was afraid.

The fear of the unknown was crushing. Would I walk, can I ran, will I fight again? The six pack that I had looked like a keg. I looked like I should belong in a log cabin by the looks of my full grown out beard. I wasn't myself-I wasn't who I was supposed to be. "What are thinking about?"

Annie's little legs kicked back and forth under her. "Nothing." I said. "Where's the kid?" I wanted to see Luke, tell him about the awesome dream that I had.

"Sorry, he has guitar lessons tonight. Day after tomorrow I'll bring him around." She hopped off the edge of the bed. "They don't pay me to hang out with you. I got to run."

"Annie." She turned. "Without sounding too needy. I really don't want you to go right now. Do you think you can hang out with me for a little bit longer, please?" I mustered up the saddest look I could think of and gave her my sad puppy dog eyes.

"Sure, goof ball. I was supposed to give Mr. Anderson a sponge bath." She shivered, then looked around the room and in a hushed voice. "He has back acne and he's super gross." She stuck her tongue out and we both laughed out loud.

"Besides me who is your worst patient and be honest?" I sat up in my bed trying to get comfortable.

Rolling her eyes. "You are my friend and no longer my patient so you don't count." She gently pinched my arm. She bit her bottom lip and put a finger to her chin. "Hands down it has to be this guy that's on my rounds. He got here a few days ago. Construction worker fell two stories off a building."

"Dang."

"He deserved it. He broke his leg in two places. If he could walk he'd be walking around thinking he's God's gift, but now he just lays around thinking so."

"So what's so bad about him?" I never considered myself a gossip but any little tidbit about the outside world got me going.

"Where do I start? He's a big baby and he thinks that I'm his personal maid or something. Beside his ass grabbing, he-"

"He touched you?" I had lost all humor that was in our conversation. This asshole put his hand on my friend.

Annie put her hand on my shoulder. "If I had a dollar for every time some guy got a little too friendly-Luke could go to any college he wanted and I would retire. Devon, its fine."

"The hell it is. Who is he?"

"Do you really think that I'm going to tell you? You just turned into the Hulk in a matter of seconds." She shook her head.

"What else did he do to you-did he say anything to you?" I was clenching the thin cover on the bed until my knuckles hurt. "Tell me Annie."

"Devon. It's really not a big deal. He's just some redneck piece of trash that thinks that every woman wants him. Guys like that are a dime of dozen, and if I worried about what he thought I would lock myself in my room and never come out. You just focus on getting better and walking again." She looked at her watch. "Mr. Back Acne needs me. I'll stop back by in a few." She began to walk out the room and looked at me again. "Devon, please don't worry about it."

I didn't say I would or wouldn't. "See you later." When I heard the door shut behind her I started to think about my plan to hurt this guy.

Chapter 4

I couldn't wait till Annie left at 3:00. I laid there waiting for what's her name to come in. In the last few weeks that I have been here I would just play sleep, let her take my vitals and wait till she left.

The door opened and I smiled. "Oh." Her eyes widened. "You're up." She began to fiddle with the leg of her scrubs.

"Yeah, I couldn't sleep my life away now could I?" I smiled. What's her name bite at her bottom lip. Got her. "So how long have you been working here?"

Her giggle was nails on a chalk board but I kept my smile up. Occasionally looking at her eyes and at her mouth. "Um, I started here about four and half months ago." Then she went into a story that I really didn't care for about her boyfriend losing his job and then some more crap. I nodded and kept my focus solely on her.

God this girl could talk. There wasn't a ton of things that I remembered but I couldn't recall a person talking while inhaling and exhaling, my goodness. She probably talked in her sleep. I cleared my throat which caught her attention. "Hey, I heard that there's come construction worker here, took a bad fall. He's on this floor right?"

"Yeah, was working on some new housing development in Mount Juliet. He should be out in a few days. Why?" I noticed that she was rubbing the hell out of my arm, slowly going up and down. Doesn't she have a boyfriend?

I put my hand over hers and looked at her intently. "When I get out of here I was thinking about doing some renovations to my place. You know I'll probably be in the chair for a bit. Thinking I may need a ramp or something." I saw her thinking about it, so I squeezed her small hand. "It would be so helpful if you could let me know where he is. I know that he will probably be out of commission for a while but I'm sure that he has a buddy or something. I would really appreciate it."

She turned to look at the closed door. "I don't think I should give out any patient information."

I nodded with her in agreement. "I totally understand I would hate to get you in any sort of trouble." I saw her body begin to lose the tension in her shoulders. "You know you look like a girl I used to know. Her name is Cassie." I waited.

She put her hand to on her heart. "Really? My name is Caren with a C."

"Yeah, the both of you two smile the same. Which I may add is a very beautiful smile." She couldn't resist in showing me her pearly whites. I looked at my lap. "You know the reason that I try to sleep when I know you are coming?"

Caren leaned in as if I was going to tell her where the Holy Grail was. "Why?"

"I know you told me that you had a boyfriend and I don't like lusting over another man's property. I just couldn't bare looking at you without being able to touch you." Her cheeks turned bright red.

"Really? Wow!" Then I had to listen to another round of how Phil, her boyfriend is this lazy piece of crap but they'd been together for like forever. Whenever she paused I would try to jump in with, "You could do better." And. "He's a fool to treat you like that."

And my personal favorite. "Someone as pretty as you shouldn't have to deal with his crap."

After what seemed like an eternity. "Caren, thank you so much with trusting me with your problems with Phil."

A small tear was creeping down her face and I wiped it off with the pad of my thumb. "Thanks, Mr. Hart you are a good guy. I hope that you get out of here and be able to fight again."

"Baby steps, right." Lightly pinching her cheek. "When I get out of here I still need to find a guy that could get my place together for my chair."

Looking at the door-she leaned down into my ear. Giving me a great view of her cleavage she gave me every bit of information that I needed.

After Caren's shift was over at 11 pm, it took a bit for the next nurse to come in so I took my time. "Now or never." I eyed the wheelchair that was next to my bed for a moment. "Look, I don't want any funny business from you. I'm going to need you just for the next few minutes so don't be a dick." Straining to pull down the rail on my bed, I swung my legs over the side of the bed and nearly pitched myself off the bed. I had to smile, I was getting stronger.

Now the hard part. First my toes, the ball of my feet and then my heels were on the cold floor. I double, then tripled checked the brace on my leg. With a strong grip on the bed I stood. I'm sure I looked like I had just been punched in my gut. I was bent over at the waist and the amount of sweat that was pouring out of me I looked like I had gone a few rounds with Cain Velasquez.

The grips on the socks were a blessing but I wanted to take the lazy route by half sliding and scooting to the chair. "Screw it." I lifted my leg up and a snap of fear made me put it back down. What if I fall? What if I black out again? I took a deep breath. I had to do this for Annie. I thought of her little round face and the messy ponytail that stood on top of her head. Looking more like an Asian version of I Dream of Genie than my nurse. She was a single mom, raising a boy. I had both my parents as a kid and I was a hellion. She didn't need any added grief. Again, lifting my leg I pushed my foot forward. Feeling my toes dragging against the linoleum floor I held my breath. I was no more than two feet away from my chair. Reluctantly, releasing the bed my arms shot out in front of me, praying that they could stand the weight if/ or when I fell.

I looked over at the chair the wheel locks were on thank you God. In the biggest face off of my life I stared down the chair. "Remember what I told you. We got to help each other." I said to the chair. If this whole ordeal was hell in its self, I had to turn and sit down. Next time, I'll walk backwards. I put my hands on the locked chair and tried to twist my waist to get into the chair, mistake of a life time. My whole left side felt like it had been ripped off my body. I collapsed, but I did it in the chair. Quick examination, nothing was bleeding or poking out so I was good.

I sat in the chair for a second to try and gather myself back together. "Let's do this." I wheeled myself to my door and peered out of it. The nurse's station was to my right, and if all the information that Caren gave me I would go to my left.

The nurses were in some sort of conversation about who was the better front man Scott Stapp from Creed or Eddie Vedder from Pearl Jam. I made the left and everyone knew that Creed was way better. There it was room 211. The door was cracked, I pushed the door open and was engulfed in darkness. I wheeled further in and saw that piece of shit on his cellphone. His left leg was on hoisted up in the air, he wasn't that big of a guy. Husky, yeah but I have beaten dudes twice his size.

"He bro you lost?" His voice was deep, I'm sure that he used it to try to intimidate people but it wasn't going to work on me.

"Nope, I'm right where I want to be." He flicked on the light by the switch on the bed. "It seems we both know a certain lady."

From what Caren told me his name is Hank Roberts. Hank looked me up and down. "Bro if I'm screwing your wife, I would say I'm sorry but-I'll say it like this. My leg will heal you on the other hand-" Giving me another hard glare. "You probably can't even get it up, huh?"

I wheeled closer to him and smiled. "Nothing like that. I just want to tell you to leave the nurses here, well one in particular."

Hank smirked. "Which one in particular are you talking about? Could it be the black chick that should be coming in soon?" He licked his lips. "I've never had a black gal before. They say they could be pretty wild in bed, but who really wants the hassle right." It was confirmed that I really hated this guy. "Not the Caren broad. She talk too damn much for me." He lifted a finger and smiled. "But I know what I could put in her mouth to keep her quiet for a while." He laughed out loud. "So it must be the slanted eye lady then, huh?" The racist term nearly had me jumping out of my chair.

"By the rage on your face I see that now we are finally talking about the same chick."

"Leave her alone and I'm not going to ask you again."

He leaned back in his bed and put his hands behind his head. No longer looking at me setting his sights to the ceiling he smirked. "Now that one…I could have fun with her all night long. That small little body, I could do some major damage. I would break that little thing in two." Looking back at me. "I'd make her enjoy every bit of it."

Before the last bit of filth came out of his mouth, I already had my elbow in the small space above his knee and between his thigh and bore down. His mouth opened in shock and in pain. "If you say another word I'll separate your knee from the rest of your body, you understand?" He nodded biting back a scream. "Now that I have your attention. Caren, if she wants to tell you her rendition of Mary had a Little Lamb, which will take about three and half hours. You listen. For Erin the night nurse that should be here in a second. You tell her what Martin Luther King, Jr. means to you." I pushed down on his leg and he yelped. "As for Annie, you don't speak when she comes into the room unless she ask you a question."

"Screw you, bro." He spat out through gritted teeth.

There was something inside of me that had prayed that he would say something crazy to me. With my elbow still digging into his leg. I took his ankle and began to bend backwards. I was trying to make his toes touch his chest. In the cage, I would have been standing, with his leg in my grip using everything I had to bend this SOB's leg back till it snapped.

"Okay, okay." He screamed out. His arm stretched out trying to reach me.

"Good." I let him go and his foot feel back on the bed. "If I hear you can't keep your hands to yourself, I will give the nurses your leg. You understand?" I wheeled myself backwards and looked him over. "And maybe your arm too." There were tears in his eyes as he sniffed snot and nodded.

I wheeled out of his room, feeling like the day that Jerry told me that I was a tournament away from being in the King of the Cage. I pushed myself back to my room my door was open, did I forget to close it behind me? Shit.

"Mr. Hart! My God I thought you went AWOL." Erin fell back on the wall out breath. "Where did you go?"

Her hazel eyes narrowed down at me. Her dark brown hair was pulled back in a ponytail. She'd put me in the mind of Thandie Newton, but instead of an English accent she had a southern drawl. "I went out for a walk."

"A walk? Mr. Hart if you need to get around you could have waited a few minutes until I came in to check on you." Putting her hands on her hips. She just shook her head and helped me back into bed. "Try and get some rest okay. I have to go and make my rounds and I promise I won't wake you if you fall asleep." And she never did.

The dream that I had last night was one of the best. I had Hank in the cage, I refused to knock him out just kept putting him in submission moves over and over again. His legs were rubber bands, his arms were more than twigs that I could have snapped at my will.

I was hurled out of the dream by a quick knock to the head. My eyes shot open. "What the hell did you do to him?" Annie's face was twisted into a snarl. The hit didn't hurt at all but more of the shock of it made me laugh. "What is so funny Devon? What did you do to Mr. Roberts?"

"Annie, it's too early in the morning for a beating you could at least wait till I've had breakfast." Rubbing the side of my head.

"You did something to him-didn't you?" She folded her little arms over her chest. Narrowing her eyes at me. "Spill it and now."

I hunched my shoulders. "I just had a talk with him man to man. Told him to leave you and all the other nurses alone, that's all." I internally told myself that this would be the first and last lie that I would tell my friend. "Why did he say something to you?"

"That's just it. I walked in expecting him to say something foul and he sits there like a statue. I asked him was he feeling ok, he says yeah. Then the worst part he tells me to have a great day." Her mouth fell open. "Can you believe that? I've had to put up with his crap for days and he does a 180 on me."

I gave her a blank look. "Well sometimes some people just need a little talking to." I gave her a big smile and her reaction wasn't what I expected. She started to cry. "Annie!"

Annie sat down in what I dubbed as her favorite chair with her face in her hands. "Thank you Devon."

"I'll do anything for my friends." I reached out to her.

"I don't want you to think that I'm weak, but after my husband passed it's just been me and Luke. It just gets hard sometimes, you know?" She wiped her wet cheeks. "Dealing with his bully at school and that pile of trash down the hall, it's just been crazy." Annie finally meet my eyes and continued. "I down played a lot of the conversations to you with that asshole. I swear if you weren't here I would have taken my vacation until he was discharged."

"Come here." I put my arms out and her little body fell on my mine. She sobbed on my chest. "It's okay babygirl. Long as I'm around you and Luke will always be safe, okay?" She sat up and smiled through tears.

"So now you're my bodyguard? Luke will love knowing that." She sat up straight. "That reminds me I will bring him in tomorrow for you."

Rubbing my hands together. "I can't wait to get started. No kid in that school will dare try to test Luke ever again when I get done with him."

She cocked her head to the side. "You must have been a saint in a passed life."

I would like to think in a passed life I was some sort of apex predator. A grizzly or gator but a saint-never. "Thanks."

Annie checked herself in the bathroom mirror. "I'll be back to take you to therapy in a few."

"Annie-what happened to Luke's dad?" Her mouth opened and like my usual self speaking before thinking. "If you don't want to talk about it I understand."

Slowly walking back to my side. "You remember me telling you about the runner, the one that had never been sick a day in his life."

"Yeah." This wasn't going to be good.

Having to hop up on the bed. "Ron was a marathon runner, he ran years before he and I met. Late November a few years ago he came down with a cough. Me being a nurse I begged him to go to the doctor." She shook her head and laughed. "You remind me so much of him, both of you are head strong and stubborn." I held her hand. "So by the first of the year he and I were at one of his co-workers house for a New Year's party. He started coughing and then there was blood on his napkin. It scared him so we went to the doctor. We were too late."

It was killing me to sit and watch my friend go through reliving this pain. "Annie, I'm so sorry."

Forcing a smile. "Devon it happens. Just like your father and my husband we have to watch as the ones we love go through hell, but everything happens for a reason that reason only God knows. Ron will forever be with me just like your dad will be with you."

"Yeah." Every thought of my father ran through my head. Taking his car out without permission when I was 15. I scooped hay until I could no longer lift my arms above my head. When I was 12, my mom asked me to help in the kitchen. So there I was washing dishes when he came in. 'No son of mine will be doing women's work.' He took the rolling pin from my mom and made me roll that sucker up and down my shins until I thought I wouldn't be able to walk again. Then I couldn't understand, later when an opponent would try to kick at my legs he would draw his foot back in pain. Everything he had ever done for me was to help me.

"Gotta run pumpkin I'll be back." She hopped down off the bed. For the first time in my life I actually love a woman that I didn't have a strong desire to sleep with. I laid back and grinned.

"Alright Hot wheels show me what you got." Tia had me flat on my back on a mat lifting myself up on a metal bar.

"I could do this all day." Honestly it took me a second I haven't done any true working out since the wreck. Tia looked down at me like a person was looking before they crossed the street. So I started to pull myself up with one hand, still no reaction. I upped my game and started to pull myself up and clapping my hands between pulls. Nothing.

She turned away slowly from me and scanned the room. "Hey Quincy come over here for a sec would you please." The guy lumbered his way towards us. He was about my height, the one arm that he did have was large and his bicep looked like a bowling ball hidden under his flesh. "Look here Q I'm going to ask you something but you have to say yes first."

Quincy looked at her then down at me and shrugged his shoulders. "Well, I guess I don't have a choice. I reckon yes then."

Tia looked down at me and I could only imagine the smile that she gave me was nothing nice. "Quincy, it looks like hot wheels here is pretty good at the bar here, so well in fact he said that he could pull up while you're sitting on his chest."

"I never said-"

"Come on hot wheels you said right here to give you a big guy." I was thinking of some horrible come back but she flashed me that smile and I forgot was I was doing. "Q, have a seat."

The big guy looked down at me and smiled. "Now don't go flopping around I just ate."

God help me. The sound from Top Gun soundtrack Take my breath away darted through my head when Quincy sat on my chest. I made no moves to reach for the bar I was finished. "You alright down there, buddy?" Quincy asked.

If there was in oxygen in my body I would told him to get the hell off of me. I saw Tia's outstretched hand lifting Quincy off me. I gasped and relished in the fact that air was finally getting to my brain. "Thanks Q." He walked off. Tia squatted to my side, I couldn't even roll over to face her. "Do you have a death wish?"

"What the hell? I didn't ask for that walking boulder to sit on me- you did that." I was beyond pisst off.

"And I didn't ask you to show off. Hot wheels I'm not impressed. You walk in here, excuse me you roll in here acting like you are so much better than everyone else, you needed to be dropped down a few pegs."

"Who the hell are you to judge me, you don't even know me." I was able to get on my elbows and look at those big blue eyes of hers.

"You just don't get it do you?"

"Get what?"

"These men in here they will never be the same. You with any luck will be walking again going on with your life, but they won't." She pointed behind herself. "Yeah, Quincy can walk and run, but ask him to open a ketchup bottle and we have a problem. Mac, has the best heart of any man I've ever met and standing straight is an everyday challenge." She rolled her eyes in the back of her head and sighed. "I don't need a show off, I need for you to listen and to focus. I respect your drive, but you rush yourself you are going to hurt yourself. So please do us all a favor and slow down."

She didn't give me a chance to have a quick come back she walked over to Mac and started talking. What the hell am I doing? I fell back to the mat and began to lift myself up slower and concentrated on my breathing. I noticed the strain in my bicep and I smiled.

By the time that Annie came to pick me up, I insisted that I push myself back to my room. "Are you sure Devon?" She asked.

"Yeah, I think I can do it." She locked the wheelchair in place as I struggled to stand up.

"You are more than four feet away from the bed. You remember last time you tried to get in the bed by yourself." I had to shove that memory out of my head of taking a face plant to the floor. I was going to walk to the bed.

"If I don't try how will I ever know that I can do it?" Leave no doubt is what my father would tell me before a fight. I lifted my leg and it did what I wanted it to. The cold floor began to bite at my sock feet which gave me more incentive to get to my bed. Before I knew it my thighs were pressed against the mattress and the plastic of the railing. Now the hard part.

"You can do it." Annie's small whisper behind me gave me the touch of strength that I needed to bend my knee. "Devon you got it, come on." Walking my hands to the center of the bed I used every bit of might I had to pull my leg off the floor. My knee was just inches away from cresting the top of the bed. I put my leg back down.

I felt Annie walking up right behind me. "No, Annie I can do it." My words came out angry and harsh. She took a step back in surprise. "I'm sorry." I was in pain and I felt more than stupid.

"Don't be sorry just do it." Looking over my shoulder my little buddy had both hands on her hips and was giving me the look that she probably gives her son when he's thrown in the towel. "Take as long as you need, I'll be right here but you get in the bed."

I gripped the mattress and exhaled. My size 12 foot felt like a ton of lead but I pulled the sucker up. After four more attempts I finally got it on the bed.

"Now use your other leg and push up." Annie coached. I grabbed at the railing at the other side of the bed and pulled my other leg into the bed. "Brace yourself with the other hand and lean back." I did what I was told. I was curled up at the top of the bed. "Relax your legs and push them out." It took me a second to catch my breath but I did it.

Annie came back to my side and pulled the covers over my legs. "Thank you."

"Don't thank me yet. Do it again."

My tiny buddy had turned into Hitler, making me get out of the bed walk to my chair and get into the bed. She and I repeated the process four more times until I nearly wore a path from the door to the bed. "You must really hate me, huh?" I huffed and collapsed in the bed.

"Wrong, I care about you." Pushing my sweaty hair off my face. "Even though, I don't like you fighting, this is what you want to do and I'm going to make sure that you reach your goal. Now get some rest. I still have other folks I gotta see."

"Annie, I really don't know what to say, but I love you." It had been forever since those words had come out of my mouth. They felt clumsier than me tumbling off my tongue. "You know as a friend."

"No need to clarify. I love you too Devon now get some rest, lunch will be coming in a sec."

I closed my eyes and thought of the last time I told someone that I loved them. Was it my dad before he died? I knew it wasn't my mom after she told me about her lies. Honestly, I couldn't remember but the feeling I had for Annie was something I'd never experienced. I wanted to protect her and Luke. Wanted her to never feel any pain.

I must have dozed off when I heard the door to my room open. "I have to stretch you out. Come on." Annie flipped the covers back to show sore and fatigued legs. "I guess when I told you to rest you actually listened."

"How long was I out?" I rubbed my eyes.

She twisted her lips and looked to the ceiling. "About 30 minutes. Didn't want to push you too hard but we have to loosen you up.

Don't want you to catch a cramp or something." She crawled up on the foot of the bed, grabbed my ankle and put it on her shoulder. Annie started to push back on my knee. "Relax Devon, and for the love of all things holy don't push back you will send me flying into next week with this big hoof you got." At a slow pace she inched herself forward. "When it gets unbearable let me know and I'll stop."

It has been over a mouth-damn almost two since I had my knee this high. Annie got my knee at a 90 degree angle and held it there for a beat and she repeated the process with the other leg. "So, I was talking to your doctor and he said that since you are progressing so well you should be released within the next few weeks." All I've wanted was to go home lay in my own bed. Go back to the gym and train but a slithering feeling of fear crept in that I couldn't explain. "Devon, there's nothing to be afraid of."

"I'm not scared." I lied.

"Whatever. You and my son get that same look on your faces when the truth is not in you. You'll be fine and you will still have appointments with Tia."

"Now that's what I'm afraid of." We both laughed.

"Ok, now give me a little pressure not a lot. Don't want my shoulder out of socket." I grabbed the railing on my bed and gave Annie a little push back. Dang, she was strong she dug in. "Promise me when you start fighting again you will be careful and-"

I no longer heard what Annie was saying. The sensation started down my spine then up my legs. Oh God! "Annie-I think you should get up."

She gave me a puzzled look and kept pressing back on me. "Am I hurting you?" She was almost on top of me, pushing up on my parted legs.

"Annie-I think you should move and now." Please God this can't be happening. My whole body was hot. "Annie. Please get up." My belly button was sinking down to my spine and my feet drew cold.

"If I'm not hurting you I don't see why you are whining." Then my friend looked down. "Oh."

"Yeah-oh."

Both of us didn't move as we both stared down at my very large erection. Annie broke the silence and smirked. "Well, that mystery has been solved."

"Annie." I covered my face with both hands.

"Pumpkin, you had a very traumatic hip injury. Doctors thought that part of you would be-well you know-lazy."

"My God Annie lazy!?"

Annie hopped off the bed. "Not lazy but like not functioning properly, but now we see that it works just fine. You should be happy." She was smiling down at me like it was my birthday and she bought me the biggest gift. "All that huffing and puffing you been doing and having a beautiful woman between your legs helped you out." She struck a pose giving me pouty lips as if standing in front of a camera.

"I'm sorry-it was disrespectful." I was probably turned eight different shades of red by now.

"No worries. It's like when you sneeze you can't do it without closing your eyes." Annie took a look behind herself. "Look, I'll leave the two of you alone-I'm sure that you have some catching up to do." She winked.

"Annie-I'm not going to do that here." I half yelled half whispered.

She put her hands on hips and cocked her head to the side making her ponytail flop to the right. "Did you forget that I have a ten year old boy? I wash his sheets and God knows those things looks like he's been eating glazed donuts in the bed. I'm sure after you rub one out you will feel tons better."

Let me die now Lord. "Annie."

"You don't have to thank me. Me love you long time." Giving me her best Asian accent she closed the door.

I sat there feeling like my mom walked in on me jacking off. "Of all the times you had to come around, you come around now." I said down at my crotch.

"Honey who are you talking to?" My door open to my mom and Anthony her new husband and just like magic the tent in my sheets deflated.

"What are you doing here?" It was more of a demand than a question. I couldn't help but snarl at Anthony with his designer suit and slicked back hair.

My mother pressed her lips together and rolled her eyes. "Devon, honey we came to check up on you. Just to see how you are doing." Her face lite up. "The doctor said that you should be going home soon and I wanted to know if you have come to a decision yet."

"There was no decision to be made mom, I'm staying here."

"Devon, please try to be respectful." Anthony stepped forward.

"And who the hell was talking to you?"

"She's my wife."

"And that's your fault." I turned and looked out the window.

"Devon Lee Hart, now you can throw insults to me all day but don't talk to Anthony like that, he has been nothing but kind to you." She sat on the corner of my bed, which pissed me even farther off. "Without Anthony you would be homeless."

I whipped my head around. "What the hell are you talking about? Homeless."

Anthony came to my mother's side and the two held hands. "He has been generous enough to pay your rent and utilities since you been in the hospital. What did you think that they just pay themselves seen you've been here? He even had someone to come and clean and dust the place."

"You've been in my apartment?"

She stood up with a shot. "I didn't raise you to be this ungrateful Devon." She threw both hands in the air. "Is that all you can say? Your step father-"

"I don't need a step father-I'm a man thank you." Looking over at Anthony who was as still as a statue. "Thank you; once I get out of here I will pay you back everything I owe. Now if the both of you don't mind I need to get some sleep-it's been a crazy day."

They both looked at each and by the way they gazed into each other's eyes, I knew my day was going to get even crazier. "We think its best that you come down to Atlanta with us. You can work for my company. You will have full benefits out the gate, vacation time-" I gave my mom's husband a blank stare as he spoke. What in the world gave him the impression that I needed to work for him?

"Anthony, look man I appreciate the offer and everything you've done but my home is here." The man looked at my mom and hunched his shoulders, probably internally relived that his grown ass step kid wouldn't have to live off of him.

"Devon, there is one other thing that I would like to discuss with you."

This day just keeps getting better. "What mom?"

I saw her squeeze Anthony's hand as if trying to draw strength from it. "Anthony and I have decided that we are going to sell the farm."

Everything in the room seemed to tilt and shake itself out. For a second there I felt my heart stop beating and there was no air in my lungs. "What about Randle where is he going to go?" He is one of the farm hands that stayed around the property after my father passed.

She smiled, how the hell can she be smiling right now? "Anthony gave him enough money and a nice place in East Tennessee closer to his family." She huffed. "Devon, the place is old and too big for Randle to handle by himself. We were planning to give the money to you after we sell it." She was talking like I'd won it. The farm was already mine.

"I'll fight it. I'll fight you both in court for it, you can't sell the place." I was fighting tears now and my voice had raised several octaves. "Don't do this."

Anthony put his hand on my shoulder. "Son, it's already in motion. It's to be auctioned off in the morning."

"I'm not your son and get your hand off me. I have a father." I shouted. "Both of you get the hell out of here now!"

My door flew open. "Devon, you okay I heard shouting?" Annie darted passed my mom and Anthony to my side. "Are you okay?"

"Nothing that a kick in the pants wouldn't fix." My mother said, starting for the door. "Devon, I know that this is going to be hard, but you have a place to stay in Atlanta." She looked back up at Anthony who was straightening his tie. "After this month, Anthony will stop paying your bills." And without a goodbye they left.

"Are you going to tell me who they were and why your blood pressure is through the roof?" Annie had her hand on my wrist and I'm sure my pulse sounded like a drum line.

"My mom and her husband. They are selling the farm that I was raised on-they're auctioning it off in the morning." I felt like I had lost my father all over again.

"Devon, pumpkin I'm so sorry." Annie wrapped her arms around my neck and squeezed.

"There's nothing I can do."

"How much are they selling it for?"

"Right now Annie it could be five dollars or a million. I have no money and my mom's husband Anthony has been paying everything for me. Now I'm in debt to this douche bag. God help me." Scream-run-throw something. All I could do was lie there, in a pathetic heap.

"Well you called on the right guy." I was totally confused. "You called on God. Try talking to him, he'll have the answers for you." She hugged me again. "Devon, you're strong so be who you are strong."

"I don't know how?" I looked down at my clenched fist.

"It's hard, I know. But I'm sure that you can overcome it." She pulled her chair to the bed. "Tell me a time that you were scared."

"Annie, I'm a man and we don't get scared like that."

"Like scared in the ring."

"You mean the cage?"

"Yeah, the cage or whatever. Scared that you were going to lose and get your butt beat but you won, tell me." She scooted closer to me.

"It was this one time. I was fighting out in Florida I was supposed to fight this local dude there, but he came down with salmonella. So not to piss off the crowd and the promoter wanted his return on the event they had me against this Japanese Jujitsu master guy. The dude was shredded. I knew I was going to lose. His form and technic were out of this world.

"Was he a big guy like you?"

"Nope, he was small but that's what scared me. He was quick as lighting. I knew if I got close to him and before I can land a punch the dude would of hit me like ten times."

"So did you take him to the ground?" Annie was on the edge of her seat.

I had to smile at her. "You have been watching MMA?"

"My son loves it so I got see what he's in to. Go on."

"Well, by the end of the second round this dude was prancing around the cage like he had just checked the mail and I'm beating half to death. Then dab in the center of the third I saw my opening, the kid is show boating and playing it up to the crowd. I hit him with a combo and did a spinning kick." I laid back and smiled.

"And then what happened?"

"Broke his jaw and knocked him out cold."

"That's it!"

Her excitement damn near knocked me out the bed. "What's it?"

"Find your opening then use it to your advantage."

"How am I going to do that?"

"Same way you beat that guy. Use your instincts, it as simple as breathing to you. Find your opening, Devon. Got to run talk to you tomorrow."

"You are the best friend a guy could have, you know that?"

"Yes, I do. Look Devon, something that my mom always told me, worrying is like a rocking chair-you're moving but you're not going anywhere. Look got to get the kid, be of good cheer my friend see you in the AM."

The sappy optimism of my buddy was encouraging and it made me feel a mountain size better, I still knew that when I got out of here the farm that I learned to fight at. The place where I milked a cow and chased chickens was going to be a home for some other family. I had to do something with my time. Caren should be here shortly and my whole body began to cringe. I had to make my great escape.

I was pretty proud of myself getting all the to the therapy room/gym all by myself. I didn't get lost one time. I knocked hard on the steel door and waited. Nothing. With the chair it was a struggle to get the door open by myself but I managed. Another small victory. Most of the lights were off and I had to search for the switch and when I did, the room looked exactly how I left it cold and bare.

I wheeled myself over to the thing that with the two rails were that helped you walk. One day I'm going to ask Annie what it's called but for now I'm going to beat this thing. I position myself on one end and locked my chair in place. The rails were bolted to the ground thank God for that and I lifted myself up in the standing position. I saw that trail between the two rails was worn. I thought how many other dudes stood exactly where I was, pushing them to get better. Willing themselves to get out of the position they were currently in. To walk to their loved ones and get back to their normal lives.

"Here we go." I said to the empty room. I held on to each rail and pushed my legs forward. The stretching from earlier helped out a lot. Mental note, thank Annie again for all her help. The small journey was only about as far as one would have to go from their bedroom to their bathroom, for me it was a hundred miles but I pushed ahead.

By the time I reached the end of the bars my hair was plastered to my forehead with sweat and my arms began to wobble, but I made it. Since I've been here I couldn't remember smiling this hard and big. Tiny visions popped into my head, me running again-maybe Annie and I could catch a movie or something. Most of all fighting, the feel and the smell of the cage is calling to me.

Remembering my mom and I having a conversation and me telling her I was a beast and she said if you are a beast why would you want to be in a cage? Wouldn't you want to be free? She made a good point, but none the less I wanted to be back. The sport, my sport was what I lived for and not my mom, the selling of the farm or my stupid therapies would stop me.

"What the hell are you doing in here?" If you would have asked me then the last thing I remember was Tia standing at the door looking pissed off as usual. I was in the middle of twisting around to go back to my chair, to be honest she startled me and I lost my balance. My big foot, or what Annie calls it my hoof got caught up in the mat and I tried to brace myself.

I heard my head crack the metal bar as I went down and the snap of my arm as I hit the floor. On my side I saw Tia's white Nikes running towards me. I imagined myself looking like a cartoon with the little birds whistling above my head. Yeah, that's all folks.

CHAPTER 5

"Mom is he dead?"

"Luke stop that, he's not dead."

I opened my eyes and like the movie Ground Hog's Day I was back in my room. Head pounding behind my eyes. "Annie?"

"Devon, my God." When I was able to focus she had Luke by her side looking down at me. "What in the hell were you thinking?"

"Mom, no bad words."

"Hell is not just a word it's a place." She corrected.

The ten year old looked up to his mother. "You don't say that to me when I say it."

"Luke!"

The boy shut it. "How long have I been out?"

Annie glanced down at her watch. "Just about 14 hours."

"What?" I went to push my overgrown hair out of my eyes and the heaviness of the cast caught me by surprise.

"You hit your head and pretty good too. They had to cut your hair and put 10 stiches in your scalp. You fell on your arm and re-broke it and twisted your ankle. Devon what were you thinking?"

That was the question of the hour. "I couldn't just sit or lay here. I had to do something." The excuse was lame I knew.

"Do you need me to bring you coloring books or cross words puzzle. Devon you could of killed yourself in there. Thank God for Tia."

"Yeah, if she didn't barge in there and scare me half to death I wouldn't be in this position now would I?" I tried to fold my arms but it wasn't working with the cast.

"Don't you go blaming her for your screw up." She pointed. "You did this to yourself and now instead of being released next week you have to monitor that head injury." She shook her head. "Why Devon you were doing fine."

"You said not to pray and worry *not* pray and don't work out." I smiled.

A flash of fury crossed Annie's face that made any able bodied man run in the other direction. "Do you think this is funny? Hitting that bar you could have lost your eye. You could have hit the base of your skull. Did you know that less than five pounds of pressure to your temple could kill you? And with that big ass rock head of yours you would have been dead before you hit the floor."

"Mom."

"Sorry Luke but your hero here." She waved her hand like swatting a fly towards me. "Is being stupid and he is making your mom very mad right now."

The kid peered over at me. "And you don't really want to see her mad, do you?"

I didn't but I was watching her fury right now. "Annie, I'm sorry."

"Really? You're sorry Devon? I'm sure that you would have been really sorry when their throwing dirt on your casket. Or you would be really sorry if you have to be in a motorized wheelchair from being paralyzed. Try thinking for once, you keep this up and you will never fight again-ever." She looked to her son. "Luke I have to get you to guitar practice. Tell Mr. Devon that you will see him later. Since he's going to be here much-much longer."

Luke waved at me and they headed for the door.

Just like the sad parts in a movie, I began to hear the soft sounds of rain tapping on the window. The tapping fell in time with the slow beating of pain behind my eyes. And just like the storm coming it matched the hurricane in my head. I've done it now, I hit a major setback.

Over the last month my hair had become a bother with the constant pushing it out of my eyes and off my face. Without a mirror I knew for sure that I was scalped. My left arm, my good one touched the tender spot. I winced at the touch of the gauze pad and drew back a pin prick of blood on my finger. Shit. The cast that seemed too heavy had just come off was now back on and there was 14 hours of my life that I could never get back.

All of a sudden I couldn't get comfortable. Granted there were no more IVs, but I had the monitor on my chest that was a bitch when I shifted, grabbing and tugging at my chest hair. What the hell was I thinking? What possessed me thinking that I could walk again? I prayed for sleep that never came that night. The rain was the only sound that I could hear and the chatter of nurses-walking and talking. Half of them talking about meaningless crap. Boyfriends, Sons of anarchy and buying some more scrubs. For whatever reason, the man upstairs deemed their lives more important than mine. I was a good person-scratch that I am a good person and in a blink of an eye I have been reduced to a lump of flesh that had to get mentally prepared to take a piss.

Seven weeks-seven long weeks and I could count on one hand all my so called friends that said had my back that never came to see. My mom who only came to deliver bad news, my trainer that had all but given up on me. The storm outside and the one inside of me began to rage. I hated them. Not because they didn't love me or care. I hated them because they were right. My mom knew that I would be nothing from the time I was born. Just some cum stain that could never be washed away in her life. Jerry, couldn't waste his time on some has been. He had to move on-trying to find the next big thing.

I was nothing. All I could do was put my head in my hands. Not used to the weight of the cast I slammed the cast into my face. I would have loved to say that the tears came because of the possible broken cheek bone, but I would be lying. My outer body was dead and my inner was dying slow.

"Devon, are you going to talk to me?" Annie stood at the foot of my bed the next morning, with that messy ponytail sitting on top of her head. "I was thinking maybe you and I can cruise the hallway, you know get you some exercise."

"I can't walk." The lack of sleep mixed with my screw the world attitude made my only friend eyes widen.

Taken a small step closer. "It's just a minor setback Devon. Besides it was your arm and your ankle was just sprained we can take it easy." She forced a weak smile.

"I'm fine Annie." I paused and finally looked at her. It seemed I had been staring out the window all night. Watching how the storm had left broken branches from last night and now how the sun was back and bright. Why couldn't I change like that? "Did you need anything else?"

"Don't do this."

"Annie, not in the mood today. Just want to be left alone, okay." I huffed and twisted the bed sheets in my unbroken hand.

Out of the corner of my eye, Annie stepped closer and rested her hand on my ankle. If I had any energy left I would have jerked away. "Don't give up and don't push me away."

"There's nothing to give up-I don't have anything! When I get out of here I won't have my apartment. My mom is selling my farm. I don't have legs and I don't have a job. I have nothing, there's nothing left to give, Annie don't you understand that!?" I was screaming at the top of my lungs. My left hand began to burn from gripping the cover so tight. "I have no one. No one. I have laid here for weeks and people that I have trained with for years haven't even called to check and see if I was alive. I could of dead that day and not one person even cared enough to see if I was okay." Annie looked to the floor. "Just go."

"Devon." She pleaded.

In that instant if I had something to throw I would have. "Get out." I barked.

Annie nodded and walked backwards out my room like she was afraid to turn her back on a savage dog.

There was no excuse for my behavior, but justification was human nature right? Annie deserved to have good people surround her, not some washed up wanna be fighter. My smile was weak when I thought it through. Annie needed someone that was good, right? Not me-I'm nothing.

I didn't see her for the rest of the afternoon and it was for the best. I must have nodded off when I heard the soft knock on the door. "I'm here to take you to therapy." Annie had the handles of the wheelchair in a vise grip.

"I'm not going."

Her posture slumped. "Devon that is the only way that you are going to get better. Please."

I knew I must have looked like a spoiled fourth grader. I folded my arms and looked out the window in defiance. "Could you please leave now?"

"I thought you were a fighter. You have to fight through this Devon, don't let this beat you."

"What the hell do you know about fighting? You allow your son to get the shit kicked out of him at school. You put up with some asshole touching and grabbing at you. You don't know anything about the sport so if you don't have an idea about a subject keep your mouth shut."

I heard her intake of breath and the slow release. "Devon, I know that you are angry but don't take it out on me." Her words were barely audible from the quivering in her voice. "Just let me help you."

"I don't need your help. I will be out of here in a week or so and you won't have to bother with me."

"You're not a bother Devon you're my friend."

"You are horrible at picking friends. Annie if you don't leave now, I will talk to the head nurse and have you removed."

I watched as the only person that gave a crap about me, the only person that kept me sane in this place seem to shrink in front of me. She left the chair in the middle of the floor and walked out of my room without a word or a second glance. Annie was stubborn, but I hoped that this would finally push her away from me. Concentrate on other patients that needed her help. I was a lost cause.

Lunch was served and I ate the crappy fruit salad and what past for steak. My door opened and every nerve in me went on high alert I was ready to attack.

"Hi, Annie told me that you wouldn't be coming to therapy today." Tia stood in my room-minus the scrubs she looked like just another beautiful woman walking in the mall.

"Wasn't up to it." Giving her the hardest stare that I could come with.

Sliding her fingers in the pockets of her scrubs she walked to my side. "Um, I really don't know how to say this but…"She bit at her bottom lip and her cheeks looking like that were on fire. "But I missed you today, Devon."

It was the first time that she ever called me by my name, and the sound was so sweet to hear.

"I usually don't do this but um…do you want to go somewhere….alone?" She looked around my bare room and smiled. "I mean if you are up to it."

My eyes narrowed. "Why?"

She giggled into her hand. "Have you ever thought that I want to get to know you better?" She looked at the door. "Maybe this was a bad idea." She started to back pedal out the room.

"No-I mean. Wait."

Tia paused with her hand on the door knob. "God, I'm coming off so forward. I just figured you hated being stuck in this room all day and maybe you and I could you know." My mind went to every far off place imaginable. Her on her back or me underneath her. Me behind her exploring what lies under those scrubs. Finally finding out what my name sounds like when she climaxes. I wanted her to scream my name, right now if she screamed hot wheels it would of tore me up.

She continued to stand there biting that bottom lip, me envying her teeth and her tongue. Giving anything to switch places. Wanting to taste those pouty pink glossed lips for myself. It had been so long since I had a woman. Just the thought of it was killing me. Now knowing that all my equipment worked, it gave me a surge of energy. "I guess." I tried to sound relaxed as if the thought of her and I alone didn't do anything to me.

"Great. Look, I know that you want to change. There is a pair of jeans and a sweatshirt that I have from lost and found that I'm sure that you can fit." Tia put her hands together in front of her face in excitement. "I'll be back."

Did she just skip out of here?

With a little tugging and a lot of pushing I got the jeans on. Which to my surprise fit, the sweatshirt that read VANDY was a little snug around the shoulders but I could live with it. I was finally outside. Not in the hallway or the breeze way but out in the air. Tia pushed me through the elevators to the hospital lobby to her car. With the gentleness you would have with a kitten she helped me into her Honda Accord.

Then silence.

I have never been the guy that asked how your day at work was or what do you like to do. I knew it was business time with Tia. She had changed clothes also, she was wearing the oversized Batman shirt and a pair of skinny jeans that let my mind wonder what was underneath them.

"So where are we going?" Rubbing my sweaty palms on my second hand jeans.

"Somewhere where the two of us can be alone." She cooed.

In laymen terms somewhere where no one can hear us enjoying each other. I couldn't help but smile. All that time she was being an ass and finally she recognized the man that was before her. Before I could get a thought out of what her breast would feel like in my mouth she was pulling up on the e-brake.

I peered over the dash and there was nothing but water in front of us.

"A buddy of mine owns this land. She won't mind if you and I have lunch out here." She hopped out of the car and retrieved the chair and proceeds to wheel me down to the dock. Lifting me out of the chair and lowering me to a waiting paddle boat. "You can swim can't you?"

"I was a lifeguard for about four summers as a teenager." I smiled and she smiled back.

With my arm in the cast I offered to help her paddle, but the independent woman that Tia is she declined my help. We made it to the center of the lake in no time. The ducks bobbed in the water as if we didn't existent and the sun sat on me and I welcomed the heat. Not like the artificial shit that pumped through the vents at the hospital, but the natural stuff that warmed my body. I stretched out and welcomed the warmth and the glow that it cast on the both of us and the water. "So." I said.

"So." Tia replied. I watched as she put her hand in the clear water and rub her hands together. "Do you like it out here, because I love it?" Smiling at me. That smile and that dimple was killing me. I wanted to touch her features. I waited for my opening, waited to get the right signal for me to make my more.

"It's beautiful but it doesn't compare to you." I heard birds laughing on the shore. Yeah, it was corny but hell she invited me out here.

Staring deep into my eyes. "Yeah." Like she caught a thought. "Do you want to come and sit by me?"

That's what I had been begging for this whole trip. I balanced myself in the tiny boat, hunched over thinking I could make the few steps to her. I looked at her smiling face which morphed into a snarl. I felt her push, then the ice cold water that was an anchor.

Instincts took over and I flapped my arms to get to the surface. Through blared vision I saw Tia begin to paddle away. "What the hell?"

"Glad I got your attention." She said pulling the ores handles back into the boat. "Are you ready?"

I kicked with everything that I had. "Ready for what?" I spit out lake water.

"Ready to tell me what happened that night." Tia spoke as if talking with girlfriends over coffee not watching me drown.

"You know what happened, you said so." I screamed out in a panic as my cast started to weight me down.

"I want to hear it from you. And the more and more you stall-I'll start to paddle away. Deal?"

"Do I really have a choice in the matter?" She put her hands on the ores. "Okay, okay, okay what do you want to know?"

"Everything." She said with her arms folded.

That whole night ran across my mind in flash. Trying to put my words together and swim with a broken arm was taken its toll. "Shit, okay. I was driving and I-"

"I know that part."

"You said everything." I watched as she put her hands on the ores and pushed forward and pull back away from me.

"Don't be a smartass-go on."

"I was coming home. It was early like 10 am or something and there were these kids." I paused remember I just hung out with Henry my sparring partner. He and I hit a club that night. There was this little red head that couldn't keep her hands off me. I remembered the smell of her hair and how she moaned when I had her hunched over some guy's car in the parking lot. I thought how mad he was going to be when he saw how her nails dug into the paint when she came all over my junk.

Henry let me crash at his places and I was going home. "Go on." Tia shouted.

"I wasn't driving fast. I know I wasn't. Out the corner of my eye the kid's ball goes bouncing into the street. I swerved."

"Then what happened?" I was watching my cast melt in front of me and I started to panic. "Focus, hot wheels. Tell me what happened."

"The kid he didn't see me but I saw him. He ran right in front of my car and I turned the wheel and I-"

"Tell me." Tia shouted threating to row farther away from me.

"I couldn't hit him so I went into the other lane. You happy now? I ran into another car."

"Hell no I'm not happy-tell me how you feel."

"I'm cold and wet. Let me get into the boat." I reached out and she rowed one stroke away from me.

"Not now then. How did you feel?"

"Like good and bad at the same time." My legs had grown tired of kicking trying to keep my heavy frame above water.

"Why bad?"

"I don't know."

"You know." Rowing away from me. "Tell me."

"Fine. I wish I would have hit the kid." There it was. The thought and the feeling that I have been holding for seven weeks was out there. My words floating around in the universe doing a better job than me staying above water. "If I would have hit him I wouldn't be this way. I would be walking and training."

"But he would be dead." With two easy strokes she was at my side. Tia's hand was out stretched to me. She bent at the knees to pull my wet body back into the body. I lay there heavy breathing my upper body face down in the boat-my tired legs still in the lake.

"You must think I'm an asshole." I panted.

"Nope, just think you are a human that's all."

Tia made me walk back to the car, the jeans heavy with lake water sloshed as I half limped back to her Honda. "Why are you looking so mad for? My car is going to smell like duck shit. Put your seat belt on."

All I wanted to do is get the hell away from her. There was a time that I could have jogged all the way back to the hospital, now I was lucky I made it to her car without passing out. "Fine you win. You finally broke the big bad guy." I said looking out the window.

"Ahh, look at you all butt hurt and feeling sorry for yourself. Get over it-move on. The whole time you've been in the hospital the sun still came up and went down. Nothing on the outside of the hospital has changed. You have so adapt." Tia rolled down her window and the smell of her hair filled the car.

"Damn, why do you have to be such a…"

"Say it!" She slammed on the brakes and I nearly went through the dashboard. "Just say it Hot Wheels." Jamming the car into park and twisting over in her seat to look me dead in the face. "I can see the word bouncing around in that big head of yours. Say it call me a bitch, I know you want to you."

The word really hadn't crossed my mind. "I was going to call you an asshole." She rolled her eyes at me and put the car back into drive. "I wouldn't call you that, that's not the type of guy I am. But if you would try to really get to know me you would know, instead of pushing me into a lake."

She didn't say a word for a long time as she continued to drive. "Why the hell would I want to get to know you? I already know you well enough."

"Whatever."

"I know that you are scared and fear brings out the true character in a man." Turning the wheel I could see the hospital in the distance.

"Just take me back to my room."

"You act all big and bad but all you are is a scared little boy."

She was right and I hated it. "I'm a good person and-"

"Yeah so good the only person that treated you with respect and kindness you talk to her like she has a tail." God, Annie. "Don't look all surprised. When you didn't come to class, I ran into her and she was all upset. Calling you a jumper."

"What I wasn't going to jump out of a window or anything."

"No dummy. In the medial field we call people like you jumpers when they jump right out of their own life. Killing themselves, like making themselves dead to everyone around them. She's scared for you. Annie said that you were jumping out of her life and it scared her. Thought you had really given up." If guilty was measured in currency I would be a rich man. "Just like I thought you have nothing to say do you?" She was right as she parked in the same spot that she pulled out of in the staff parking.

"If you think I'm such a bad guy why even take the time to go through all of this?" I threw my hands around. Looking at the completely dissolved cast. "Were you trying to drown me?"

Tia hunched her shoulders. "One I did all of this to wake you up and two if I were trying to kill you it would be bloody and slow." She leaned in, inches from my face.

"Would it creep you out if I told you that I'm kinda got turned on by that?"

"Why did you think I said it?"

For the next week I would go to my physical therapy sessions, it was hard I had to admit. Then after that Tia would take me to the lake and make me walk around in the shallow end of course. I was tired and sore but by the end of the week I was walking again.

"Are you serious?" I almost shouted.

Tia shrugged her shoulders. "Yeah, I talked to Annie last night; she said that she is taking the rest of her vacation in California with her son. Said that she just wanted to get away for a while."

I stood on the side of my bed with my discharge papers in my hand. No doubt I was feeling happy that I was getting out of here, but the one person that I wanted to share my happiness with was in California. "When you talk to her could you tell her to give me a call? I miss her." I sounded like a love sick teenager. Annie had stuck by me for eight weeks. Putting up with my attitude and temper tantrums. I guess I had finally done it, finally pushed her away.

"Hot wheels, Annie had more going on in her life than you. I'll let her know that you asked about her." Tia looked around the room and smiled. "You're getting out this is what you been bitchin about for the last few weeks, but I'm happy for you. Take this opportunity to do something big with your life."

All I could do was look into those big blue eyes and wonder, could she be my next opportunity. Forcing a smile on my face. "You're right." Indeed she was but I had nowhere to start this new road that I was on, no direction.

Chapter 5

"Devon, honey there is more food on the stove. You are more than welcome to have as much as you would like." Maggie, my old trainer's wife put her hand on mine and smiled.

I had made arrangements to camp over their place until I knew what I wanted to do with my life. Jerry wouldn't have any other way.

"Maggie, this boy is hungry." Slapping me on my back. "If the wreck didn't kill him that hospital food would have." Jerry laughed and took my plate. Putting some more mac and cheese on it.

There was a look that passed between the old couple, something that I couldn't decipher. "Well, I'll leave you two boys to talk." Maggie wiped her mouth, cleared the table and disappeared down the hall.

My belly was full from the carb overload but it still didn't fill the nagging void inside. "Devon, you can stay here as long as you like. Hell, you were always Maggie's favorite. Just want you to be relaxed here, make yourself at home."

A week before a fight I would bunk with Jerry and Maggie. Jerry is a hands on trainer, making sure that we would eat right, train hard and go to bed early. "I know. I promise you that once I get back on my feet, I'll be out of your hair."

"There is no rush son. Me and your old man were close and if me and Maggie weren't here I know that he would take care of my girls. So you don't worry about a thing, okay? You stay here rent free; you come and help me out at the gym. I'll keep some cash in your pocket."

There was sense of relief that he didn't say anything about me fighting again. Those days were all behind me now. I won't lie and say that I don't miss it; I miss it like I miss my dad. I guess in a poetic sense they both died with me standing outside of the cage unable for me to get in there and save either of them.

That night I stood in my new/old bedroom and didn't know what to do what myself. The bed was perfect; Maggie knew the needs of all of the fighters and purchased an extra-long bed. Just the thought of lying down made me want to run scream out of Jerry's house.

For damn near two months I was laying on my back. I felt phantom pin pricks on my back, like spiders with razor sharp appendages running from the base of my skull to the small of my back. I was tired and the more I stood looking at the mattress that seemed to be calling my name the more I wanted to wonder, could I fall asleep standing up.

"Son, I almost forgot." The bedroom door opened. "I went to your place and got some of your things." Jerry had a boxed tucked under his arm. "I talked to the leasing agent at your apartment and he said that at the end of this month he will have to re-rent your place. So you have just a few weeks. You are more than welcome to use the pickup and if you need some help I'll get the guys to give you a hand."

I must of looked like a fool just standing there nodding. Jerry put the box down at my feet and closed the bedroom door.

I couldn't help but draw the lines between myself Aaron. We both had our lives stuffed into a little box and we were both dead.

Jerry tried to ignore the grumbling of my stomach as we drove in the world's oldest Ford pickup truck. I have rode in this truck, travelled this road more times that I could count but not like this. My head wasn't right; I didn't have the excitement that I once had returning to the gym. I felt bad because I didn't feel bad about it.

It was five am, the time the gym rats would start to scurry up here to hit something and Jerry killed the engine. "You want to sit a second before you go in?"

Getting back on the horse wasn't the part that literally terrified me; it was the people that were watching me. "No better time than the present right? We're here now." In my mind I would like to think that I was half walking half running to my once sanctuary, but reality bites. I still had a slight limp that I was doing everything in my power to hide.

Pushing the glass door open Jerry gave me a nod to take the first step in. Time waited for no man it seemed. Marcus was still at the bag punching away with dreams of being the next Sugar Ray Leonard. Corey was dancing around the ring giving his sparring partner Felix a hard time, as usual.

Less than four months ago I was the man to beat. We were all brothers but I was the big brother. I had earned the respect from every soul in here and I couldn't make eye contact with any of them.

"Devon you can go and into the office and fill out an application." Jerry still standing behind me.

I want to advance further into my second home, but the feeling that I no longer belonged here was crushing me. Like the song when you heard as a kid on Sesame Street. One of things doesn't belong. And I was one of those things.

"Hey slacker glad to see that you up and moving. Thought when they announcement that you were fighting in the King of Cage you ran and headed for the hills". Marcus nearly ran me over, pulling his gloves off by his teeth.

Marcus wasn't as tall as me, he was cut better. Way better than me know. Damn hospital food. "Yeah, I had to bow out try to give you young boys a chance." I smiled.

Patting my shoulder Marcus took a step closer to me. It wasn't even 5:30 and he already smelled like the gym. "Look man, if you need anything-"

"I'm good. But thank you." I cut him off. "Henry here?"

A flash of confusion passed his face. "Bro Hen hasn't been here in months. You should probably call him."

"Ok, ladies enough with the beauty shop gossip. Marcus go hit the bag. Devon come on. Let's get you situated." Marcus put his gloves back on and I couldn't help but watch him trot back and give the bag no mercy.

I felt naked with my gym bag with all my gear in it. I shoved my hands deep in my sweat shirt pockets. Wanting to pull the hood over my head and hide.

Jerry gave me a quick look and opened his office door. "Devon, now if you feel uncomfortable here I know that you would tell me, right."

The sweat shirt that had become my security blanket had now become too hot and sticky. I wanted to rip it off my body. "I'm fine." Taking a seat in one of the two steel chairs. Even with the door closed I could still hear the grunts of my brothers working.

"Now, all I need you to do is just get in where you fit in. Help some of the new guys with their form. And I need you to-"

I couldn't listen to him anymore. I never wanted to disappoint any one in my entire life. If my father could see me now. All hunched over trying to make my 6'5" frame smaller. Twisting my fingers around in my pocket. In my head I had the showdown with my dead father in my head.

"I didn't raise a quitter. Once upon a time you walked in this gym like you owned the place. Now look at you." I see him in my mind shaking his head back and forth so hard, the beer in his hand began to foam. "You look as scared a virgin on her wedding night."

"Dad." I whispered to him.

"D, you better put some strength in your voice when you talk to me. Talk to me man to man."

"It hurts. Everybody in here thinks I'm weak."

I could see my old man standing there in his work boots with more dirt on him to pave our walk way. Coming home from working the grave yard shift, tired as all get out. "Let them think you are."

"Devon. Son do you hear me?" Jerry was looking at me the same way you look at an injured animal on the side of the road. But you keep driving, praying that someone would just put the animal out of its misery.

"Yeah. Just thinking of the old man."

Jerry leaned back in the worn leather chair. "Your father, now you talking about a fighter. I've seen him put men out for just looking at him crazy." Jerry shook his head and smiled. "Danny was a good man God bless his soul. And he loved you more than this world. I know that you won't forget your first fight."

My cheeks began to burn. "That was a disaster. I forgot just about everything you and Dad showed me. I was shaking like a leaf out there." Both of us laughed. "I didn't think that I was going to last the first round."

"Yeah, with all that puking you did in the locker room. But you won…you won. It took you two more rounds." He put two fingers up and leaned over his desk. "Just two and you were fighting like your life depended on."

"Hell, dad took off work and invited half the plant there to watch me. If I didn't win he would have killed me." Remembering before they could open the cage door my dad picked me up off the ground and swung me around. He had his chest poked out for weeks after that fight.

"Son, that's where you're wrong, if you would have got the shit kicked out of you that night. Your father would still push passed me and hugged you. That man thought ever move you made was perfect." I could see in Jerry's eyes that we were sharing the same memory of my dad lifting me above the crowd. "Where ever your father is he is smiling down at you, you know that? And you have me and Maggie in your corner."

"Why didn't you tell me Henry's been MIA?"

Jerry shook his head and sighed. "After your accident, he damn near fell apart. He blames himself for your accident."

"Why? He had nothing to do with it. I swerved so I wouldn't road kill a kid. He was at home in the bed."

Jerry gave me a hard stare. "You really got knocked around in that pickup didn't ya?" I shrugged. "You really don't remember do you?" He narrowed his eyes like as if doing so would make and deceit poor out of me."

"I swear." I went back to the night in my mind. "We got smashed at some club, there was this redhead and then. I woke up and went home, right?"

Shifting to his side and slide his truck keys to me. "Go"

Chapter 6

I was several blocks from the gym when it finally dawned on me that I was behind the wheel again. I started to pray that I didn't have a panic attack or come down with some form of PTSD. By the time I got to Amen, I was parked outside of Henry's house. His car was still in the driveway so I knew he was there.

If my failing memory served my correctly, Henry didn't hit the gym till later in the evening when he got off work. I turned the truck off and put Jerry's keys back in my pocket. Its early May the cherry blossoms in his yard were at full bloom. The smell of spring made me want to run like me and Henry used to do.

I rung the bell and waited. I turned and watched kids starting to take their post on the corner waiting for the school bus and then I was feeling a PTSD moment was about to occur, Henry's front door opened.

I looked at my best friend of five years in his eyes. He looked me dead in the face like he had seen a ghost holding his breath. "Hey."

"Um. Hey. Didn't know you were getting out today." Henry stood damn near eye to eye with me. His dark brown skin had a soft sheen of sweat around his collar in his police uniform.

"Got out a few days ago." My hip was starting to hurt a bit, so leaning not on my good leg but not as bad leg. "You gonna invite me in or do you still have company in there." I smiled. I think and again my memory apparent isn't the best but I think Henry and I had gone through just about every unmarried and married woman on this side of Tennessee.

"Nah, come on in." He took a step back and let me enter the house that I have drunk fools under the table in. The house that I have sleighed many a fine women at.

Months ago, if I wasn't training I would make a bee line right to the kitchen grab a beer flop on his couch and talk shop. Now it felt like I was no longer welcome. "So how's it going?"

"Really D? You gonna come in here like that?" I could see his fist ball up at his side and his nostrils flare. We didn't give him the name Ox for nothing.

Putting my hands up. "Bro, I came over here because Marcus said you haven't been in the gym since my wreck." I wanted to add and you never came to see me, but I guessed he and I would swing to that part later.

"There's nothing there for me anymore. I got promoted I'm a sergeant now and my priorities have changed. Why are you really here?"

"Well, because I thought we were friends and friends check up on each other. So I'm here." I walked passed him and sat on the couch. "Now are you going to tell me what I did to you to make you so mad at me?"

He sat across from me and looked me over and gave me a sick smile. "You don't remember?" I shook my head no. "My God, D." I watched as my brother biceps began to swell in his uniform. As if he was going to bust right out of it.

"Hen whatever happened that night we can talk about it."

"There times that I wanted to come to the hospital and see you, you know? But I'd get to the door and I just couldn't do it."

"Bro, if I did something just tell me."

"You cut me out."

"What?" I had no idea what the hell he was talking about. I was forcing every detail of the night in my head and I was drawing up a blank.

"Damn, The King of the Cage, you cut me out." All I could do was shake my head. "We came back here to sleep off the liquor that night. You-"He pointed. "You let it slip that you were going to take Ronnie with you to Vegas as your sparring partner." Henry stood and paced around his living room. "Ronnie, really. I've been hitting mitts with you like forever. Bro you know me, and I know you. I know exactly where you going to land punches and you know were my mitts are. I thought whenever you are I made it we'd make it together."

If I could trade places with my former self from a few months ago I would. Lying flat on my back in gut tearing pain, I would switch places right now if I could. "I'm sorry. I'm a dick and that was a dick move." I shook my head again trying to rattle around any sort of recollection.

"No, I'm sorry. We fought that night." Just then I notice that the lamp the Henry's mom bought him when he first moved into his place wasn't there. Did we break it? And no longer was the coffee table. Damn. "You really don't remember, huh?"

I made a gun with my finger and pointed to my head. "Nothing."

"I kicked your ass too." He smiled.

"Nah, I would have remembered that."

"I told you to get the hell out of my house. We exchanged a few more words and you were gone." He paused and closed his eyes. "Jerry called about an hour later telling me that you got hurt real bad. If I wasn't acting all butt hurt you wouldn't have been on the road that morning."

"I shouldn't been an asshole and picked Ronnie over you." What the hell was I thinking? Ronnie wasn't worthy of tying Henry's laces.

"You forgive me?" My buddy's features relaxed.

"Forgive me?"

"Of course who else is going to listen to my police stories and watch UFC on Saturday nights with?"

We hugged it out.

"Henry, baby you off to work?" A very sleepy and very pretty girl walked out of Henry's bedroom with nothing on but his Tap Out shirt on.

"Dirty dog." I whispered to him.

"Yeah, I was just about to head out. Devon this is…um this is-" He began to snap his fingers like the snapping would make her name pop into his mind.

"Nicole." She said not the slightest embarrassed that she spent the night with a man that didn't even remember her name.

"Sure. Yeah. Nicole this is Devon, my best friend. And Devon this is Nicole."

Nicole's chocolate legs which seemed to go on forever pranced over to me. "Best friend, huh?" She said pressing against my now heaving chest. "Maybe later we can all be best friends."

I couldn't help but give Henry a smile. "Maybe another time baby girl gotta run."

Nicole put her hand over her mouth to conceal a yawn. "I'm patient." And I couldn't help watch those legs go back into his bed room.

"I guess the more things change."

"The more they stay the same." Henry laughed.

He promised that he would stop by the gym after his shift was over and we would talk some more. Henry turned out of his driveway and made the left as I made the right back to the gym. Please don't get me wrong falling back into my best friend's graces was a blessing, but I had one more friend that seemed to be somewhere in California.

"Bout time you get back here, you and Ox make up?" Jerry yelled over at me.

"Yeah, me and that big bovine are back in business again." I rubbed my hands together and smiled. My first smile back in the gym and it felt wonderful.

"Lord God, please hide every woman in this state and all neighboring states from these two idiots on the loose. Amen." Jerry gave up a mock prayer. "Good, now Hart and Ox will be back in my gym and everything will be set right in the world." Jerry began to walk on to the other side of gym and all I could do was follow behind him. "Devon, this is Parker. He just came in here a few weeks ago and I need for you to give him a hand."

I crashed back down to earth. This Parker kid looked like he couldn't fight his way out of a paper bag let alone fight another human being. The kid was scrawny, nothing but bones with a thin layer of the pasties skin as cover. He had to be in his late teens, all goofy looking.

"What you trying to accomplish kid?" Giving Jerry a quick nod letting him know that I had it from here.

"You're in good hands kid." Jerry said to Parker with a wink and he stalked around the gym.

The kid gulped and I saw his very large Adam's apple bob up and down. "I'm… well I want to try and build some muscle up. Starting my senior year in the fall and I just thought I needed to change, you know look like you."

I couldn't help but cut the tough guy routine. "Parker, abs don't just come from the gym they come from the kitchen. Whatcha eaten?"

"In general?"

I rolled my eyes. "Like what did you eat this morning before you came here?" I got on the other side of the punching bag.

His mouth drop. "I'm supposed to eat?"

Lord take me now

I just about collapsed in my bed when I got home. I can't remember being this tired coming home from the gym. Hell, I didn't do anything but stand. Henry came by as promised and we hide out in the locker rooms like we used to and did our score card of every one currently training.

Jerry really had some good up and comers. All parts of me were happy for them, Jerry, my brothers and even Parker. If Jerry produces the next big thing he'll get the notoriety that he deserves. And the already crowded gym would be busting out the seams. That made me smile.

I had a restless and dreamless sleep that night. My legs were throbbing and my feet felt way too big for my body. I felt like I had the flu not the sick feeling but I had the aches all over.

I think I probably dug a permanent grove in the bed from all the tossing and turning I was doing. When morning finally came I was still wrapped up in covers not even catching a bit of sleep. It was Saturday morning and the gym didn't open until 7, so I knew I had a few hours to lay there uncomfortable in my own skin.

I heard the soft tapping on my door. "Come in."

Maggie opened the door slowly and peeked in. "Devon, honey you have a guest waiting for you in the kitchen."

Henry knew better than to come to Jerry's house unannounced. The old man would kill him. I rolled out of bed and took what seemed like a thousand steps back downstairs.

Randle sat at the kitchen table talking to Jerry. My heart sank. "Randle. How you doing?" That was the dumbest question that I could muster up. How well could the old guy being doing? He'd just been let go from the farm that my mother sold.

And just like old Randle he was all smiles. "Fine son and how are you?"

"I'm good."

"Randy was just talking about the farm and all." Jerry was nursing a bottled water in his hand.

I put my head down. "Randle, I'm sorry how things went down. My mom had the farm auctioned off; I thought you'd be in East Tennessee by now." Pulling up a chair next to him.

He still had on his overalls. "That's what I came over here to talk to you about." It took him a moment to pull an envelope out of his pocket and hand it to me.

"What is this?"

Randle looked over to Jerry. "Open it." Jerry said taking a long swig of water.

I tore the large manila envelope and legal documents slipped out in my hands. "Am I being sued or something."

"Forgive him Randle you know he has taken a few bonks on the head." Jerry said twirling his pointer finger on the side of his head to indicate that I was crazy.

Randle shifted in his seat and started. "Your mother did auction off the place." I started to cringe. "But some wonderful woman came back and bought it and paid cash too. And she turned around and gave you the deed to the place." My head was swimming. Who would do this and for me no less? She told me that you would be here, so I wanted you to receive it from me in person. So I guess you are my new boss." Both the older men laughed.

"Who did this?" I was rummaging through the documents.

"Little tiny thing. Oriental gal, ponytail that stood on her head as tall as she was. Cute as a button."

"Annie."

Chapter 7

Jerry already had his keys in his hands before I could ask him. Just with an undershirt and jeans I pulled out the driveway headed to the hospital.

I would have loved to say that I ran to the hospital doors, but it was more of like a skip but it was the fastest that I've gone in a long time.

I came to the nurse station out of breath and then I saw her. Head down looking at some poor bastard's chart, ponytail flopping around. I ran to her a picked her up off her feet, she screamed bloody murder and swatted at my arms. "Let me go you big goofball. Put me down."

I kissed her on the forehead. "Annie, why? Why would you do that? Buy the farm." I was out of breath and my words were extremely loud and choppy. "I treated you so…"

"Shitty, yeah." Annie was pulling at her scrubs getting them back into place from my assault. "First don't say I bought the farm it's like I died or something. Goofball, you're a good guy and everything you did and said I knew you didn't mean. I did it so you can start a brand new life." Annie spotted all the onlookers. She took my hand and pulled me into an unoccupied room. I saw the look on your face when your mom was here the last time. It broke my heart."

"Then I stomped on it when I spoke to you like that. I'm sorry."

She waved her hand. "No worries. I may be little but I'm tough. I knew that you didn't mean it. Besides Luke thinks the world of you and children are great judges of character. Go back to your home, Devon. This place…" She looked around the hospital room. "This place isn't for well people it's for the sick. Go home.

I didn't go home. I took the left made another left through the breezeway and was facing the steel doors. I wasn't seeing Tia every other day anymore, but once a week now. Half a day in therapy the other half in the lake.

But I had to admit it felt great standing pushing the door open instead of having Annie do it or do in a chair.

I totally expected her to be sitting at her desk, face down in a pile of paperwork. Instead her right leg was fully extended above her head. She's a dancer and the thought of that leg being so high up I thought I heard my crotch moan. Tia's left leg planted on the floor and I watched as she struggled for a moment as she raised her body off the ground on to her toes. She's beautiful, I couldn't help but stare. Her right leg was coming down slowly, her shoulders back chin high. I could watch her all day long.

Once her right foot was back on the ground, I heard her take a deep breath and relax her shoulders. She ground her right foot on the mat and began to raise her left leg. Tia's leg wasn't fully extended when I saw her right begin to wobble.

Slamming her left leg down and putting her hands on her knees. "Shit." Then she saw me. "What?"

"You a dancer?" I wanted to look at her in pure astonishment but I'm sure I had my stupid lustful grin on.

Her cute little butt was poking out, when she snarled. "What do you want?"

"Wow, didn't know that you could do that. That's amazing. Were you a dancer or a gymnast? I'm betting dancer you looked really graceful."

"Devon, we are supposed to meet up tomorrow. Why are you here?"

To be honest I truly couldn't remember why I was here. "I guess out of habit. But you looked-"

"Stop!" She put her hand up." You shouldn't be here. Devon, you should go home." Her cheeks were good and rosy. Sure I guess it would take a lot out of you kicking the sky like that but was she embarrassed?"

"Speaking of homes." I smiled. "Annie bought my farm. So I don't have to live with my trainer any more. Isn't that great."

Tia gave me a blank look. "Good for you. Maybe you should go there and celebrate." Her back was tense as she straightened up to stand. On one wobbly leg she tried to walk back to her desk. And I'm using the word *tried* loosely. Tia knew I was watching her as her right leg looked like a flimsy noodle under her scrubs. Over her shoulder, "Devon, just go."

"Not before you tell me why you are so pisst off. I tell you the best news and you act like…"I was getting more and more frustrated standing there talking to her back. "You know what forget it. Bye Tia."

Those strong shoulders of hers slumped and she leaned against the wall. "Yeah, just get the hell out of here." I was no more than a foot from the door when I heard her slide down the wall to the ground.

I wanted to run back to her and drill her till she gave me some answers. I refused to let my mood be dampened by her crazy temper.

I was at Jerry's in no time flat. I tucked my box under my arm, shook Jerry's hand telling him that I would be in the gym this Monday, kissed Maggie on the forehead and waved. I was going home.

Henry came and got me and we rode back to the farm, my farm. "Then she flips out about me being there after I told her that I finally have a place to stay. Man, this chick is crazy." I threw my head back on the passenger side seat, telling Henry about Tia and all her madness."

"Yeah, you really fell and bumped your head." Henry said weaving through Nashville traffic.

"Bro, could you turn that rap shit off or down. I can't even concentrate in being temporarily pisst off." I wasn't really all that mad just a bit disrespected was all.

"Hey respect Tupac." He turned the dial down from 10 to 7. "This is classic stuff we are listening to. And I said, you really bumped your head if you are fazed by some girl that you haven't claimed as one of your victims or is it because you like her and she doesn't like you back?" He looked over to me and stuck his bottom lip out and gave me sad eyes.

"Hell naw I don't like her. I mean I would bang the hell out of her if I was bored and didn't have anything better to hit." That long leg high in the air was damn near begging for me to get in between them.

I heard Henry suck his teeth. "It looks like somebody's got a crush and don't know what to do with themselves. Guaranteed once she lets you hit it you wouldn't be wound up so tight." I saw the wheels turning in Henry's big head. "Matter fact, I was gonna invite this chick over tonight and I'm pretty sure she has a friend. You down?"

Right now all I needed was a woman; no really I needed a girl with no strings attached. I needed to relieve this tension. It's been months since I ate pie. But my heart wasn't truly in it. "I have a thousand and one things to do with the farm. Maybe next weekend or something."

"This Tia girl really got you twisted. She ain't even your old lady and she already got you staying home." I gave him a sharp look and he busted up laughing. "Dude I'm pressing your buttons. I know that you got a load of stuff at the farm. Maybe tomorrow we can move the rest of your stuff over, keep it in the barn."

"Now that is the smartest thing you've said all day."

Henry took the windy dirt road up to the farm house and like a child on Christmas day I sat up in the car seat and watched as my home got closer and closer.

"You coming in?"

"Naw, I told you I got a lady coming over today and I have to wash sheets, if you know what I mean. Did I tell you that she's a pole fitness instructor?" He bit his bottom lip and closed his eyes. "Man, I'm praying that she does tricks on my pole tonight. You sure you don't want to come through. I know that she got a home girl or something."

"I'm good." Henry waited for me to get inside the house before he drove off. Randle kept the place the same. This is the first time since I've been out the hospital that I felt myself breath. Not the gasping for air that I've been doing but really take it all in.

The house looked the exact same way when I left it months ago. Since my father passed and my mom got remarried I would try to check up on old Randle. Always smiling, he'd reassure me that all was well on the home front and to go and do what young men my age did. Party, drink, fight and get some tail. Believe me I did all that and then some.

I took the box up to my old room. Nights when I was so smashed and didn't feel like being alone I would come here and fall asleep. Randle had his own home on the other side of the property and the house was quiet like a church mouse. I never felt alone.

I would have liked to make a list of things that I needed, but the comforts of home was pulling me away from what I needed to do. Fully clothed I just kicked off my tennis shoes and got under the covers and fell asleep.

The next time I opened my eyes the sun had went down and my stomach was thinking that my throat was slit. I didn't grab any breakfast at Jerry's and by the way things looked outside lunch time had come and gone.

The stiffness in my hip and both of my legs nearly brought me to tears as I stood. This has to get better, I thought as I walked in socked feet to the kitchen. Half expecting my dad to be there, with a Miller High Life in his hand. Bitchin about the pitcher of the Atlanta Braves and why the Titans couldn't win a game even if the other team forfeited. I shook my head even though he's dead and gone I could still hear him. I smiled.

I looked around the kitchen and shrugged. I wasn't training anymore so why not? I took out everything I needed for my famous triple decker meat sandwich. I began to cut the tomatoes and wash off the lettuce then the house phone rang.

The kitchen phone buzzed on the wall. "Hello."

"How's our farm doing?" Annie laughed over the phone and I couldn't help but laugh too.

"It's going great boss. How's it going?"

"All is good. Just wanted to check up on you see how you were feeling?"

It felt great to be missed. "Um…all is great. I'm on my feet." I looked down at my socks. "Hey look, I'm making sandwiches tonight if you and Luke want to swing by I have more than enough." Please say yes, please say yes.

"Sorry goofball, I promised the kid that I would watch Guardians of the Galaxy with him. But I'll be down there some time this coming week to check up on you. Don't worry I'll call before I come.

I took the phone away from my ear and looked at it. "What's that supposed to mean?"

Hearing her take a deep breath over the phone. "Devon, the place is yours now. I'm not going to just barge into your house. And besides, I'm sure you want to test out your junk. And your old nurse and her 10 year old may cramp your style."

"You are being ridiculous right now you know that?" I hated to admit I did want to test out my junk. And as heated I was over Tia and her bipolar I wanted to test it out on her. "You and the kid are always welcomed here. If it wasn't for you I wouldn't be standing, for one and for two I wouldn't be standing here in my place." I paused and thought over the last two months. "Did I ever thank you for everything? If I hadn't I want to say it, thank you. You and this." I looked around the kitchen. "Are amazing. Thank you."

"Now look at you being all nice and sweet. No worries buddy, that's what friends do, right? We take care of each other. So keep plugging away at your recovery and I'll talk to you later, have a good night."

My buddy hung up and I ate my sandwich in complete silence. I still had a few clothes here from my hang over days in the closet and drawers. Took a long hot shower and turned in for the night.

I saw myself gripping the steering and in my mind I was trying to be mindful that it was Monday morning and I had to get to the gym and there were nothing but kids in Henry's neighborhood. I was turning the corner and I was doused with anger and grief. I was thinking of something but what it was I couldn't remember. Then I saw it. The ball bounced in the middle of the street and in the second I turned to my right and there he was a little boy. His features at this moment I can't place but his blonde hair was all over the place from playing I suppose.

Maybe 8 or 9 years old without a care in the world just the thought that his ball was in the street. Maybe it was a ball that his parents got him or something. Could be something that an older brother or sister had let him borrow. Who knows? My foot jammed on the brake so hard and fast the thought of my whole foot going through my pick up and stopping like a Flintstone shot across my mind.

But this time the brakes didn't work, the more I stomped the car just seem to accelerate. The kid snatched the ball from the street and looked at it and smiled. Totally unaware that I was coming straight for him in a Ford 150 King cab. All I could do was close my eyes as the truck bounced up and down. Running over the kid, my foot felt like it was imbedded in the trucks under carriage.

I heard sirens-a woman running out of her house, I could only guess it was his mother. Screaming at the top of her lungs. "My baby, my baby you killed my baby." My truck slow rolled to the curb and by then the whole neighborhood had come out of their homes to look at the guy that killed a child.

The boy's mom came around to my side of truck and bang on the window. The mother of the boy wasn't his, but my own. Banging on the truck window. "It should have been you!" She screamed. My mother's brunette hair was in a braided ponytail that hung low down her back, the way she used to wear it when I was a kid. "Devon, you should have died. You should be under this truck."

I looked around through the windshield and the neighborhood was watching. Housewives still with their bathrobes on and curlers in their hair, covering their gapping mouths. Men half dressed, some still holding shaving razors in their hands. Other with car keys dangling from their finger trying to start their day but it had been permanently marred by me. The wrong person under my truck. Even Henry came around the corner, standing on the sideway, looking at me totally disgusted. All eyes were on me.

"I'm sorry. I didn't mean…"

"Son, you got to wake up." Randle had a hold to both my shoulders and shook the hell out of me till my eyes opened. "I can hear you hollering clear cross the property. You all right?"

I didn't kill the boy. He was alive, more than likely chasing a ball in the street. "I'm good." Sunshine engulfed my room. I had to shield my eyes from the window. "What time is it?"

Randle gave me another look and stood up straight. "Half past noon. Boy, you done slept the better part of the day away. Now get your sorry tail up, got a stale pot of coffee down stairs with your name on it." Without further words, Randle walked out my bedroom and down the hall.

I hadn't had a nightmare like that since I was in the hospital. I thought all that was behind me, but I knew different when I tried to stand up and my leg threatened to give out on me. One day at a time, right?

I had to grip the railing coming down the steps, Randle looking out the kitchen window. "I never goes away." It took a second for me to pick up what he was talking about. I took a seat at the table and waited. "I was 19 years old." Randle closed his eyes, I guess trying to recall the memory or push it away. "It was August of 1970 it smelled like hell over there. Some nights I could still hear the screams of the men that lost their lives over there in that country." Randle continued to gaze out the window. Knuckles turning white from gripping the sink. "Nothing to be shamed about, it gets better but it never really goes away." I knew that Randle was in the Vietnam War but this is the first that he ever talked about it.

Finally turning to me wiping from what I believed to be sore hands on his coveralls, he smiled. "They didn't have a name for it then, but I think they call it PTSD. Boys came back broken. More ways than you can imagine." He paused. "Get the help you need." He turned his back on me and walked out the back door.

I struggled to stand and watched my father's best friend walk back into the barn.

Randle wasn't lying about how bad the coffee was, so after only two sips I poured the rest down the sink. After a shit, shower and shave I took my dad's Silverado out and drove. With no particular destination, I just need to get away.

Trying to stir up the mental image of the cupboard in the kitchen, might as well stop at the store and pick up a few things. I was only a few blocks from Miller's a local corner store that my father used to go to when he was kid.

"What up Mill?" I shouted to the kid over the register. Seth was probably the great-great-great grandkid of the original Mr. Miller that opened the store forever go.

Snatching the earbuds out his head. "Devon, bro is that you?" Seth ran around the register and gave me a hug. "Man, I heard about your accident." He looked me up and down. "Sorry, that it happened to you, you gonna get back in the cage soon?" The young man that was just a few years younger than myself put his fist up and danced around.

"Naw, done with that part of my life, but if you want to hit the bag around I'll still be over at Jerry's."

Seth stopped dancing and gave me a look like I told him that I once was a woman. "Why, you were the best?" Seth walked slowly back around to the register and sat back on his stool.

I hunched my shoulders. "The wreck messed up my leg pretty bad. I'd rather train, you know?" The words fell out of my mouth like they were true.

"Nope, I don't know what you mean." Seth leaned over the counter between the penny candy and headache medicine. "Look, word on the street is that Michael has your invite to the King of the Cage." He shook his head. "That second string bastard is bragging like he really did something. Only reason he's even fighting is because you won't"

"I can't." I corrected.

"Whatever, on your worst day you would mop him up."

Months ago, I would have totally agreed with him, not today. Michael would probably lay me out right about now. "Well, that is something we will never find out. Look Seth let me pick up some stuff and get out of here."

Seth waved me off and put his earbuds back in and went back to what he was doing before I came, which was probably nothing. I went to the back of the store and got anything better than that store brand crap that Randle insisted getting.

It felt like a lifetime since I've been in here last, it had only been a few months.

With an arm full of stuff that I really didn't need, I stopped cold. Seth's reaction time wasn't like mine, but with my leg in the condition that it was in I couldn't get to him in time.

The double barrel sawed off shot gun was in Seth's face before I could say rear naked choke.

"Dude, I'm not playing empty the register and NOW!" The gunmen said. And all I could do was stand in the middle of the aisle with a ton of crap in my hands. Was this asshole jacked up on something, if so he could be jumpy? The shotgun was pointed dead center of Seth's chest and trying to stand still was killing my balance. I was feeling the jar of jelly begin to slip. My mouth opened to say something like please don't shot a cripple guy the jar and all its contents were on the floor.

The gunmen turned quickly and let a round loose. I hit the floor. Laying on glass and jelly. I have went rounds with pure meatheads, survived a car wreck and a crazy chick named Tia and now I was going to get blown away from some crack head.

"Devon?" Great killed by a crack head that's a fan. I lifted my head up with jelly on my cheek. Removing his ski mask, the face was oddly familiar but I couldn't place him. "Devon, what the hell are you doing here?" I strained to look up; the gunmen put his gun on the floor and helped me up. "Devon, it's me. Ed…Eddie Kingsford. Remember we used to train together."

I know that my memory was shot and I was out of commission for a few months, but the Eddie Kingsford was one of the best amateur welterweight fighters that I've ever meet. What stood before me was just a shadow of the man I used to know. He had a three day old bruise on his left jaw and was skinny as a rail.

"You know this guy?" Seth had his own shotgun in his hands.

"Whoa, this is turning into the OK Corral. Seth put your down." Turning back to Eddie. "What the hell? Why aren't you somewhere else, like not knocking over a mini-mart?"

His body sunk in like if he were a turtle I wouldn't be able to see his head. "Got into some trouble. But you look good….concerting all that's happened to you." Life as a fighter you go into the cage with injuries and you come out with some new ones. This guy looked like he was in a continuous battle.

I took Eddie under his arm and ushered him to the front of the store. "Seth, I'll come back and clean this mess up." Seth agreed as his heart rate went back to its regular rest rate.

Once outside in the parking lot, it took everything in me not to grab Ed by his neck. "Dude you could of put a hole in me." I made a very large circle in the middle of my chest. "What in the hell are you in to?"

Ed shifted to one leg and then the other, until finally leaning against my dad's pick up. "I needed the money." He cried. "I took the gamble. Dude said he was going to lay out in the second round and I had big money on it." He shrugged and put those bony fingers back into his worn jean pockets. "I guess the dudes pride got in the way and I wasn't prepared. He put me down in the third." Eddie cursed. "I got into a bind and I needed a way out. I just dug the hole a hell of a lot deeper.

In the fighting game there are sharks out there to prey on the weak, and not just in the ring. They eat you alive. "Who's the shark?"

Ed shook his head, "Not your problem."

"You're damn right it's not, but I'm curious."

Ed wiped sweaty palms on his nasty jeans then wiped his eyes. "Barry Washington."

Oh damn.

Chapter 8

"So you want me to do what?" Henry paced in my parent's kitchen going over Ed's dilemma. "I just can't go in there and arrest this guy. I don't have any proof of any wrong doing.

Eddie had his head down in my last beer. "Last week I went to my son's school and one of Barry's guys has his arm around my boy, walking him to the car." He wiped his tears. "He's threating my family, man. Ox we've been friends for years. I just need a little help man please."

Henry finally sat down and exhaled. "Look, if you can get Washington on tape any sort of proof then I can rock with that. Right now, there is nothing I can about. I'm sorry." Both men looked at me as if I had some answers which I didn't.

"Ed, you can stay here for the night and we-"I looked to Henry. "Will try to figure something out."

Ed twisted in his chair. "Naw thanks Devon but I think that I'll just go home." Ed stood and made his way to the door.

"Wait, at least let me give you ride." Henry said.

"Don't worry about it; I'll need the time to think. Besides, Jennie and my son are at her mother's house in North Carolina. Don't worry you guys, I'll be fine." Then he was gone.

"You know this is garbage right?"

Henry's mouth opened. "What do you think I can do, huh? Just walk up in Washington's operations making accusations. I'll be fired and on Washington's shit list. D, good cops and bad have been trying to stick it to Washington for like forever. The man washes his hands of things and leaves not one trace. He's a ghost."

Maybe because I was bored or maybe at this particular moment I have nothing to fight for, but I wanted to be in Eddie's corner on this. "We'll find a way out of this."

Henry twisted his lips at me. "You keep saying we, do you have a mouse in your pocket or something? I will do what I can. I know that your memory is shot to hell, but we haven't seen Eddie way before your wreck."

"What happened to him? He looks like he's been living off meth and water for months."

"Heard he was messing with some enhancement drugs that weren't any good. Then he started owe everybody around town. Jerry banned him so he starts taken non sanctioned fights, then the bottom fell out."

"And he landed right into Washington's lap."

"Pretty much. Devon, please don't start taken in strays. You get fleas that way. Leave Eddie alone, the guy is like the plague. Just his presence only will destroy you and you are still on the mend."

"Hen, you are Johnny on the spot." Switching gears. "So how was last night?" Since all I got last night was the world's worst nightmare.

Big smile graced my buddies face. "Look I called her, right. She says some stuff like, 'Well, I promised my home girl that I was going to go out with her. And blah, blah, blah'. So I say what about you and your friend come over my place, have a few drinks maybe a little pre-funk before you two hit the club."

"Got'em." I laughed

"Got'em like Jordan's on sale. Man, they come over there and looking all cute and what not. Dude, they were baking pies faster than I could eat them."

"You bang?"

He put up two fingers. "Yes, both of them…twice."

"Lucky bastard."

"You were invited. I told you that you could have come through but noooooo, you want to sit at home and think about Tiffany."

"Her name is Tia and I wasn't thinking about her. I was tired. Bro don't you realize that I had a very traumatic experience. An experience that could of left me paralyzed or worse." I turned my head.

"You must have forgot who you are talking to that pity shit don't work on me. Now next time I tell you to bring your scrawny white ass to get some, you just tell me what time, okay."

We both stood from the table, Henry getting up a bit faster than me. "I got it. Whatever you can do for Eddie will be greatly appreciated."

"I'll put my fellers out. If I hear anything I will let you know." We walked to the door, and I had to jump back from Henry turning around so fast. "Another thing, please wash that shirt. It's making me want a PB&J something awful"

I looked down and I was still covered with jelly from this afternoon. I was going to tell him to kiss my ass, but Henry was already in the car…laughing

---

"Come on Parker get your ass off that mat. Get your feet in the diamond position. Come on, kid you're killing me here." I'm sure he said something like I'm trying but his mouth piece made his words all grumbly. It was damn near painful to watch. "Get back in to his guard Johnny, let's do this again."

"Damn, Ike Turner. Keep pushing the kid he's either going to kill someone or himself." Henry said carrying his gear in.

I looked at the clock. "Bro, you playing hooky from work? It's not six yet."

"Changed my shift. Thought I needed my time in the gym and keep an eye on you."

"On me?"

"Yeah, on you." He pointed. "I need to get you back in shape."

"For what? I'm done Hen."

Henry took a look at my body. "You got to get back into fighting shape even if you aren't fighting; I have a reputation to up hold. And if I'm going to try and get you laid sometime in the near future, that gut is not going to work." My red and black Affliction shirt was a bit snug around the midsection. "So instead of the beating the kid up, what about you and me play a bit."

Parker came up behind. "Do you think you can win?"

I smirked. "Against this loser, I will destroy him."

Henry was only using 10% speed and strength on me but he kicked my ass all over that mat. He put me in every submission hold in the book. I've never tapped out that much in my life. Any other person would have been embarrassed, I was just lucky to be alive against the Ox. "You had enough?" Henry grunted in my ear. I was winded from the D'Arce choke hold he had me. I had to tap out. Henry pulled me off the ground. "Good job, we'll rock out tomorrow."

"That was awesome." Parker sounded way too excited to see me get my ass handed to me.

"Yeah-awesome. Shouldn't you be in school are something." Rubbing my neck.

"It's an in service day so no. I get to hang out with you guys all day." He smiled and I didn't.

"Now your turn." His smiled vanished. "You are going to learn to do a triangle choke before this day is done, understand?"

"Yes, sir."

"Go stretch I'll get Johnny to help you." Johnny had probably left hours ago, but I needed the excuse to stretch my legs before I caught a cramp.

"Umm. Are you going to move or am I going to have to make you?" I heard the small voice come from the other side of Henry.

Annie still in her scrubs with Luke in tow. "Annie what are you doing here, you shouldn't be here."

"Your friend mule here wouldn't let me get in." Rolling her eyes at Henry.

"Friend of yours?" Henry's eyebrows raised and I knew exactly what he was thinking.

"Yeah, watch the kid I have to speak to Annie." I yanked Annie and we went right into the locker. Some guys were in there half naked and Annie shielded her eyes. "Out now!" I growled. After the last guy walked out with a grumble. "Why the hell are you here you can't be here."

She put her hands on her hips and she and her high ponytail flopped to one side. "Why because I'm a girl?"

"Exactly, you can get hurt in here. There's a ton of testosterone fueling this place and I don't want you to be here. Some ass hole may start something and I'll have to finish it."

"So that's what that smell is? I thought it was corn chips and butt."

"Annie."

"Look, Luke had one of those stupid days off and I couldn't find a sitter so he and I have been cruising around. Thought you'd be here so we dropped by is all. Me and the little monster can be on our way, no big deal."

She turned. Annie, I'm not trying to hurt your feelings, it's just this place." I exhaled. "This place some of the guys don't have filters here. They just come straight out there mouths with some foul stuff and you are too good and too attractive to be in here."

"You think I'm attractive?" She pinched my cheeks. "Flattery will get you everywhere. Look tomorrow dinner either it be at my place or yours but you need a home cooked meal. And I will not take no for an answers."

Annie walked out and all the cat calls and the whistles started. "Hey!" Henry's voice boomed and bounced off the walls of the gym. "Show this young mother some respect, her son is here for Christ's sake." Everyone turned back to what they were doing. Henry stuck his hand out. "Let's start over. Everybody calls me Ox, what's your name." I had to stop this before it starts.

"Why do they call you ox, because you're dumb like one?" No need to stop it Annie finished it. "Luke tell Mr. Hart goodbye."

"See ya Mr. Hart. Can we come to the farm and have dinner please mom." He whined.

I answered first. "Yes, I will have the place spic and span for the both of you. Let's say around 6?"

"That will be perfect."

"See ya Annie." Looking at Henry who was transfixed on the glass doors. "Don't even think about it. I can't fight you head on in my condition so I will kill you in your sleep. Annie is a good girl not those sluts that you and I deal with. Leave her alone."

"I think I'm in love. And you know I have a thing for tiny women. I'd toss her around."

I gave him a harsh look. "Ox, I mean it leave her alone. Without her I would of went crazy in that place, I owe her everything. So don't screw it up, please. You hurt her and she'll hate me."

"She a good girl then?" I nodded. "I won't promise you anything but if she keeps popping up over here…she won't be able to resist all this chocolaty goodness." He rubbed his large hands over his wide chest. "Once she sees all this dark chocolate she is subject to lose her mind and I can't be blamed for that.

"Just stay away from her."

"Hell you tell her to stay away from me. I've been known to give chicks diabetes with all this chocolate."

And to think I nearly killed myself to get out of the hospital for this. I must be crazy.

Me and Henry started to clear out the Gym at around 10 to seven. "Look bro, I'll see you tomorrow, got ta hit the sack my graveyard shift starts tomorrow."

I turned out the last light, set the alarm and headed out. Parker was still standing outside on the curb with his cellphone to his head. "Their locking up now dad, when are you coming?" The kid looked more scared now than he did on the mats. "Just hurry." He hung up and put the phone back into his gym bag.

"You need a ride?"

Parker looked like he lost his last dollar. "Naw, it's cool dad said that he'll be here in an hour or so. Meeting of his is running over."

I looked at Henry and gave out a long exaggerated sigh. "Come on." He turned right back around and we headed back into the gym.

"You guys don't have to do this for me. I mean I'll be okay."

"Parker shut up and get in here." Henry took the back of the kid's head and pushed him in.

"Besides you won't be okay, you can't fight." The kid smiled.

I turned on a few lights and we all took seats on the mat. Henry started, "So kid what you like to do?"

"Well um…I like MMA and I like video games and-"

I put my hand up, "Stop please don't ever put the words MMA and video games together again. You are mixing a sport with sitting on your ass. Oil and water don't mix."

"So what do you like to do?" He sat up straight.

"I like to do women and a lot of them. Sometimes at the same time, but I would give it all up for this one girl." Henry smiled over at me.

"Don't start this shit again. You are not going to touch Annie and that's final."

Henry gave me a wink and smile. "So Parks and Rec, do have a girl you been dealing with? Strapping young man like yourself should have a boat load."

"Naw, my dad says that I should focus on school and working on bettering myself."

Henry leaned back on the mat on his elbows. "Your dad is full of shit. Get as much tail as you can get."

"Ox, lay off him. He's a kid."

"I've seen a boob before." He perked up and smiled.

"What on television?" Henry said unimpressed.

Parker shook his head. "This girl named Hailey she's in my Algebra class and she raises her hand to answer a question and she has this half shirt on and it goes up and she doesn't even have a bra on." He smiled as his cheeks turned red.

"So you saw bottom boob. Well you are headed in the right direction. Your next step is pray that the teacher ask a simply question she raises her hand and you palm that bad boy with all you got."

"Ox, you know that is classified as sexual assault right? Parks and Rec will be in pokey being somebody's bitch and you can't fight…yet." I winked at him.

Parker shook his head. "What Parks and Rec?" Looking at Henry. "And Ox, where do you guys come up with these names.

"Hell if I know. Henry's always been Ox. Maybe because he smells like one and he does resemble a hairy cow."

"Yo momma is a hairy cow."

"I'll drink to that." I smiled. "Naw, Hen's last name is Oxford so we just shortened it up. For the longest time dudes used to call me Art."

"Art, why?"

Henry chimed in. "His last name is Hart, like the heart the one that beats in your chest. So a heart is linked in to arteries in your body. Arteries-Art."

"Also Art sounds like Hart so there. By next week everyone is going to start calling you Ralph."

Henry looked over to me and busted out laughing he knew where I was going with it. Parker had no clue. "Kid, okay. You name is Parker, which goes into Parks and recreations. That's too long so the gym rats will start calling you Rec, then it will turn into Wreck it Ralph, then just Ralph. Get it?"

"Well no but I guess I could live with it."

"This whole things started with Uncle Becky."

"Is that man or woman?" Parker wrinkled his nose.

"It's a guy. His name is Alex." I said

"Really? All these years I had no clue what he's name was." He shrugged crossing his ankles. "Continue."

"Thanks bro, well Alex or Uncle Becky was this old school boxer and-"

"Was- is he dead?" Parker's eyes widened.

"One, don't interrupt my story and two he's not dead he's back in Knoxville with his grandchildren. But anyway, really old school boxed all his life. Would come in here and show the new school how to dance, ya know." The kid was lost. "Not ballroom, how to get around in the ring. Uncle Becky could have gone all the way, but he had a bad eye so he trained with us knuckle heads. So one day one of the guys asked what hell did his name mean."

"We assumed that his dad named him that to make him tough or something. Like Johnny Cash, a Boy Named Sue."

"That reminds me, Johnny the kid you were working out with today. His name isn't Johnny its Phil. First day he walks in he's wearing black from head to toe with cowboy boots. So we named him after the man in black." Parker had no idea what the hell I was talking about. "Johnny Cash, Parker damn. But anyway, Uncle Becky tells us that his name is really Alex, and this other guy starts calling him Alex Tribek from Jeopardy. So Tribek turned into Bek then Becky then they added the uncle for whatever reason and now you have Uncle Becky"

"I got it." The kid smiled.

"Remember that time that Uncle Becky almost killed us?" Henry laughed out loud. "That old fart almost burned us alive one night."

I couldn't stop laughing just thinking about it. "Bro, I'm afraid of propane tanks to this very day messing with Uncle Becky."

"I want to know what happened too." Parker scooting closer to the circle.

Henry was wiping his eyes from crying laughing tears. "Like we said, Uncle Becky is old school. So this dingle berry had to make weight." Henry pointing at me.

"I was shredded." Damn I looked so good but it didn't do me one bit of good now.

"Yeah, he looked like a tall Marky Mark but anyway. Chubby Checker is like seven pounds over-"

Looking at Parker, "Bro I was six."

Henry waved me off. "Whatever with your fat ass. So this dude had to lose six pounds in 14 hours or they were going to cancel the fight."

"Hey, you know I'm sensitive about me weight. So, Uncle Becky comes up with this plan for me to sweat it out. So me and Henry here build this tent thing in my barn. Secured it to the ground and everything, put the tanks up to full blast."

"Fats Dominoes over here has then sauna suit on looking like a garbage bag. Mind you its dead winter and we know that Nashville winters are no joke. So there we were sweating like pigs. Until-"

"Until the poles started to melt. There we were the tent collapsed on us and we are half delirious and trying to get the tarp off the propane before we go up in a blaze of glory."

"Daaaaaang. That's crazy." Parker said.

I put my hand up. "Wait there's more."

"Yeah, we go back into his house hit the scale and Thickey Ricardo gained weight. So now we have less than ten hours to get this fool to make weight."

"So we broke into the gym, with the tanks and put towels under the door in the locker room and did the whole thing all over again."

"I was sweating like a slave in there. Every bit of moisture left my body I couldn't blink for like two days." Henry shook his head.

"But it paid off in the end right? All that hard work."

"Man, I got my ass handed to me. I had no power at all. I was milked dry as a bone. It was a rookie mistake, you live and you learn." I stretched out my tired legs. "Got a concussion and broke a toe. Uncle Becky is the anti-Christ I swear."

All of our heads turned to the glass front door. "Parker, I'm so sorry son." A guy that it was safe to assume was Parker's dad raced into the gym. His shoes and suit were designer, the dude reeked of money. He extended his hand to me. "Thank you so much for watching Parker for me. I have a very large merger going on and- I'm sorry to inconvenience you both."

"Parker is a cool kid. And it isn't a bother. Now, you remember what I showed you. We are going to go over it tomorrow." The kid's head bobbed up and down. Grabbing his bag and throwing it over his shoulder.

"Have a good night Ralph I'll see ya in the morning." Henry waved.

The kid turned to us with the biggest smile. "You too Ox."

Parker's father turned to him confused. "Who is Ralph and why did you call that man an animal?"

"Well, dad it all started with this guy named Uncle Becky, I'll explain in the car."

Henry and I stood on the curb and watched as father and son drove off in his E Class Mercedes Benz. "That's going to be a very interesting conversation on the way home." Henry laughed and patted me on the back

"And who says that you don't have a soft spot?" I poked Henry in his side.

"Ox loves the kids."

Parker was doing pretty well. The kid was breaking holds and getting around on the mats. With some more work and dedication he could be a good little scrapper.

"Hey Devon, you want to run a couple errands for me?" Jerry came up behind me.

"No problem, Parker is about done just give me a second."

"I think you should probably get going. I need this deposit to go to the bank ASAP, totally forgot about it yesterday there some checks in there." I followed Jerry's eyes to the wall clock.

"Jerry, it's not even 7am. There is no bank that's open."

The old man bit his lip. "Devon, maybe you should just take the rest of the day off. You know gets some rest, don't you think you may be over doing it.

"What gives Jer? I'm feeling fine. Why do you want me out of here so bad?"

Jerry forced a smile and looked at the ground. "I just don't want you to get hurt, kid. Your old man and I go way back and you getting hurt." He shook his head at me and grimaced. "I won't allow you to suffer any more than you already have."

"What the hell are you talking about?" The answer came from the door in engulfed in an entourage of morons.

"Oh yeah, baby the champ is here!" Michael Harris and all his glory stepped into the gym and everyone gathered around him like he was the Messiah or something.

Putting an iron clad grip on my arm, Jerry squeezed. "Go out through the back. He hasn't seen you."

"Even if I could run, I'm not running away from this guy." I pointed. "He keeps his mouth shut and he works out and I do my job, we're all good."

Jerry looked at me like I was his only son going off to war. "Devon, Michael's changed. He's not the same kid that you once knew." Jerry took a quick look behind him to look at the fanfare. "He's trained like an animal in the months you were gone. The guy turned from Cringer to Battle Cat in a few months and he's gunning for you." Poking me in the center of my chest.

"Me? What the hell for? I never did a thing to him. Granted I didn't like him then." This asshole had the nerve to start flexing in here like he's the first guy to ever win a match. "And I damn sure don't like him now, but there are only a few people that I really do like."

"I'm just saying, I got the call this morning he won big in Charlotte this weekend. Put down a big guy. He ran his mouth the whole time you were out and he wants to show everyone, more so his self that he can put you down."

"Jerry, I'm not worried."

"He's going to call you out and you are in no condition to dance with him not now anyway."

Jerry didn't take any shit from any of us. If one guy has a problem with another they settle it on the mat. I watched as this jack ass was eating up all the attention. I looked down at Jerry, "Tell him to take a walk." I turned and watched Parker take down Johnny. "Good job, Ralph. Now do it again."

"Hey kid you shouldn't be getting any sort of training from this guy. Come get on the team of winners." Michael stood right behind me barely touching my shoulder.

"Keep focus Ralph." I turned around and looked down at Michael. "Heard you won, good job." I turned back to Parker who was trying to keep an eye on me and on Johnny.

"You healed up pretty nice, huh? Look at you, but you could probably spare a few pounds." Michael took one step back to look me in the eyes. The kid got jacked since the last time I saw him. He shaved his Goldie locks for a sharp crew cut packed on major muscle, he was lean as hell. I looked like a slob standing next to him.

"Well, a hungry man got to eat, right. Happy for your win it will put major shine on the gym." There was nothing left to say and the fakeness that was oozing out of my body was slowly making me sick.

He put his slightly bruised fists up and threw a few jabs at me. I didn't flinch. "So when you want to dance?"

I couldn't help but notice the gym rats had formed a school yard fight circle around us. I smiled. "Man, I'm injured. You'd kill me on the mats." I put my hands up. "Bro, you win, okay." Of all my 26 years of my life I have never back out of a fight, not once. And this was killing me.

"Where's your heart, Hart. I know that a big guy like you isn't afraid of a guy like me right? You said so yourself that you could kick my ass and now you have the forum to do so." He spread his arms out wide. Some idiots that stood behind him were staring a little too hard at me and threw a "Yeah." To every word he said. What world did *I* step into.

My spotty memory has put me in another pickle. I remembered that I couldn't stand this guy and that his skill and technique were just okay. But saying I was going to kick his ass and by the way that he said it I must of said it in front of a crowd of people. I must have called him out just like he's calling me out right now. "Michael, look honest to God I don't remember going after you. But if it means anything to you I'm sorry. It wouldn't be a match it would be a massacre. Plus, I don't want to fight. Heard you took down a big man and I don't want any parts of you. So again, I'm sorry for any harm I may have caused you in the past."

"You're right your sorry means nothing. Devon one way or another you are going to fight me and I will win and everybody in this gym will know who the real king of the cage is."

His, for lack of a better work, his evil minions got a kick out that. They all started to cheer for him and laugh at me.

Parker stood next to me. "Only reason he got the invite was because you were in the hospital." Jesus kid you're killing me.

"The hell did you say?" Michael stood toe to toe with Parker. "What you say kid?"

Stepping in between them. "Parker get your stuff and get ready for school." The kid didn't move and my respect level when up a few notches. "Not going to tell you again, your dad will be here in a second to pick you up. Go hit the showers, now." Turning my attention back to Michael. "He's a kid leave him alone."

"Or what?" He smirked.

I turned on my heels went to Jerry's office and took the deposit bag of his desk. "I'll be back tomorrow morning."

The crowd dispersed and started to work out again as if the most humiliating experience of my life didn't just happened. I had my hand on the door then I heard behind me, "Don't race out of here too fast you might actually kill a kid this time." I heard Michael and his bag of dummies laugh behind me and I let the door close behind me.

I drove down the street it was almost seven am when I saw the Mercedes shot pass me, Parker's father. The kid probably thinks I'm some hack or something. Probably tells his father that I'm a loser and there was no way in hell he would allow me to train him. I drove the streets of Nashville until I found a Pinnacle bank that was open.

Here I was divided again. A part of me wanted to drive right back there and beat the snot out of Michael. The other part was saying to stay low, he'll get tired of me and just leave me alone. But how long would I have to put up with his drama?

I found myself parked in front of my house, truck engine still running. This is how I usually acted when I had to tell my father that I lost a fight. I sit here and go over the fight blow by blow. What I did wrong what the other kid right. What the kid did wrong and what I did right. My father and I would go over it until we figured out what happened. Was my opponent better than me? Did I lose power in the last round?

I slapped the radio off from NASH 103.3 and leaned back in my truck seat. All I could hear was the rustle of the trees behind me. The warm sun was beaming through the windshield and I let the warmth take over. Even though, I'm not fighting my fighting nature was taking over me. I wanted to run back to the gym and take off his arm.

Most likely Michael had to jab at the guy, if he was as big as he said he was. I knew that Michel's ground game was trash, but who knows now. He could be superman now. I would pound at his already fatigued shoulder; I would beat it until it was ground hamburger. I opened my eyes and remembered that I could barely walk on the mats without a small form of losing my balance. The only that I could beat Michael was as if he lay on the mat and let me.

I got out the truck my legs grew tired from siting in the cramp space for too long. I hobbled to the front door. "Ah there you are, you home early." Randle came around from the back of the farm house.

"Yeah, um…thought I take the rest of the off you know catch up on things, ya know?" I commanded my legs to keep moving. Moving away from Randle's all-knowing eyes.

"Glad to hear it. You need the rest. But before you do could you do me a favor?" He took his old Atlanta Braves hat off and wiped his forehead. I have a little bit of wood in the back that needs cutting." He put his thumb and index finger about a centimeter apart and squinted. "My arms aren't like they used to be." Nodding to come around back I followed.

There stood or lay before was a mountain of lumber. "Randle, a little bit?"

His rough hand hit my shoulder. "Nothing that you can't handle. I remember a time you would do twice as much for your old man. Now get to it, it's not going to cut itself you standing there looking at it."

Looking at the ax worn handle poking out the box made me long for to go back to the gym and continue for another round of verbal assault from Michael. I took off my Jerry's Gym shirt and tossed it on the porch. Lifted my arms over my head and stretched. This is going to be hell.

Lifting the ax above my head over and over again wasn't the crazy part; it was I was doing it better than I thought I would. I had to admire myself looking down at my biceps and I'm sure that my upper back muscles were looking pretty good too.

Randle would creep around the back every few hours to make sure that I didn't accidentally cut of my leg from swinging the ax. He put bottle water on the porch railing and whisper, good job.

"Is anybody here?" I thought I was hallucinating the voice. Randle had already gone up the hill to his side of the property hours ago. The sun was nowhere to be found, and I was still chopping wood by the porch light outside. Annie came around the corner carrying Tupperware in plastic bags. "I've been ringing the doorbell and knocking forever."

"Damn, dinner tonight. Annie I'm sorry I totally forgot." I went to get my shirt of the porch steps where I threw it earlier.

"Dang, Devon you don't have to rush…..to put that shirt on. Wow, you look good." She took a few steps closer to me and covered her nose. "You look good but you don't smell that great. You smell like beaver."

I busted out laughing. "Really? Beaver? Think about it for a second."

She shook her head and that ponytail went wild. "Not beaver like that, but because you been working all this hard wood." She closed her eyes. "You know what I'm trying to say, just forget it and take a shower."

By the time I washed the 'beaver' smell off me and down the steps. Annie had the table set with a large green salad in the middle of the table. "Take a seat the bread is in the oven." Luke looked like he was going to die of starvation, but perked up when he saw me coming around the corner.

"Mr. Devon, you look nice." Luke gave that silly toothy grin that made me smile. I looked down at myself and I didn't have on anything special just a Batman shirt, jeans and socks.

"Thanks Luke. How's school going? Nobody bothering you still?" I remembered the black eye he was sporting a month ago.

He shrugged. "Not really, I'm in music class and I play pretty well so some of kids think it's pretty cool."

I pointed at him taking a seat at the head of the table. "Guitar right?"

"Yup, right now we are going through the best guitar players and their styles. Two weeks ago we studied Eddie Van Halen, this week Muddy Waters."

"Impressive. So in your option who's the best guitar player ever?" It felt great to have a normal conversation that didn't have anything to do with fighting.

Luke looked up and thought. "Hands down Hendrix. Now he's a mix of a ton of musical skill and showmanship, that guy is the best. I've been begging mom for us to take a trip to Washington State, I want to visit his grave site. Did you know that Bruce Lee is buried there too?"

"No I didn't. Whenever you want to go let me know I want to go too." Anywhere but here.

Annie struggled to get the plates out the cupboard and served me and her little man, lasagna, with extra parmesan cheese. Warm bread sticks and diet Coke. I had died and went to heaven with this meal. From hospital food to sandwiches and Hot Pockets to this was a dream come true. "Annie I had no idea that you could cook. This is amazing."

"Mom is an awesome cook." Luke smiled over to his mom.

"When you have a kid you got to make sure that he goes to bed full and with a balanced meal. I want my guy to grow to be big and strong."

"Just like Mr. Devon."

"Naw, kid you don't want to be like me. Be better -your smart and you got talent. Don't want to be big for nothing." I put my huge hand over his head and gave it shake. "And always love your mom."

"That's easy." Luke gulped at the Diet Coke.

My front door flew open. "Asshole why didn't you tell me you left early. I've been looking for you-"Henry stopped dead in this tracks when he saw Annie. His whole demeanor changed. "Well, how's my little cherry blossom doing this fine evening?"

Annie looked at me and then back Henry. "Seriously, cherry blossom. I'm Korean not Japanese. Besides I'm not *your* anything."

"Henry what up?"

He gave one quick look to Annie and at me. "Not really important, we can talk later."

"Are you hungry?" The back of Luke's head was nearly touching his spine trying to look up to Henry.

"Thank you little man, but I'm good." Henry patted his pockets and removed a cellphone from the back of his buckle jeans. "Here, this is for you. I've been trying to call you but it said that your number was disconnected. Thank me later." Looking back down to Annie, who wasn't pleased by being placed under the big Ox's microscope.

My mom's husband stopped paying my cell bill weeks ago. "Thanks bro, I'll get you back when I get my check from Jerry in a couple of weeks."

Not even looking at me-eyes still trained on Annie. "Like I said you can thank me later."

Annie looked down at her wrist watch. "Devon, it's been great catching up with you. Luke's got school and I have to hit it myself in the morning." She stood and Luke whined.

"You don't have to run off so soon." Giving Henry an evil glare.

"What about you two stay and I go." Henry began to walk backwards slowly.

"What about we all just stay." Luke forked another mouth full of food.

"Lucas Abel, school will be there tomorrow and you will be in the seat ready to learn."

"Shit just got real-your mom is using your middle name little bro." Luke pouted and stood put his empty can in the garbage and plate in the sink.

"Next time we do this at my house, there will be less interruption." Giving Henry the side eye. "And you don't know where I live." She said putting on her coat.

"There is not a lot a place that love can't find you girl." Henry took his two fingers and put them to his eyes then back in her direction. Signaling that he has his eyes on her.

I sighed, Annie moaned and Luke laughed. I walked Annie to the door and kissed her on her forehead. "Sorry, next time I'll cook promise."

"Don't please I want my son to live to see 11 years old. I'll talk to you later have a good night." I watched as my tiny buddy got in her car they drove off down the dirt road.

Walking back into the kitchen, Henry already had a fork full of lasagna in his mouth. "Yeah, I'm gonna have to wife her. She can cook."

"What's going on? Dude you knew that I was having dinner with Annie and Luke tonight."

"Honest, I forgot. I heard what happened at the gym this morning. I overslept, remember I'm on graveyard now and by the time I got there you were gone. Jerry filled me in, so what are we going to do?"

"You got a mouse in your pocket with this *we* stuff. Only thing we are going to do is clean this kitchen up and then I'm going to go to sleep." I said clearing off the table.

Taking the plate from my hand and running hot water over it. "You got to knock this asshole out, if not he's gonna torture you. I would beat his ass, but you are going to have to be the one to do it."

Henry was right, I'm a grown man and I can't have someone else fight my battles for me. Even if Henry destroyed Michael I would never hear the end of it. "I'm just gonna do my job, keep my head down and go home."

"What about I help you get you back to where you need to be? Turn those love handles into some meat that a chick could hang on to, you know what I mean. Get you back into fighting shape." Henry was nodding his head at me praying that I would agree with him.

"He's not worth it."

Henry tossed his clean shaven head back. "Dude people that say that are the people that know that they aren't going to win. You can win, and be done with it. You can be the champion of the gym like before when everything was right in the world."

"I still wouldn't be able to go to the King of Cage, it would be pointless. And what if I get hurt, what then? Weeks of physical therapy would be down the tubes just to say that I won against this asshole. No thanks."

Putting the last fork into the dishwasher Henry patted a wet hand on my back. "Dude, I'm not going to hound you about it. Just think of it like this. What would your father say if he were alive right now?"

"Thanks for using the dead dad card, Bro"

I hated to admit it but I was overjoyed to see Parker hitting the bag the next morning. Thought he had wised up and left for the 'winning' team. But he was there long arms and all. "Today Ralph we are going to work on your speed. Come on let's go hit the bag." Parker put his gloves on. "Start off slow, no need in making a fool of yourself right now. Go slow find your tempo. It's just like your favorite song. You got the verse then go into your chorus." The kid was a natural, he was punishing the speed bag, and then without warning he stopped.

"Are you going to fight him or what?" Parker looked up at the clock. Michael should be coming within the hour.

"Your only concern is getting that muscle we talked about. You eaten right?" Changing the subject.

"Yeah, eaten the brown rice and chicken breast like you told me." He mumbled.

"Good now start off slow again and build come on kid. Think of that favorite song." I stood back and watched him as I could tell his heart and mind wasn't into." I sighed. "Parker stop." The kid's glove went to his sides and he stared up at me. "There are things about this sport that you can't understand, but if you stick with it one day you will."

I ushered him to the rear of the gym to some jump ropes. Parker picked them up and started. He looks like a school girl at recess. "Parker, once upon a time Michael wouldn't even dare in his wildest dreams to step to me. He knew that I would murder him. Right now, I'm injured and he wants to exploit it. I won't give him a chance to do it." Parker continued to bounce around skipping from one to leg to the other. "Listen do you have any little brothers or sisters or a cousin. Someone smaller than you?"

"Yeah, I have a little cousin Samantha why?" He said already out of breath.

"Would you challenge her to a foot race, let's say 40 meters?" The kid shook his head no. "You would win and what would be the reward in that? You beat someone that can't win against you."

Parker stopped jumping and looked at me. "Are you talking about him or you? Because you would kill him in the cage. Like me beating my five year old cousin. Taking candy from a baby, Devon you can win and everybody know it but you."

"Hey Devon, you are turning this place into a Curves not an all-male gym." I heard Marcus yell over at me.

Of all days, why did Tia come in here? "Tia you have to go. I don't have time for you right now."

She was wearing a pair of dark blue skinny jeans and Captain America shirt. Her long blonde hair was twisted over in a long ponytail that hung across her shoulder. "You haven't been in class."

"Well, I've been busy, you need to leave." I took a step closer to her my chin touching my chest to look down in those big blues of hers. I pointed to the door. "Go and now." Behind me I could hear the whispers and I could only guess what the gym rats were thinking. "Not going to say it again, go."

"I just wanted to say that I was sorry for the way that I treated you. Annie told me that you were doing well. Just wanted to see how my patient was doing, is all. Devon I'm sorry."

God please forgive me. I bent down in her face to drive my point home. "Tia." I said slowly. "I don't give a damn about your sorry. I don't ever want to see you again. Seeing you is like reliving a nightmare. Now I have to do some real work, not that pansy shit you had me doing with you. Now go." I turned my back and slow walked back to Parker.

"Asshole." She shouted.

"Been called worse by better looking chicks, keep it moving Tia." In my heart I knew I did the right thing getting her out of here before the wolves came in.

I was still walking when I felt a body collide into mine from the back. I spun around and it was Tia gripping the back of my shirt. Was she trying to hit me? My first emotion was anger, but the look in her eyes was something else.

"Where you going blondie? How rude of you not to introduce me to your little piece of ass." Michael and his cronies were walking towards Tia and me. One of his guys was making kissy noises at her and she nearly ran up under my shirt.

"Parker take Tia in the locker room don't let anyone in." The boy nodded but Tia kept hold of my shirt and wouldn't let go. "Michael you proved your point, you are the bigger stronger guy. Leave her alone and let her leave."

"You just don't want to get your ass kicked in front of your bitch." I jumped toward him, Marcus was there standing in between us and Tia still holding on for dear life.

"Devon, you know the rules, you come at him first and the two of you have to hit the mat." Marcus said looking for Jerry I presumed.

I tried to relax but I had a scared beautiful woman clinging on to me and my instincts were beginning to take over.

Marcus was being sandwiched between me and Michael. "He's not worth it. Any man that would go after a woman is worth shit on a shoe."

Michael looked down at the feather weight. "How bout I wipe you up first boy then I'll make you watch me kick the crude out your friend and make blondie here scream.

"Devon." Tia whispered her face pressed against my back trembling.

Where the hell was Jerry? "Michael, I'm not going to fight you. Just let her leave and we can talk this out, okay?" I put my hands up in surrender.

Michael looked to the three other men at his side and shrugged. "We are going to fight, but not today. Let her go." The four guys parted like the Rea Sea.

"Tia go straight home and I'll call you later, okay?"

She didn't say a word but walked between the men. I wanted to kill each and every one of them and their families. Michael gave me a smile and smacked Tia's behind. "Giddy up there girl." She screamed not in pain but in fear and the devil in hell couldn't stop me.

I had Michael by his throat and rammed him back first into the wall. I squeezed until his tongue sprang out of his mouth. "I'll kill you."

Parker pulled and yanked at my arm. "Devon, no." It was Henry behind me that had to bear hug me to release Michael. "Devon what the hell are you doing?" All I wanted to do is bury Michael.

Michael rubbed his neck and caught his breath. "See you in 48 hours." He winked and he and his buddies walked out the gym.

Chapter 9

"What's in 48 hours?" Tia said sitting on the floor next to me in the locker room.

"Jerry doesn't allow us to just to get into brawls in the gym. If you have beef with someone you handle it on the mat. You can't set foot in the gym for 48 hours. So you can't train or get coached. It makes it a level playing field. The better fighter comes out on top." Henry said.

"Have you got a hold of Jerry yet?" I looked over to Parker

He waved his cellphone up at me. "That was my forth message."

Henry extended both his hands to me and Tia and helped us off the ground. "We got less than five minutes to get out of here."

Tia looked to me. "You have 10 minutes to get everything you need out of the gym since I'm not allowed back in two days."

"Well Parker and I will help you train for the next 48 that's not a problem. I don't know Michael's game, so we will go over strategies tonight and then we work those muscle and you end this asshole." Henry said.

"Parker, you need to go to school. Don't worry about me I'll be fine." It took a crowbar named Henry to get the kid to leave my side.

Once we were all outside Tia limped to her Honda. "I'm sorry that all this went down." I said watching her.

She smirked up at me. "All I wanted was to apologize to you and I dug a deeper hole for you. I'm sorry….again." Tia wrapped her arms around herself and I wanted to touch her.

The desire to coo in her neck and let her know that I was going to defend her honor was on me like a sheet. "It's not you. This guy's been on me since I got out of the hospital. He kinda used you to get at me."

"And it worked." She put her head down.

"Don't want you to beat yourself up about it. It happened and-"

"And you are going to get hurt. Your hip-"She shook her head. "Devon, there is still a bracket in there. If just one piece of bone is broken around it the bone could lose blood flow. The bone will die. Then hip replacement and then-"

I took her shoulders and rubbed them softly. "I'll cross that bridge when I come to it. Right now I want you to go home and rest and don't worry about me, okay." I let her arms go and she sunk back unto the driver door. I started to walk away. "I didn't mean to yell at you like that. I was trying to get you out there."

"I know now. The second you turned around they were standing there. They heard everything. Devon." She called out to me. "First thing in the morning you meet me at the lake, we got training to do."

"And there is no one prettier than you that's ever called me and asshole."

Later that night, Parker's dad had another merger meeting so Henry picked him up and we all sat around the kitchen table. "Dude, I don't know about his ground game. Your best chance is to knock him out."

Henry was right if he gets me to the ground I'm done. "You do have size on your side though." Parker said.

"Should you or should I." I said to Henry.

"I got it. Young grass hopper, size is not a thing in this fight. Yeah, D has the size and reach on him but as we speak we don't have the speed." Henry banged his hand on the table. "Damn, I wished he wasn't such a bum before I would have watched him closer. Right now I don't know any of his weaknesses."

"And he knows all of mine. I can't defend and block all day. The knock out is going to be my best and only option."

"Let's go hit the bag."

The three of went out in to the spring night to the mini gym that my dad made for me growing up. It has a weight bench, speed bag a few mats and punching bag. Parker and Henry took turns as I did combos all night.

I felt like a teenager, instead of my dad holding the bag it was Henry. Randle came down the hill and poked his head to check on us. "You got to give me some kicks man. Michael won't be expecting it." Henry barked. "Come on stop playing with the bag and give it to me."

Out of breath. "I can't. I'll lose my balance."

"Don't give me excuse-give me results. I swear D if you don't get one of those legs off the ground. Ooohh boy, we gonna be at this all night." I danced a bit around the bag and kicked. It was low, I know but it had some power to it. "You like that?"

"Are you kicking your shoes off or knocking Michael's head off? Pick one, now give it to me."

Now or never I thought. I did a spinning kick and the next thing I know I was on the side on the ground. "D, you aight?"

Henry came to my side and I pushed him. "Well at least I know what to work on." I smiled.

"Guys, I think we have another problem." Parker looked shell shocked staring down at his smartphone. "Look." He turned the phone around so we can see.

There was Michael and the rest of his crew. Parker pushed play. *"Hey yo, Devon Hart. This time Thursday you would have thought your time in the hospital was rough wait till I get my hands on you."* His buddies fell out laughing. *"Let's make this interesting. If I win, you can never show your mug in the gym ever. But the small chance that you pull one over on me; I will give you my invite to the King of Cage."*

"This guy is crazy as hell." Henry looked at the phone in disbelief.

Before the end of the video Michael did the same spinning kick perfectly like he invented the move. "We still have forty hours, bro."

"Henry could you take Ralph home. I'm gonna need some sleep. First thing in the morning I'm training." I tried my best not to look worried. Tried to brush it all off, but the feeling of impending death was seeking me out to destroy me and his name was Michael.

I was tired as hell, I hadn't slept all night. Every time I would start to dose off I'd see Michael's big, ugly foot coming across my jaw and crushing it. Tia was sitting in her Honda when I pulled up.

I wore a pair of basketball shorts and tank top, she got out of her car without a word and headed straight for the dock. Her right leg wasn't as wobbly was it was yesterday, she must be keeping it together. She got in the boat and began to paddle, leaving me standing there. "Um…did you forget something?"

"Nope. Swim to me." There it was the Crazy Tia again. I kicked off my Nikes and got in the cold water. "Swim to the point where you are still able to stand up. Have the water to at least your shoulders."

I swam with ease at least 50 or so yards from the dock. Bobbing to keep my head above water. "What now?"

"Kick."

"Okay, then what?"

"Kick some more. Remember you are weightless out here. Do all your combos."

"You know anything about MMA?" I spit out lake water and started to kick my legs out.

She shrugged her shoulders. "Enough to know that if you don't keep focus you are going to get your butt handed to you. So get to kicking."

"Why do you do that? Act all nice one day and then the next you turn into a drill sergeant." She pulled a fashion magazine out of her purse and ignored me. "So this is how we are going to play it, huh? You boss me around and treat me like garbage then ignore me. Okay, I got I'll just talk to myself then."

I started to talk like a 5th grader on speed. I talked about just about every fight that I've been into. What my first kiss was like, the night I met Henry. "Do the spinning kick." She finally said.

"You must have seen Michael do it last night, huh?" No answer. I pushed through the water and thank God I can float because I would have gone under.

"Instead of talking, do your jab combo and kick. Do it till you perfect it." She flipped another page in the magazine. "The only muscle you are working right now is your jaw muscle. Kick."

"Yes, sir."

I don't know how long we'd been out here but every inch of my body had pruned and the sun was high in the sky. "Let's go." She rowed over to me and helped me in the boat. "Thank God this time you will be in your own car with that smell.

"Let me paddle back."

Her eyebrows went up in surprise. "I've worked you for three and half hours straight."

"Give me the oars please." Tia handed them to me and we paddled the few remaining yards back to the dock. I jumped out the boat and tied it to the dock. I pulled Tia out and smiled.

"What are you so smiley about?" She started to walk away. My legs felt like jelly trying to keep up.

"I want to thank you for helping me. Maybe you and I could have dinner or something to show my gratitude.

She stopped and turned to face me. "Look Devon don't think that since you saw me in a vulnerable state yesterday means I need you. Because I don't. I got you into this mess and I'm gonna do everything I can to try and get you out. Understand?" I nodded. "Good. Work on the kick.

"I never thought you were weak, just scared."

"I wasn't scared." She shouted then began to fiddle with the ties to her sweat pants. "Look, if you want to show me some gratitude give me that guy's head in a box."

"It can be arranged." I smiled back at her and like a miracle I saw that rough exterior of hers melt away.

"He's weak on his right side, just thought you should now." Grinning back at me.

I cleared the distance between the two of us in a second. "How do you know?"

"When he ass grabbed me he turned nearly half way around to do it. He could have easily got me with his right but he did it with his left.

You didn't notice?" I shook my head no. "He held his arm like this the whole time." Tia bent here elbow and kept it close to her. "I would guess a hair line fracture in his radius. When was the last time he fought?"

"Last weekend."

"Yeah, it's probably giving him the blues right about now. He's pushing that thing and he's not even aware of the tiny break." She hunched her shoulders. "Tiny breaks burst damns right?"

Henry and I had crammed enough fight scenarios it wasn't even funny. We went over every possible up and down of the fight. I was going through every single one of them as I bounced around the mat.

"Has anybody seen Jerry?" I said over to Henry. "It's literally been 48 hours sense anyone has heard from him.

"Right now, you can't worry about Jerry. Once this is over win or lose we are going to his place."

Tia and Parker were standing in my corner and it felt like a real fight. Granted there was a no cage but large octagon shaped mat. Johnny came forward and checked my gloves and then Michael's. The arrogant little shit didn't even look like he had broken a sweat. He was coming to the mat cold. My goodness.

"Fighters are you both aware of the rules?" Johnny looked at the both of us on opposite sides of the mat. "UFC rules are used, win by knock out or submission. May the best fighter come out victorious.

The bell rung and just like I thought he would be a lion out of gate, he charged at me. Swinging coming at me with brute strength. There was no cage to catch me so Michael pushed me off the mat. Johnny stepped in and let us go. I blocked everything his kicks and his punches. I could hear Henry shouting behind me to attack. But Michael was too quick. All I knew was I needed to find my opening and get in there. And there it was.

Once he pulled back and charged I hit him with an upper cut to the jaw. It stunned the hell out of him. "NOW!" Henry yelled and I set up for the kick, but Michael must have seen it coming a mile away because he dodged before I connected. At least this time I didn't fall flat on my face, but my recovery was too long and he caught me with a few body shots.

Michael cradled his arms again and stepped back and gave me some room. I came at him again and we traded jabs. I could hear Tia's voice over the crowd; I dare not look at her. I had to keep focus. I could see Tia move around through the crowd trying to get my attention.

Michael charged and got a lock on the back of my neck and delivered some knees to my stomach and chest. Then he let go. He couldn't be tired; he could have finished me if he wanted to. Was he trying to prolong the fight for some sick desire of his?

Tia got directly behind Michael and pointed to her side. She shook her hands wildly in front of her face and shook her head no. Not his arm. I tried to keep both Michael and Tia in my line of sight. Tia kept pointing to his right side.

He's ribs.

With new found information I beat the right side of his upper body like a drum. Michael nearly crumbled to the mat. "Give me his head, Hot Wheels." Tia shouted.

I gripped Michael with my right arm by his shoulder, pulling him forward as he cradled his right side. With my left I gave that shoulder another yank. Henry knew exactly where I was going and I hear him screaming yes, yes.

With my right I tucked his head down, sliding my left over the top of his head. I pivoted around and gave him the standing choke. My knee was barely on the ground and I felt that familiar tap on my elbow.

Chapter 10

There was no time to celebrate; Tia, Henry, Parker and I were in the car headed to Jerry's. "If you think if something happened don't you think he would call?" Parker asked.

"You would think. I just hope he's alright." Henry and Parker took the front seat of his King Cab F250 while Tia and I sat in the back.

"I'm sorry I got it wrong the other day. I should have guessed it was his ribs that were killing him."

"Are you serious? You won that fight for me. Thank you." In the movies this is that part that you kiss the girl at the end. But I was sore as hell and I really didn't feel like getting my ass kicked by a girl.

"His car is in the driveway." Parker pointed.

We jumped, well they jumped out of the truck and raced to the door. I hobbled and made it just in time for Jerry to open the door. "You gave us a scare. Where have you been?" Henry asked.

Any other day Jerry would of told him to mind his damn business, but he looked haggard and tired. "I gotta go back to the hospital. It's Maggie."

I rode with Jerry back to the hospital while the others followed. "She had stroke the other night." He paused to wipe his eyes. "We were getting ready for bed like always and her words, they were just nonsense. Just jumbled up words thrown together she wasn't making any sense." Then she fell before I could catch her."

"Jerry why didn't you tell me? You've been there for me so many times you and Maggie."

"Everything happened so fast." He patted my knee. "I heard about you Michael at the gym. How did you fair?"

"He tapped out but that's not really important-"

"Son, humor an all guy okay? I need to hear some good news." I told him about what Michael said and did to Tia. The fight itself, the tap out. I thought I would be more excited in retelling it. "I will be the first to admit that I doubt that you could come back. That spark inside of you just couldn't be put out, could it?"

"Jerry it's not like I'm making some sort of a comeback. I'm finished. Me and Henry will probably hang at the farm for a bit toss back a few. Then I'll get up in the morning and work with Parker. No big deal."

Jerry just shook his head. "When something is in you son, it just doesn't go away."

"I just texted my dad to let him know that I was hanging out with you guys for a bit." I totally forgot that we were accomplices to the truancies of a minor. The kid would be oh so absent today at school.

"Please let your dad know that we are sorry that you missed school today." I said to Parker.

"No worries, dad's cool and he understands."

We sat outside of ICU while Jerry went in and talked to the doctors. "Do you think that she's gonna make it through?" I looked to the only one with any type of medical experience, Tia.

"It's hard to tell." Tia said. "I'm not a specialist in brain trauma but she is in good hands here. Hey, I have my card and if you want to get something to eat in the cafeteria it's on the house." Henry and Parker jumped at the chance for free food. I sat back and watched the door to Maggie's room.

To my surprise, Tia hung back and sat next to me. "You really did well today you should be proud of yourself."

"I owe a lot of people for that win. You for pushing me, Henry and Parker all of you guys. From the bottom of my heart thank you." I closed my eyes and it seemed to be a struggle to open them back up.

"You need more work on your cardio; it helps your recovery time out. You need to be in the bed, your body is probably going through shock. Remember you've been pretty much immobile for months. Take it easy."

"Who are you?" Tia rocked back in her chair. "The Tia that I know would be drilling my ass about something. Which Tia are you?" I smiled.

"Today I'm the Tia that's in your corner. Now tomorrow you may get the Tia that tells you to piss off, who knows which Tia may show up."

"Would you mind if I wanted to wait around and see?" I was hunched over my elbows on my knees. Swaying my body closer to hers.

"No."

"Why?"

"Because I said so that's why?" She sat up straight. "Just leave it only Devon."

"Maybe I don't want to leave it only. I want to get to know all the Tias that resident in the pretty little head of yours." It felt like I was no longer sitting down but floating closer to her and I couldn't nor did I want to stop.

"Guys like you don't really like girls like me."

Before I could tell her that whoever told her that needed to go kill themselves like right now. Jerry appeared and took in a deep breath. "She's gonna be alright." Now that was the excitement in my day that was missing.

Coming back to the gym, I felt almost like the old me. Pats on the back, the guys going over their favorite parts of the fight it felt great, but short lived. "Ronnie, let me holler at you for a second." Ronnie like most guys here came to the gym to impress their girlfriends and coworkers with a bit of knowledge about MMA. He had a regular 9-5, he's occupation escapes me at the moment. Hardcore gym rats call dudes like him 'baggers' they hit the bag for a bit talk junk and then they go on their merry way.

"What up bro, glad to see you on your feet." He leaned in closer to me. "Heard you put a hurting on ol Mikey there. Between you and me I'm glad you did, that guys a dick." Ronnie was you mid-thirties, guy that thought he still had it. Balding up top and red faced all the time.

"Ronnie, as you know I took a few bonks to the head. Do you remember why I wanted you to come with me to The King of the Cage?" I didn't know what his reaction was going to be like.

"Oh, yeah you needed a sponsor. We talked about it, you needed the company that I worked for to sponsor your trip to Vegas and in return you take me as your mitt holder."

"Well, I'm not going. So sorry about that." The conversation was over in my mind.

"Wait, Michael gave the invite back to you. You're not gonna go? I mean I stuck my neck out for you. The least you can do is take the chance."

The nerve of this bastard. "Ronnie, I'm done. I don't want the King of Cage fights." I looked around. "If Michael is here I'll let him know myself. Maybe he'll take you up on the offer." I walked away and prayed that I didn't have to knock his ass out. Like a good boy Ronnie stood there still red faced with his mouth open.

I went to the locker room to get the rest of my gear. Henry had us out of there so quick I'd left my keys behind.

"Devon, man I'm sorry."

Standing behind me was Eddie Kingsford in all his absent non glory. "Sorry for almost killing me? Dude that feels like a million years ago don't worry about it."

Eddie sniffed snot and all that he didn't get he wiped it on his sleeve. "Sorry for that and this too."

The sound of the locker room doors whistled open and standing there in all his criminal, sleaze ball glory was Barry Washington. Washington from all accounts was always a good for nothing piece of trash. I'd never been this close to him, because people always said if you were this close he was close enough to kill you. He stood about 6 feet tall, medium build. Heard he used to be a fighter, but he got caught up in the under belly of it. Starting throwing fights and all that.

"Devon, I heard you had a wonderful fight today." I looked between the both of them. "I see that you and Mr. Kingsford have known each other for some time now. Some would say that the two of you are friends."

"What's this about?" Looking at Eddie who was looking at the tops of his shoes.

Washington smiled. "I'll get to it then. I have placed you in Beast Wars Tournament that will be taken place in three weeks in Daytona. There will be 4 fights-"

"I know about the Beast Wars." The Wars was another invitation only event for all the fighters before King of the Cage. It was basically a show and tell for all the competitors and coaches to see what they will be up against in Vegas. "What round do you want me to go down in?" Washington smiled. "That's the reason that you are here right, let the money ride on the other guy."

"Frankly, the opposite. You will win all four fights or our friend here wife and son will be in a place that animals won't be able to sniff them out.

In life you will have extreme ups and extremely lows, but not in the same day.

Chapter 11

"So we have three weeks to get you ready for The Wars." Henry held a beer in his hands.

"Bro, you have to get this guy. I don't think that I will be able to do this -four more times in four days. Washington is going to kill me and Eddie, I can't take days of pure fighting and then win them all." I stood and walked over to the kitchen sink and looked out the window. The light was still on up at Randle's place.

Before Washington left me detail for The Wars I instantly thought about running. But there was Randle, Henry, Jerry and Parker that I would leave behind and God knows what Washington would do to them if I took off.

"I'll take some time off so we can train." He stood beside me.

"No, you just got promoted. You told me not to get tangled up with Eddie, now here I am covered in fleas." There were only few people in my life and those few I wanted to keep alive.

"Well, Jerry has his hands tied with Maggie; there is no way that he's leaving her side."

"I wouldn't ask him to." Even though I wanted to. Jerry has been my trainer since I was 18 years old. My father had given me all he had to offer in the boxing world. He knew that Jerry would have the connections to get me into bigger fights, get my name out there. Going into any sort of fight without him was like Johnny without June. This wasn't right.

"Bro, I can take the time off. Hell I worked for it. I mean, I've held mitts with you for years. I'm no Jerry by any stretch of the imagination but I can try."

I loved Henry for everything he's done and currently doing for me. "Now just try to find a way for me to get out of his mess. Find some charges on Washington or something."

Slapping my shoulder, "Looking I got to get some sleep, gotta go to work tonight. I'm still working on getting something on Washington that sticks. We always find a way to get out of a pickle you know? It wouldn't be the first."

"And damn sure won't be the last." Henry poured the rest of his beer down the sink and said he would see me in the morning to train.

Randle came through the back door, smiling as usual. "Heard you kicked the crude of the boy today. Happy for you son."

"Yeah."

"Well you don't look so happy about it."

"Randle, have you had everything in your life go so good and then BAM it just hits the wall. It's like you try so hard then it just crumbles apart in your hands." I looked to one of my surrogate fathers for guidance.

Randle turned the kitchen chair around and sat wide legged with his arms on the back of the chair. "D, that is what us old people call living. You win some days then you lose others. Not because the good Lord is cruel, but He wants you strong. When your father died the man left the earth with regrets, as strong as he was those regrets weaken you. He's won a lot but the few he lost were great. Leave this world with no debt in your leger, son. You live life to the fullest, don't worry what tomorrow brings. Let God worry about that." He stood. "Get some rest and for the love God please put an ice back on your eye. It's my own eye squint.

After taking a shower, I changed into a pair of my Sprawl shorts and wife beater. I reached in the icebox and took a pack of peas over my eye. The ringing of the phone in the kitchen was a God spent.

"Hello."

"Devon you had a fight today and didn't tell me. The least I could have done was cheer you on or something. I mean come on. Wait, are you hurt? How's your leg? Do you need me to come over? Are you experiencing any light headedness, what year is it? Who is the president of the United States?"

"Annie! I'm fine." I could see her now pacing around-her hair a mess all over her head in the cute little way that only she could pull off. "It was nothing. I had to stand up for myself, so I did. Hold on, how do you know?"

"I ran into Tia today at work and she told me."

"Oh."

"Just, oh? You want to know what she said."

God yes. "No."

"Whatever. She said that you were amazing out there. That guy you fought didn't stand a chance, you put him in some sort of move and it was a wrap she was really impressed."

Impressed. "Wow, really?"

"No, I was lying. She said that you were getting pretty beat up and she had to save your bacon."

"Well, that about sums it up."

"Devon, are you going to tell me or am I going to have to yank it out of you?"

"Well, the guy called me out the other day, I grabbed him by the neck. But the rules say that I have 48 hours to-"

Annie exhaled loudly. "No you goofball. Are you going to tell me about you and Tia?"

"There is no such thing as a me and Tia. She's over there doing her thing and I'm doing mine. I mean she helped me out but that's it."

"If I was standing right in front of you right now, you know what I would do?"

"What?"

"Punch you in the face."

I had to laugh. "Annie you would have to stand on a stool then get on a stack of phonebooks to punch me in the face. Even then I would still have to help you get on the chair. How tall are you anyway?"

"Tall enough to know that you and Tia like each other."

I knew that I was attracted to her, but I couldn't see her digging me at all. "What makes you think that?"

"Oh now you want to talk about it."

"Annie, if you don't tell me I will ball you up and put you in a sling shot. So spill it."

Annie cleared her throat. "She likes you and a lot. Women can just tell. But don't jump all over her; you'll scare the hell out of her."

Just thinking how scared she was when Michael and his crew came in made me furious all over again. I wanted to literally give Tia his head. "So how should I play it then Ms. Cupid?"

"Look Tia is a good friend of mine. Just be yourself, no wait. Don't be yourself."

"Annie come on."

"No seriously, she already likes you. Just letting you know she's been hurt a lot in the past by butt face guys that didn't know how to handle her heart. Take care of it and if you think you can't handle it leave her and her heart alone."

"Shoot I can say the same thing about Henry." I couldn't help but laugh out loud on that. Henry was the Tin man…no heart."

"No thank you. That part of my life is pretty much done."

She sounded like me talking about fighting. "What you think that you will never marry again?"

"When you marry a man like my late husband, the next guy has some very big shoes to fill. Ron was caring and understanding but at the same time strong and protective. I just don't want to get into the crazy dating game again. But if a man finds me he finds a good thing."

"That he will."

"So look, here it is 615-555-"

"What?"

"Giving you Tia's number. Call her tonight. I think that she would like that."

I wrote down the number and put it on the counter. I washed the one dish-one fork-and one glass. I was trying to busy myself or give myself an excuse not to call her.

Finally, I sat down and took a deep breath.

"Were you sleeping?" It was just a courtesy to ask she sounded knocked out.

I heard the rumpling of sheets and heard her trying to get her bearings. "I must of dosed off. What time is it?

"It's a little past 10 'clock at night." Dang like she didn't have to get up early. "Look, I'm sorry to have disturbed you but I have to ask you a question, I guess it's more of a favor."

"What is it?" Tia said clearing her throat. I could imagine her hair all messy and her eyes all red and watery from sleep. She still looked gorgeous.

"Well, I think I have entered The Beast Wars and I think I need you to train me?"

"You think or you know?"

"I know."

"Which part?"

"All of it. I just gonna need your help. You know Jerry is out with Maggie and Henry has crazy hours. You right now are my only hope. Could you help me please?" Yeah, I know that I was begging but drastic times call for drastic measures.

I could hear sigh and imagine her sitting up in her bed. "Devon, I'm sorry but I won't do it."

"Won't or can't?"

"Won't. The only reason that I helped you last time was because I kind of got you in it. I'm sure after the fight the other day trainers and coaches will be swarming to help you." She paused and I was at a loss for words. I really thought that she liked me and would at least help me.

"Well, um I guess then goodnight. And thank you again for all your help before."

I heard her say something but my finger was already on the END button. The phone buzzed in my hand, it was Tia for a second I thought maybe she reconsidered, but I doubted and pressed the ignore button.

I ended up turning the phone off and looking around my room. I found myself downstairs wondering throughout the house in the dark. I rechecked locks and windows downstairs. I had three more weeks to The Beast Wars, so why the hell not.

Rounding the corner to the kitchen my stomach was now begging for a triple decker sandwich. My toes were on the threshold of the kitchen entrance. Then I felt it, a presence of another person. My ears perked and my eyes narrowed in the dark. I nearly missed the switch to turn the light on with my hand tightened in a fist. I kicked on the light and there sat Barry Washington.

I wasn't surprised by the intrusion. Almost relieved in fact, Washington needed to know exactly where I stood in getting his money back. "Why are you in my house?" Every muscle in my body was wound tight, even my jaw that made it hard to speak.

Washington scooted back out of the chair and stood. He took a long look at every single item, every nook and cranny of the kitchen and smiled. "Nice house. Now since I've seen yours what about you come with me and I'll show you mine."

"I'd rather not." My back up against the wall. Did he have other men with him? Right now, was there another man right outside of Randle's house on the other side of the property? Just waiting for me to 'hulk' out and put a bullet in Randle's head. "Whatever you have to say to me you can save yourself the trouble and say it here and now." I believe that every human being is born with that rational side of them, the side that tells you to shut the hell in situations like this. I think I left mine in the hospital.

Washington smiled at me. "But Devon, I insist."

The ride from my farm to Brentwood this time of night was easy, but I knew the remainder of the night wouldn't be. Washington and I rode in silence all the way to his home. For whatever reason I thought if the day would come that I had to go see the home of a crime lord one of his goons would hassle me and throw me in the trunk of his car and introduce a tire iron to my knee.

But here I was in riding shoot gun in his modest Yukon Denali. We drove up the long paved driveway and he stopped at the very well lite front door. "All out."

When Washington insisted that I see his place I just had on old pair of Sprawl shorts Jerry's Gym tank top and ADIDAS flip flops. The night air was biting at my calves and either it was just the wind picking up or my nerves that had every one of senses on high alert.

"Devon you can go into my office. It's at the end of the hall, straight ahead."

The house was beautiful; it's something that you would see in a movie. High vaulted ceilings, black leather furniture. The doors that I passed to get to his office were all that hard, dark wood. But I guess when you run half of the city or maybe even the state you throw money out like rice.

I walked in the room and too very tall and broad men stood and looked right through me. They resembled the guards that stood out in all kinds of weather at Buckingham palace. But these guys wore Italian suits and very large weapons that hung on their waist.

"Devon, please have a seat." Washington came behind me carrying a glass from what I could tell of Brandy.

I was irritated and sleepy. "Mr. Washington if you don't mind I would rather stand."

He flashed a million dollar smile. "Suit yourself. " He took a seat behind a large granite top desk and leaned back in his leather high back chair. "So how's the training going?"

"I thought I would rest today and then tomorrow I would hit it." I should of took the offer to sit, my hip felt like it was going to fall off my waist at any given second.

"Well, I'm glad to hear that you are taking this opportunity seriously. Lives depend on you." He took a sip of Brandy and swirled it around in his glass. "What all do you know of me?" He looked down into this glass. "Tell me what people whisper about me when I'm out of ear shot." I didn't know where to start. "Come on, I can guarantee that my feelings won't be hurt."

Maybe it was a lack of sleep or the fact that not only was my hip throbbing but my lower back felt like I was one step away of breaking in half. "You prey on the weak."

"And?" He pressed.

"And you can be crueler than any son of a cuss. I guess that really sums it all up." I tried to lean on my other leg, but the shifting of weight was still murder.

"Well, I guess it does now Devon. I think that people that don't really understand my, what would you call it my profession get confused. You see, I don't prey on the weak. Those lost souls seek me out. I give them every opportunity to make it right. And for the most part they screw me. Like Kingsford for example, he needed some money and I gave it to him. I set it up so that he could pay me in installments, because I'm fair that way." He smiled. "He screwed up the money and just like anyone else I want what he owes." He stood and walked around the desk and sat on the edge. "All I want Devon is my return. Don't you think that's fair?" I didn't reply but he didn't really need it. "Now you." He clapped his hands together.

"What about me?"

"You are what we call collateral. You winning these fights will put Eddie back on track and back in the green. I will have my money back and then some and then you are free to do whatever you please. You understand? You know what I could probably show you better than I can tell you." He looked to the guy who was closer to my height with a black buzz cut. "Martin could you please get Sophia for me." The goon walked right passed and all I could do was watch.

I've watched a mountain of movies in my lifetime. Was Sophia a portable saw, or a very large automatic weapon? The soft breeze behind indicated that the door was open and fearing the worst I turned to look at my fate.

"Sophia could you say hello to Mr. Hart? He is my special guest for the night."

I stared down at a little girl skin the color of coffee mixed with cream. Big brown eyes rimmed red. The girl, Sophia stood in front of me. "Hello, Mr. Hart." Her voice was low and too raspy for her age. She must have cried out her voice.

"You see Devon, little Sophia here is what you call a long term collateral. Her brother got himself in a jam and came to me. And instead of paying me back, he ran but we caught little Sophia didn't we?"

Like a puppet the child nodded her head in agreement. The big guy behind me that was my height; I knew that I would make short work out him. The smaller one was a brute; you could take a look at his knuckles that were banged all the way up.

Sophia's arms were black and blue from recent and day old bruises. A very large hand print was on her neck. The smaller one did this to her and I started to sweat and my fist were getting tight. "Sophia, could you please show Mr. Devon how we greet our special guest." He gave her a little nudge in her back.

Her brown eyes met mine and she shut them tight. I saw a little girl slowly go down to her knees and reach for my waistband. Out of pure rage I pushed her and she fell flat on her rear, looking up to Washington. "What Devon you don't like colored girls?"

"I enjoy the comforts of woman…a woman that is willing." I growled.

Washington stepped over the girl like you would step over gum in the street and he waved a finger at me. "See Devon that is where you are wrong. Little Sophia here can do things women twice her age can do. And believe me, she will enjoy every second of it. Won't you?" He looked down at the girl in her hot pink Converse and she nodded. My primal instinct was taking over and I felt every bit of rage building in my chest. "Or do you like something more blonde." My heart stopped beating in my chest. "That got you going didn't it?"

"You wouldn't dare." I said through clenched teeth.

"Don't what? Turn Tia into long term collateral? That is all up to you, Devon. Get my money back or your physical therapist will be the one giving any man I want her to blow jobs. My reach goes further than you will ever know." He smiled.

I stepped around Washington and picked up the little girl off the ground. "How old are you?" I asked.

She looked up to Washington for approval, which he gave with a soft nod. "Eleven." Her voice barely a whisper.

Washington picked the girl up off her feet and walked her to his desk placing her in his lap. "Now you have training to do. Flex-"The short one. "Could you take Devon home, please?" With a hairy knuckle, Washington traced the length of the girl's arm. She sat there motionless; they had beaten the fight out of her. "Oh before I forget." Putting his arm around her waist so she wouldn't tip over as he reached under his desk. "Here's walking around money." It was large leather duffel. Before I could protest. Washington rubbed the girl's neck and smiled. "I insist."

One last look at Sophia who was perched up on this monster lap left me feeling like I had failed the universe. Her brown eyes begged me to stay or take her with me. I was pushed from behind to exit the Washington's office.

That roaring lion that I keep caged until fight night, had scratched and clawed his way to the surface. The short one that had put his hands on this child was first.

His hand on my shoulder, I hip tossed him. Using his right arm as leverage I dropped 215 pounds of raw, untamed rage into his ribs. I heard them splinter and I smiled. The goon didn't have chance to scream out in shock or pain before I landed punch after punch into this face.

I was no longer in Washington's well-manicured home, I was in the cage again in my mind. Trying to punish to remove this man from the earth.

The vibration of the big guy's steps behind me turn. The gun in his hand was no deterrent for me. I charged him full on, he fell backwards and the hard clank of the gun hit and skid on the hardwood floor. Punish him, I thought. While this girl was living in a nightmare this piece of shit watched.

He and I tussled a bit until I gave him one punch to the throat. Both of his hands sprang to his neck and he wheezed. My leg was no longer fatigue and I inwardly smiled as I took his ankle and pulled back on it. The man's scream became a wonderful symphony for me. I closed my eyes, bared down and leaned back. Feeling the pulling and the separation of his fibula from his knee just made me hungry for more.

I was almost squatted to the floor with a tight grip on his leg and I knew I was almost there. The thud of a man's lower leg separating from his knee cap wasn't justice but it was a start.

I had one more to go, the lion inside of my wasn't quite full. I turned to Washington who sat there smiling and laughing with a .50 Desert Eagle resting on Sophia's temple. "And you said that you were just going to rest today." He laughed.

My chest was still heaving, the little girl looked as if she was watching her favorite show on television. Looked right through me as if one of the world's most powerful handguns weren't at her head.

"Devon, I'm afraid that you incapacitated my men. Now there is no one to drive you home tonight." He lowered the gun from the child's head. "And I'm a tad bit tired, I hope that you can find your way home safely."

I turned on my heels and made my way out to his office door. "Devon." I turned to the madman. He pointed the gun in my direction. "Short term collateral." Then to Sophia that sat on his lap. "Long term, understood."

I neither confirmed, but his message was pretty clear. I wasn't even half way down the hall before I heard Sophia's screams for help.

"Why the hell didn't you call me? He could have killed you." I was standing in Henry's office at the police station. Walking around like a possessed man.

"Screw me! That little girl is in there. We have to go in there and get her now Henry." The whole night ran across my mind, like a horrible song suck on repeat. "He's…he's hurting her. Please Henry. God we have to get to her now!"

Henry did something that I never thought he would do. He grabbed me and hugged me. "We go in there guns blazing, he'll kill her." Henry took a step back. "If she is as petrified as you say, she won't turn against him. He'll get out and you already said he threatened Tia. He will kill her, then Jerry and Maggie." I couldn't take the truth he was telling me. I turned my back. "Then Parker and his dad, Annie and Luke, until there is no one in this world that you have left." He sighed. "Don't you think they know that I'm an officer? Washington probably knows that you are sitting here right now and I can't do a damn thing about it.

"How can you be so callous? There is someone's little girl in there with him. He is doing things to her; he's allowing other men to do things. Henry." I was out of breath and my chest was tighter than a knot. If I hadn't of chopped most of my hair off I would have been pulling it out.

Henry closed his eyes and ran his hand over his bald head. "I'm not callous. I'm used to it. Devon, I know what you are going through. Last night I had to throw a 15 year old pregnant girl in lock up so she would stop shooting up. You think that I sit in this room and play Barney Fife. I've seen things that would make you never want to close your eyes and go to sleep ever." He put his hand on my shoulder. "We are going to get this guy, but it has to be right. He won't get away, I swear to you and that little girl."

When I finally made it home it was close to 1 in the morning. I felt guilty that I was able to go sleep knowing the things that went on outside my door. I got dressed and drove to the gym, the dream that I had that night was playing over and over in my head. I dreamt that

Luke was playing his guitar in my kitchen and Sophia would call out a song and he would play it. The two of them would laugh themselves silly. Her hot pink Converse danced all around me table. She had no bruises or scars. Her voice was high pitched and squeaky like a kid's is supposed to be.

Tears fell down my face all the way to the gym. I tried to focus on the work out as much as possible with Parker, but my head and my heart weren't in it. Most of the guys there were still talking about the fight that me and Michael had. I tried to smile it was so hard to grin.

Henry came by but he told me there was nothing he could say to me, because they were starting to build a case against Washington and the less I knew the better. Parker got picked up by his dad, I hit the bag and sparred with Henry for a bit, but I was tired and my thoughts always went back to hot pink Converse.

I saw the leather duffel bag on the floor of the truck. I forgot that child rapist gave it to me and I threw it in the truck when I went to go see Henry. Putting my hand on the zipper, I prayed it wouldn't be a head of someone's child in there. Instead it was a bag full of money.

Stacks of it, wads of $100 bills wrapped together, with a bit of quick math I was holding maybe a little bit over or under $100,000.

I dropped the money back in the bag and wiped my hand on my shirt. How many lives were lost because of this money? How many children lost parents, how many parents have lost children from this money? It was dirty, downright filthy.

I sat in the parking lot of the gym well over an hour before I decided what I wanted to do with it.

Chapter 12

I peeked inside of the physical therapy room. Memory served me correctly class just got over with. Tia and Mac were standing at her desk talking. "What up champ, Tia told me how you beat the snot of out that guy yesterday. Hey you still owe me a lesson." Mac smiled from ear to ear. The young vet looked to Tia and then back at me. "Well, I will leave you two alone." Was it that obvious that I liked her?

"Mac, I didn't come to see her. Matter of fact I came to see you." I saw Tia's face and was that disappointment that I saw?

"Me? What do you need to see me for?" He gave a nervous laugh and looked between Tia and me.

"Don't look at me, I have no idea what Hot Wheels is up to." She threw her hands up.

"You were nice to me and in the position that I was in a few months ago that means a lot. So can I show a token of my appreciation?"

"Sure man. I guess." He stuttered, poor guy so excited he was tripping over his own tongue.

I put one finger up. "Wait here." I ran and opened the steel door and picked up the box that I left. "Here man. You deserve it."

"Wow thanks man. You didn't have to do this."

"You don't even know what I got you. Open it up."

Mac balanced the long box on his hip. I saw how he struggled to stand up. He opened the box and his mouth drop. "Devon." He whispered. "You didn't have to do this."

Tia was trying to sneak a peek of over Mac's shoulder. "Let me see." Once she saw the contents of the box her head sprang up and her lips parted. "You…you-"

"You got me a new leg." Mac shouted. Like a kid on his birthday that opened the best gift of the day. Mac sat on the floor. He raised his pant leg up and took of the uncomfortable straps on his upper leg and placed the new one on.

He took my hand and I pulled himself up. Mac stood tall. "I can't believe it. Devon. Do you know how much these cost?" Pointing down to his brand new limb.

"Yeah." A little over $25k to be exact. "I guessed your height and your weight. If it doesn't fit right let me know and we can get it adjusted for you.

"No it's perfect. Thank you."

"Now in the next three to five years you let me know and we get it readjust for you."

Tia was wiping happy tears from her eyes. "You're not as big of an asshole as I thought."

"Well, the day is not over yet."

I gave Mac all needed information about his leg and if he had any questions to let me know.

I ran by Millers and got some jelly without incident. It was a bit after five, I called Jerry he was still at the hospital with Maggie. He reassured me that they would both be coming home in the next few days. Maggie was a having a little trouble with her speech and that with a bit of therapy she would be fine.

I carried the groceries in to the farm house and put the bags on the table. I tried to keep focus on Mac's face, how happy he was and not my encounter with Washington.

I was feeling good and my day was going well. Then the knock on the door. I walked to the front door with caution and opened it slowly. Tia stood looking as beautiful as she did an hour ago.

"Hey can I come in?"

"Yeah, sure. Umm…how did you know where I lived?" She looked surprised then nerves. "No, no I don't mind just curious."

"A mutual friend that happens to be a nurse gave me directions. If you were busy I mean I could go." She took a step backwards towards the door.

"No, I want you to stay. Please. Do you want a PB&J?"

"No thank you. I don't want to take up any of your time." She followed me to the kitchen and I tried to put my groceries away so I wouldn't just stare at her. "I really respect what you did for Mac. He's a good guy and he deserves it, you know? Thank you."

"It's not a problem. I mean if it wasn't for him I probably would have wheeled myself out of therapy screaming and crying."

"About that-"

"No need to explain. I get it. You have to be tough on us guys, if not we would be just that-guys. Doing and saying stupid things. Thank you for all you've done to get me where I need to be recovery wise. I hated it then but it paid off right?"

"Well, you kicked that dude's butt so I guess it paid off." She shoved her hands in the pockets of her dark purple scrubs. "Devon, I want to help you."

"Tia, you already have."

Her gold colored hair fell over her shoulder when she shook her head. "I want to help you train."

"Tia, I don't want you to think that I did that for Mac so that you would help me. I did it so his outward appearance would match is inward, which is outstanding and amazing. Like you said if he kept going on that leg he would have all other problems with his back."

"I know. I just…well. Damn." She rolled the big baby blues in her head and sighed. Tia pulled out the ties of her drawstring scrubs that were tucked in. She gave a look around the kitchen and pulled her pants straight down to her knees.

"Whoa, whoa I haven't even bought you dinner yet." I closed my eyes and turned completely around.

Pulling at the sleeve of my shirt. "Like you never seen one before."

"I've seen a few but not yours." My eyes still closed and I couldn't help but laugh.

"Turn around you nerd burger."

I opened my eyes and all the air left the room. Down the length of Tia's right leg was a hideous scar. Her tanned leg looked Frankensteined together. The skin was pulled and puckered running down passed the side of her knee. Tia's scrub top covered her rear and from what I could see the scar snaked its way all the way up. "My God."

"No, it was the other guy that did it." She pulled her pants up. "Devon, I want to help you get your dream. Go to the Wars and go to the King of the Cage. You can do it and I will do everything in my power to get you there."

"What happened?" My voice shook.

"When I lived up in Michigan I dated this guy in high school. He was everything. Tall, smart and he loved me so I thought." She rolled her eyes and took a seat at the kitchen table. "I thought that I was going to marry him. But he started to change after we graduated."

"Like how?"

"You were right. I was a dancer, I was chosen to go to New York and dance in a small company there. It wasn't Juilliard but it was my first break you know? So my life was going great and he's not so much. He had the grades and the smarts but not the money to go college. He was young and frustrated." She rubbed her face with her hand. "I reassured him over and over again that we would still be together and that I was going not to leave him but to build a foundation for us. Isn't that silly?"

"No not at all. You loved him."

"Well, that quickly faded. He started drinking and the months before I was getting ready to live he grew jealous. Every time I walked out the house, he thought I was cheating on him. I tried to stick it out. But…"

"What happened?"

"The night before I was going to leave for New York. He invited me over to his folk's house. His parents both worked so, it gave us some alone time before I left. You know our last hoorah before I left." Tia paused and gave a strained look. "That night he beat the living hell out of me. He stomped my leg in and out. I must have blacked out and when I woke up he was still booting my leg. He told me that he did it so we would always be together and that I would never leave him."

"What's his name?" I grew tense.

Tia smiled. "Who cares? That night my dream ended of being a professional dancer. But you can reach your goal. I was being an asshole when I didn't want to help you. Why should I stop you from reaching your goal?"

I stood there looking at an angel. And from all accounts was sent from Heaven to help me. I didn't deserve her kindness and I didn't deserve this second chance. What I was going to do was make the best of what has been given to me.

Chapter 13

It was in the wee hours of the night that Tia and I turned in for the night. I begged her to stay, with Washington's threat bouncing around in my head I needed her close to me. After about thirty minutes of pleading with her and telling her when I used to train with Jerry we lived under the same roof. She agreed.

She took my bed and I was on the couch. It had to be a little after 4 in the morning when my phone buzzed. I rolled over, wiped crude out my eye to focus and it was one text message it read. *For I know the plans I have for you, declares the Lord, plans to prosper you and not to harm you, plans to give you hope and a future. Jeremiah 29:11.*

The phone dinged again. *Thought you would need a pick me up this morning. Hope all is well. –Annie.*

If she only knew.

With a bit of soreness I went upstairs and showered. Tia was still in my bed. She looked like a baby in a queen sized bed as she lay in the center. "Tia, wake up. I gotta go to work and I have to train." I nudged at her shoulder.

Her sleepy eyes fluttered open and she smiled. "What time is it?" She sat up her scrub top wrinkled and twisted.

"A quarter to five. I need to open up the gym. You can stay here until you go to work if you like. Randle, will probably come down off the hill in a few hours if you need something to eat."

Tia smiled at me that did something to me. I wanted to lay her back down and get under the covers with her. Touch that angel face of hers. Make love to her. Wait? What? I've had plenty of sex, but making love? I must still be sleepy. Her voice broke me out of my trance. "I think I'll head home, get a few more hours in. Go to therapy then we go to the lake."

"Sounds like a plan coach." I stood and started for the door.

"Could you hand me my pants please." Great now I have to walk around for the remainder of the day knowing that the object of my affection was in my bed all night without anything covering the perfect behind. Help me God.

Before I could open the gym doors, Parker was standing on my heels. "Today we work on legs. You're pushing 150 today on the leg machine. Can't have you looking like Popeye up top and Olive Oyl on the bottom." The kid did his stretches and worked on his breathing like I taught him. Man, if I was that young again, I wouldn't have taken everything up until my wreck for granted.

Henry came in about an hour and half later and we did some mitt work. "Parker you got any homies that you really trust?" Henry still throwing punches at me.

It took him less and a second to shake his head. Henry and I both stopped and put our hands down. "Wait, you're telling us you don't have any friends."

"Well, I have a ton a Facebook friends and guys that I play online games with, but none at my school." Parker replied not really looking at either one of us.

"Why the hell is that? I mean you seem like a pretty decent guy, you're a junior in high school right?" Parker nodded. "There shouldn't be any reason that you don't have your own crew."

"In my own defense, the kids think that I'm some spoiled rich kid. My dad is successful not me." Parker bowed his head.

"One day kid you'll be, just keep practicing-keep getting stronger and every girl is gonna want you to be in your bed and every guy is going to want to be just like you, just watch." I said.

"How did you and two become friends?"

Henry and I looked at each other and smiled. "Well, once upon a time I use to drink a lot." Four months ago. "So I just won a match in Kentucky so instead of going home I wanted to celebrate, so I went to this local bar." I said looking at Henry to continue.

"At that time I just moved here from Atlanta and I needed something a little extra to take care of some bills that I left back there. So I was bouncing at said bar." Henry taking off his mitts and me doing the same.

"I was completely unaware that UK had won a division championship that night-"

"Plus we weren't that far from a military base. Some of military guys were sour the Kentucky won, some diehard fans egged it on-" All three of us sat on the mat

"Fight broke out." I said. "Henry and this other guy had to try and get a bar under control, bottles and punches were flying like crazy. Ox over there was trying to pick up some kid off the ground so he wouldn't get trampled to death. I was still living off the high of the win and-"

"And a few Miller lights." Henry laughed.

"This kid had his face painted blue and white had a beer bottle in his hand ready to ring Henry's bell."

"And my knight in shining armor tore the kid apart. We've been friends ever since that day."

"Wow, that's crazy. One day I'll get some friends like that, some cool guy that I know has my back, ya know?"

Henry looked over to me and smiled. "What if it doesn't work?" I said.

"It will work-it will be fool proof-promise." Henry smiling.

"Um, did I miss something? What are we talking about?" Parker confused.

Henry clapped his massive hands together. "Kid you've ever been in a Knoxville Knock out before?"

"Um, no I don't think so." The kid was squinting his eyes trying to recall.

Henry wrapped his arm around Parker's neck. "You would know if you were." Henry took a quick look around the gym. "Johnny would be perfect for this."

"I don't know. We can get a lawsuit tagged to us and in my position I don't need any more drama." Who in the world was I fooling, I lived for the Knoxville Knock out.

"Parker call your dad and tell him that we are going to take you to school today."

Parker did what he was told. He and I sparred while Henry went over the Knoxville Knock out with Johnny until it was time to get Parker to school.

This was going to be so much fun.

"Hey you up?"

"Yeah, just got out the shower." Tia was killing me with her declarations of nudity. "We're still on for this afternoon right?"

"Yeah, I just want to-" I don't know why I called her. Maybe it was to make sure that she was real. Maybe to hear that voice of hers. "I was just confirming our workout for this afternoon was all. Um, just do what you have to do today and I guess I will see you later." That came off real stupid.

"I'm glad that you called. I just want to thank you for giving me a chance to help, you know."

"You are doing me the biggest favor of all time. I should be kissing the ground you walk on right now." I heard her laugh and I wanted to kiss everything on her. Her neck, her face and everything that her clothes covered. Everything in my mouth tasting her.

"Devon, let me talk to you later, I'm standing here dripping on my carpet." If she would just give me a chance I would have her dripping on the carpet, bed, and hallway and anywhere she wanted.

"Sure, I'll see you in a few." I hung up and put the cellphone in my gym bag. I stepped out the locker room and all the players were ready.

"While, you were in there talking to your girlfriend, everyone knows their position." Henry said.

"Kid you ride with me and Ox. Johnny you can take your own car." Johnny's who was only 20 smiled at all of us. "This is going to be awesome."

Parker's school was nothing but a few miles down the road and I could see in my rearview mirror that the kid was a ball of nerves. "Buck up Parker. You'll be fine just remember everything that I taught you." Parker nodded and looked out the back window.

The three of us sat in sat in Porter's a local teeny bopper diner. It was the redneck version of 90210's Peach Pit. They had dirt cheap breakfast and lunch for the high schoolers. "Is she here?" All you could see was Henry's eyes peeking over the flimsy menu.

"Yeah, Hailey's over there with the rest of the cheerleaders. So what do we do now?"

I put my arm over his shoulder. "We wait." I texted Johnny who was sitting at the other side of the dinner. *Tall brunette-cheerleader sitting on the end of the booth.* Once Johnny got the text he nodded at our table. "It's in motion." I tried to my hardest not to laugh.

Johnny, was what you would call a big kid. For as big as he is you never hear him coming like he was part hillbilly and part ninja. "Hey, I think I like you. I want to talk." Johnny gripped the teenagers arm.

Her eyes went wide. "Stop let me go." The girl squealed and batted at his unyielding fist.

"You're on Parker. Make us proud." Henry said trying his hardest not to get too excited.

"Hey bro, let her go." Parker voice cracked. "Let her go now."

Johnny snarled down at Parker. "What are you going to do about it, huh?"

I couldn't have done it better myself, Parker tackled Johnny and with the speed of a cheetah had him in an arm bar. Thumb up to the ceiling. I saw Parker's heel dig in. I wanted to jump up and shout. "Tap or snap, bitch." Parker growled.

"I'm sorry, I'm sorry." Johnny yelped.

"Now get out of here." Johnny scurried to the front door and off in his Camaro.

"Are you okay?" Parker said turning to Hailey who was still rubbing her lightly bruised arm.

"Yeah, I'm good thank you. Parker, right?" The kid smiled.
"You're in my algebra class right."

"Our work here is done." Henry taking one last look at the teenagers.

"Yup." Now if my life was as easy as Knoxville Knock out I'd have it made.

For some reason the lake felt a little warm this afternoon. The sun was shining over me and Tia like were the only two people that the sun cared about.

Unlike the other times her and I been to the lake, she talked more gave me more direction. Pushed me harder but she wasn't her mean self, she just verbally assaulted me but did it with a smile on her face.

Tia began to row towards me and I lifted myself in the boat this time without her help and rowed back to the dock. "So what are you doing later?" She asked me.

"Nothing, really. Probably go home hit the bag a little get some sleep and do it all over again in the morning, why?"

She hunched her shoulders. "Just thinking maybe we can spend a bit more time out here. It feels good."

I stopped rowing and narrowed my eyes. "Last time you were nice and lured me out her you threw me in."

"About that, I'm sorry. I had to wake you up. Annie and I were afraid that we were losing you."

"So you do care about me." I smiled and her smile was warmer than the sun.

"I'm not that crazy. I care about all my patients. Some won't have the best quality of life once they leave therapy, but I try to instill in them that it's still life and to make the best of it."

The up and down motion of her body on the water was twisting me. I wanted her so bad I had to stop looking at her. "So, um how did you start you know doing therapy and all."

"After what my ex did to me. I was like you angry, depressed. I went through every negative emotion in the book. My dream of dancing was finished. Then I went to therapy." Tia shook her head and laughed. "My therapies had to me the oldest, meanest man on the planet. You thought I was rough this guy made me look like a kitten. He pushed me to my limit and then some. I cried rivers those two months learning to walk again. But I owe him everything. Brett Green, was his name. He passed a few years ago."

"I'm sorry to hear that."

"You would have thought the pope died or something. There were hundreds of people there. The church was standing room only. He helped so many people in his life. I remember when I was back on my feet, he'd still call me and say, "Blondie, get that tissue out 'cause you're gonna need it." We both laughed. "I loved him and hated him. He was the one that advised me to get out of Michigan. Saying that if I'd stay my ex would do me more harm than good. Came here to Tennessee went to school with the money I'd saved to go to New York and got hooked up with the hospital and here I am."

And here you are….with me, I thought.

Tia was the total package. Smart, funny and beautiful. I had to the luckiest guy walking, well hobbling around.

I would do everything possible to make this work.

Chapter 14

"Can I ask you what the hell you are doing?"

Henry had both hands deep into my luggage. "Did you take my shorts? I swear the last time I had them on I was with you."

"Is there something going on between the two of you that I may need to know about?" Tia laughed, both of us gave her a look and she laughed harder. "I mean if you y'all need a special moment before we get on the plane I can give you that."

Before I could protest she was already in Nashville International Airport. "Look, I will try to get there by Friday to see your last fight." Henry smirked. "Just kick a ton of ass before I get there, okay?"

"You mean not get my ass kicked." I said watching the traffic pass in the departure lane.

"You'll be fine. You got cutie pie in there that will keep you on the straight and narrow. Just relax you've done this a thousand times, you'll be fine." Henry took a step back. "Your dad is smiling down from Heaven right now at you."

Like Annie said that we carry those that have went on before us in our hearts, I knew that my father was somewhere in Heaven gathering the saints to watch me. It gave me the spark that I needed. "Yeah, the old man wouldn't miss this for the world."

"Be a beast bro." Henry gave me the peace sign and jumped back into his running car. It took me a second to find Delta Airlines and I excused myself through a crowd of people to stand by Tia's side at the ticket line.

"You two kiss goodbye?"

"Something like that." I'd rather kiss you in the morning and night.

"Okay, we should be there in the next three hours. So take the opportunity to rest. The next four days are going to be grueling exceptionally for you. So take it now."

I picked up her bag. "Dang, what all do you have in here your car?"

Rolling her eyes at me. "I didn't know what to wear at these type of things. Maybe there was a meet and greet or a dinner or something. Didn't want your coach to look like a bum."

I bent down in her ear. "You could wear a potato sack and look gorgeous."

Once we boarded the plane I ran threw everything. The last three weeks has been hard. I trained from the time I woke up in the morning at the gym. Leave go to the lake put in hours there. Before Henry went to work and did more mitt work.

Then when night fell I fought the urge not to kick my bedroom door and land kisses on the angel that laid in my bed. That was probably the hardest part of my training, training my crotch to go to sleep.

Tia was flipping through The Beast Wars itinerary, writing notes. "What you doing coach?" Trying to get comfortable in this tiny seat.

"Just looking at your competition. Like this guy, Newton Moon. He's in your weight class. He's left handed so I want you to be aware of him, he doesn't have your reach but his legs, dang." I looked at the photo of him and his legs looked like two wide trees sticking out his shorts.

"Tia, there are seven other guys here. I'll only fight four of them. The other guys I probably won't even see. This is no elimination or winner. The Wars are just to boast the MMA name. That's why they have the fights right on the beach, it just sparks interest is all. There is no ranking, it's just putting everybody's cards on the table before the King of Cage." She nodded.

"I want you to win it all." Tia grinned.

"Me too." If she only knew what these fights meant. "And we will." I leaned back as best as I could and closed my eyes. I have to win.

I thanked Parker, well his dad for letting me and Tia stay at his beach house for the next few days and nights. Tia went into her room to change. I stood on the balcony and watched as guys with EVENT written on yellow vest erecting the cages on the beach. Nine octagons stood stretching down the beach and my heart began to pump. This is where I belonged.

"Hey there, shouldn't you get some rest. The next few days are going-"

I put my hand up. "I know rough. Tia, for the first time in a long while I'm in my element." I looked back to the beach. "I'm in my wheelhouse. This is home for me."

She folded her arms. I'd just noticed that she had on a pair of shorts that barely covered her scar on her leg. She looked so cute with her dark blue tank top. "I'm glad that you are finally realizing that." She stepped closer to me. "You didn't need me when you beat that asshole. You would have figured it out all by yourself. I'm just your crutch."

I took her hand in mine. "You are more to me than that, you know that? One day *you* will realize that."

My confidence soared when she wrapped her arms around my waist. Putting her head on my chest. "Why can't one day be today?"

I stroked her long blonde hair. "After my win tomorrow. I will tell you everything you want to know."

Her slim fingers were on my chest. "I'm going to walk the board walk. And since you are not resting. You hit the beach, you need to get some sun you're looking rather pasty there."

I dropped my jaw in mock offense. "I'm not pasty. Just a little un-tan."

"Honey, if you were anymore white I would be able to see through you. A good tan will define your muscles and that is an order." She pointed and put on her tennis shoes. "Before you forget, we come back here hit mitts and then all participants meet on the beach. We rock out first thing in the morning; your first match is at 11:00am.

Tia let the door slam behind her and I stood alone in the beach house.

I changed quickly to a pair of jean shorts and tank and hit the beach. At six o'clock and the sun was scorching, the water was blue and the women were plenty.

Months ago I would have ate up the attention that I was getting. It should have been illegal from what some of these girls were wearing. I saw every color of swimsuit imaginable with every chest size too.

I waved and made small talk with some guys that I knew from my years of fighting. I was relieved that none of them mentioned my wreck. The less people knew about it the better.

"You must be a fighter with arms like that." Some girl with fire engine red hair glued herself to my arm. Slowly stroking it.

"Yeah, I'll be fighting tomorrow." I felt extremely uncomfortable.

"If you don't have anything to do later on tonight, I'm at the Lexington Inn." She pointed up to the large hotel on the strip. "Me and my best friend are in room 1219. Or is three a crowd for you?"

"Um…I…Well."

"Beat it or you will be eating and crapping through a tube, Red." Tia stepped in between the two us and growled. "Leave now while you still have legs."

The red head stumbled backward in the sand. "I'm sorry I didn't know that he was taken."

Tia stood there and glared at the poor girl until she walked away. "I had no idea that you were so protective."

Tia relaxed. "I just don't need you to go fooling around, I need you focused." Was she jealous? Tia turned and made her way back to beach house and I couldn't help but watch that perfect behind switch back and forth in those shorts.

Don't get me wrong, the last time that I worked mitts with Tia I just about fractured her wrist and she broke a nail which we both walked away with a learning experience. She learned to relax her elbows; I learned how much a manicure cost.

"Are you going like that?" She said with only twenty minutes before we hit the beach for our fighting assignments and weight in.

I looked down at myself. I had on a pair of Venom shorts and Jerry's Gym shirt. "What? This is what you wear to these types of things."

Tia gave me a blank stare and went back to her room. She came back out with a pink box with a long cord on it. "What is that?"

"Devon you look like you are hiding hamsters under your shirt." I looked down at myself and realized that I hadn't shaved my chest in months. "Now take off your shirt, we don't have a lot of time."

I tossed the shirt on the floor and waited. Tia starting pulling out long strips of cloth and I heard the little pink box begin to hiss. "You've waxed before?"

"I usually do it in the shower." She picked up my shirt and handed it to me. "You should put this in your mouth then."

Tia took what looked like a Popsicle stick and dipped it into the wax, the stick looked gobbled over with what looked like honey. She blew on it, I'm assuming to cool it down. Running the stick from the center of my sternum to my navel, she looked back up at me. "Put the shirt in your mouth." She put a long clothe strip on my chest.

"Tia, I've nearly lost a toe. I've had two fingers broken so I think- MY GOD! What the hell?" Tia ripped the waxing strip from my chest and I thought she pulled my heart out. "What you trying to do give me open heart surgery?" My hand went to my chest and felt the smoothness of my skin.

"Put your shirt in your mouth, before someone hears you screaming like a little girl. Now I have to do this like four more times-"

"Four more!"

"I didn't know that you were coming all the way here looking like a bear." She took the shirt from my hands and jammed in my mouth. One for the money-two for the show." She winked at me.

There are worst things than death and they come in a little pink waxing kit.

The event book that Tia was carrying around for the last day looked worn and tattered. "Ok, you'll be fighting Justin Wahl. He's from Mobile, AL. looks pretty tough with a 28-4-9 record. You got this."

I nodded to her and put my ear buds in. I had to drown out everything around. Tia and I were on the beach at 10, one full hour before the fight. The tent that we were in was big enough for at least twenty people, I was able to jog around it and throw punches. Visualize, is what my dad told me before a fight. Play the whole fight out in your head. I knew nothing about this Wahl kid, last night he looked way too confident. I was planning to take that confidence and shove it down his throat.

Tia stood at the front of the tent, not knowing what to do with herself. I couldn't think about her and her uneasiness right now.

I never had any sort of love for rap music, but Tupac was doing it for me right now. I kicked up my IPod a few notches and ran through my combos.

I was completely in the zone now; this was second nature to me. The warm sand under my feet was giving me the surge, the spark that I craved. This was my air that I was meant to breath. I jabbed and kicked. I was suffocating all those weeks in the hospital, I'm actually breathing now. I started to believe that I could make it to the King of the Cage. I could really win this thing. Tupac was chanting that he was about to Bring the Pain and so was I.

Tia stood in front of me and smiled. I took the ear buds out. "Yeah?"

"Let's go win this."

Chapter 15

I came out of the tent and I hadn't realized it was so dark in there. The sun was beating down on us and I had to squint to see where I was going. I felt Tia's hands on my back digging into my shoulders. Everything was right.

My name was announced and I jogged up to the octagon. "You got this. Wahl's doesn't have anything on you, okay. You've trained all your life for this and here is your moment, take it." Tia was practically screaming over the crowd. "Devon, I'm proud of you. You have more fight in you that I could ever imagine."

There was some local band that was playing walk out music that I really didn't have time to pay a lot of attention to. Wahl was announced; undeniably it was the same guy that leered at me all night at the weight in. But today he seemed different.

Sure, I could tell he built up his own lather of sweat in his own tent. His eyes, they weren't screaming hungry like most fighters they were whimpering in surrender.

The official checked us out and asked his questions to both of us. Wahl and I meet in the center; I was so ready I thought I was going to blow up from the inside out. But I couldn't neglect the way Wahl looked. Was he going to take me lightly? Did he think that my injuries had made me soft in the cage? There was nothing for me to do but to answer those questions the bell rung.

Wahl, came at me like a wild man arms swinging. He rammed me into the cage; he twisted his mouth piece to let it hang half out his mouth. "They have my girls. Take me out."

Was he joking? "What?"

He had me in a bear hug, pushing me off the ground. "Hit me as hard as you can. You have to win."

This couldn't be happening, the day I was ready more than ever, Washington took this chance away from me. I shoved Wahl off of me and he had his hands up. I reared back and gave him what everyone was asking for.

I hit him in the nose and I watched it exploded under my fist. Wahl's eyes rolled towards the back of his head and before he hit the ground he whispered, "Thank you."

I didn't wait for my name to be called, I pushed the cage doors open took Tia by the hand and dragged her from the crowd.

"Are you going to tell me what the hell is going on? I mean, Wahl just laid down." Tia shouted and the crowd that we just left behind was no gathering around us to watch round two.

I took her by her waist and pulled her close to me. "Tia, please trust me."

She fought and wiggled out of my arms. "Trust you? You had that fight thrown, didn't you? How in the world could I be so stupid?"

"Tia, it's not what you think. I swear to you." I was pleading with her.

"Bye, Devon." Tia left like a hurricane leaving me behind in her aftermath.

I reckon I walked the strip, up and down. Watching the other fights taken place the rest of that day.

It had to be around eight that evening when I finally made it back to the beach house. I assumed that since the front door was wide open, Tia must have left in a huff.

"We thought that you ran, Mr. Hart." Said an overly dressed man. He must be one of Washington's men.

"Yeah, where was I going to go?" I plopped down on the couch.

Another man came out of the kitchen drinking my orange juice straight out the carton. "I was kinda hoping that you skipped, it would have been a pleasure hunting the great Devon Hart down." Juice running down the side of his mouth.

The other one stepped forward. "Mr. Washington wanted to convey to you that his reach is just about everywhere-"

"I figured that. With you taking a man's girlfriend or wife hostage, to guarantee that I win today."

He smiled. "Look we are working with you not against you. We want you to win just as bad as you want to. Washington, just wanted to let you know-

"Yeah, he's everywhere and he wanted to scare me. Look I have a fight at noon tomorrow. I'm gonna need my rest, so if you would excuse me." I stood and he gripped my arm. "If I were you I would let go." I smirked. "I'm sure you saw how I left your boys over at Washington's place. And I wasn't even warmed up."

Orange juice mouth came over to my other side. "And I'm sure you saw what they do to little girls, hate for your blonde to be next on her knees. By the way, where is Tia?" He turned and scanned the room.

I lunged at him and felt the cool steel of the barrel of a gun to the base of my skull. "Mr. Hart we aren't here to aggravate you in anyway. Just here to let you know that we are taking care of things. You do your part and we will do ours."

He motioned for juicy to leave while he still had the gun to the back of my head. "Devon, I don't have time to explain but my name is Detective Warren Lock. I'm a friend of Henry's he told me to keep an eye on you. Believe me you are safe; just don't go against these guys, okay. I've been tracking you since you got off the plane. I've been in Washington's operation for over a year now working undercover. Be safe." He took the gun from the back of my head and walked to the door.

I couldn't breathe. There was too much going on right now for me to try and take it all in. I opened my mouth to speak. Detective Lock turned to me and put his finger to his lips. "Wahl's wife and daughter have been returned to him unharmed. Go get some rest." He shut the door.

I walked to the balcony and stared out at to the rushing water. The sounds of celebration for winners and the smell of the defeat mixed with the salt water was making me dizzy.

A tingle went up my spine, I wasn't alone. I turned and the mountain of rage took over me and I rushed forward, knocking Tia right on her behind. "I'm sorry." I shouted and lifted her with one arm off the marble floor.

"I heard. What type of trouble are we in." The way that she said we made my hand go up and move her bangs out of her face from the fall.

"You were here all this time…with them?" My mind raced to every ugly, damaging and hurtful scenario.

"I heard the door open and I was about to let you have it and I heard two voices and neither were yours. So I hid in the closet."

"Good girl." I picked her up in my arms and held her. "I would have died if something happened to you." I put her back on the ground. "I should have told you everything from the beginning, I should have been honest with you about The Beast Wars and all of it."

I lead Tia to the couch and told her everything from the beginning. Almost being shot by Eddie Kingsford at Miller's, Washington and his mansion and little Sophia. She sat there and nodded like I was telling her a bedtime story.

"Wow, so now you have to win."

"Yeah, I do. Tia I would understand if you want to get back on the plane back to Nashville and forget that you ever met me. Honestly, it would be for the best." I didn't want her to go.

"We came down here as a team and we are going to leave here the same." She looked past me out the balcony windows as the sun was no longer seen. "We need to go to sleep. You have a hometown favorite that you are up against in the morning. Dude hails from Ft. Lauderdale and he's a mean one."

I prayed that there would be no interference from Washington and let me win a clean fight. Tia had showered and gave me orders that we will be up no later than nine am to hit mitts.

I stayed up looking out at the water. How beautiful it was but how the waves crashed down without mercy onto the sand over and over. I wondered in life who was the water and who was the sand? Was the sand Tia, being beaten and smacked around. Or was it me, hit and knocked from here to there. Who knew?

I took a long hot shower and my eyes could barely stay open as I dried off and lay face down in the soft duvet.

One eye popped open when I heard the knock on my bedroom door. "Come in." I groaned.

Tia stood in my door way. I had to crane my next to see her, her features were covered by the dark. "Can I come in?"

I rolled over on my back and she tumbled in the bed beside me. Granted my memory was pretty much in the dirt, but I couldn't recall a time that I had a beautiful woman in my bed and didn't know what to do. "So couldn't sleep?"

"I just wanted to know if you wanted to do this now or later." Tia said in the dark. "I mean if you want to at all, you're the expert in this."

I chuckled. "Well, I wouldn't call myself an expert but I get the job done. I think I leave those pretty satisfied." I turned over towards her; even in the dark she was gorgeous. Her blonde hair brought light in the dark room as it fanned over the pillow.

"Well, I know that silly. I just want you to kinda satisfy my curiosity is all. Again, if you want to do this later or before the fight in the morning is fine with me."

There was no way in the world that I was going to pass up this chance. "I mean it all depends on you. Do you want to do this?" I whispered to her in the dark. Leaning closer to her smelling her hair and neck.

Her eyes still looked up to the ceiling. "I want to get started as soon as possible. I think us getting all of it out of the way will bring us a little closer, ya know?"

"Defiantly." I put my hand on her flat stomach and rubbed.

She giggled a bit and I groaned. "Your hands feel so good." I know something else that would feel wonderful I thought. "Now about the fight tomorrow. The Ft. Lauderdale guy, I've been reading that he was in the military and boxed there so his ground game isn't what yours is like."

"What?" I was seconds away from rolling on top of her when she brings up this guy.

"Huh? I mean we can talk about the fight in the morning if you're tired." She sat straight up in the bed.

I had to recover quickly. "Yeah, I guess. I mean what's this guy's game Tia?"

I laid there in the bed as Tia went on about tomorrow's strategy against Richard Ley. It was all so new for Tia; I had already known the guy from the fighting circles that I ran in.

"Devon are you listening to me?" She rolled over and put her arm under the pillow. "I mean if you want to do this later-"

"No, we can do it now." I listened as she talked with so much excitement. It made fighting brand new again for me.

Here I was again, under the tent with Tia and Tupac. I scanned the crowd for any of Washington's men or the detective, but I only saw beach bums, groupies and diehard fans. "Am I going to get any surprises today?" Tia pulled off my shirt over my head.

"Not that I'm aware of. Hell, at this point and time anything could happen." I danced around my side of the cage.

Ley entered and the hometown favorite was eating up the love he was getting from the fans. Whatever, hopefully they will carry this guy out on a stretcher when I'm done with him.

The bell rung and Ley pranced to me. If Tia was right this guy had no ground game and from what I could remember he liked to knock his opponents out first chance he gets. I be damned if he try that with me.

I pushed off on the ball of my foot, my arms up I watched as Ley stabbed a fist at me and I slipped him and in doing so the ball of my foot no longer had traction.

I hit the mat on my shoulder and I heard the crowd go crazy that I was down. Think the mat was still slick from the previous fight. I should have thought of that, if I wasn't on the ground already I would kicked my own ass.

Ley, showed his mouth piece which was red and white with the Florida state shape on it. I was planning to kick Miami back to his tonsils.

He was over me and like I thought he was going to try and pound me. I knew that I couldn't make another mistake, I couldn't afford and neither could Kingsford and his family. Once Ley's knees hit the mat I knew that I had him.

He drew back with his right to punch me and I walled giving me the opening that I needed to take his wrist. Snatching him off balance, his eyes widened and he knew that he was in trouble. Taking his wrist with my right, I grabbed his bare shoulder and pulled him into me.

I cocked my leg over his back, let go off his shoulder and pushed his neck away from me. The mat was already slick from some other meat heads feet, so I used it to my advantage and rotated away from Ley.

I could hear Tia screaming and clapping behind me, my girl. With his elbow between my legs I put my foot under his chin for leverage. Ley was flexing and wiggling but I held on to his wrist with pure adrenaline pumping through me. "Come on Devon!" She shouted and that gave me everything that I needed. I pushed off on his face, got my other leg from under him. Ley's arm was extended and twisted in my lap. I pointed my knees to the very disappointed crowd and smiled.

Some may say it was cocky but at this point I didn't care. I winked at Tia and blew her a kiss before I took Ley's shorts and pulled it towards me, rising up on my knees. I had to admit the guy tried to hang on but when you are in *my* omoplata from guard you either leave with your arm in a sling or your ass in one.

Chapter 16

"Devon, are you sure you are okay? I mean you were amazing today, but your leg." Pulling up on my knees the move that finished Ley had about finished me. My hip was tired and worn out; I tried everything that I could to not limp back to the beach house.

But she caught me. "I'm good. Just need to get some food in me and rest a bit. I'll be fine and don't worry so much; you're acting like my mother." I lay on the sofa and smiled.

"Really?" Tossing a sofa pillow at my head. "I just don't want to see you hurt is all. Man." She looked down at me and smiled.

"What?"

"You were amazing out there. You just about took that guys shoulder out. I should be passing out business cards out here. Half these guys are going to need a physical therapist if you keep fighting like this." She turned to walk back to her room on the other side of the beach house and stopped. "Hey what was that wink and kiss about?"

"Well, it was a very hot brunette standing behind you and I had to let her know that her hometown favorite just got handled." I smiled.

Her cheeks turned pink. "Oh." Tia went back to her room and shut the door before I could tell her that it was all for her.

My cell phone jiggled in my bag. "Look at you big winner and thangs. Boy, you killing them out there." Henry hollered over the phone.

"How do you know?" Trying to concentrate on what he was saying. Think of a way to tell Tia that I was winking at her and get some ice on my hip.

"Online fool. They just posted your win online. Just want to congratulate you is all. Go get some rest and I know that you are going to want a burger and fries after the fight so I will leave you to it. Hey how are things going with Tia?"

"What do you mean?" I stood looking down the hall at her door.

I heard him exhale loudly. "You like her and everyone in the world knows it. Why don't you just tell her and get it over with?" Henry was right I should just tell her. "You're scared aren't you?"

"Naw, I'm not scared. It's just she's my trainer and I don't want to make things weird between us. After Vegas I'll say something but until then it's all business."

"Whatever, bro. I heard that you met a buddy of mine." He had to be talking about Det. Lock. Before I could confirm or deny, Henry said. "Yeah, there is no need for you to go on about it. Just wanted to let you know that since I wasn't there someone that I trust is. Thank me later."

Was my phone tapped? Was the beach house bugged? "I'll thank you now, thanks bro. Look a cheese burger is calling my name so I got to run okay?" We signed off the call and I hobbled down the hall to Tia's room her door slightly cracked. She was sitting on the bed back away from me on the phone.

"Yeah, it would be awkward you know. I'm his trainer and besides guys like him don't really like chicks like me." Tia said to the other person on the phone.

I couldn't make out if this person on the phone was in my corner or totally working against me. "He's like you know, all good looking and charming in his own kinda way." She giggled and I wanted to do so many naughty things to her. "Guys like him have women falling over themselves to get to him. I guess it was some chick there that he was making eyes with at the fight, so to save myself a load of embarrassment I will let sleeping dogs lie."

I hurt her feelings, now my chest was in a pain competition with my leg. I knocked on the door softly. Tia about jumped straight off the bed. "Can I come in?"

Her smiled was strained. "Annie, let me call you back." She hung up and turned to me. Well, I know that Annie has my back on this one. "What's up?" Her look was pressed like me being on the other side of the room was too close for her.

"I don't think that I every told you that I appreciate you coming all the way down here to help out. I know that you took some time off of work to do this and it means a lot." I took a few steps closer and I saw her clutch the bed comforter.

"It's not a big deal." Her smile was fake. "You're a winner- winner chicken dinner. Speaking of which you said that you were hungry, I'm sure that I can find you something to eat on the strip. She put on her flip flops and tried to bolt pass me to the door.

I caught her arm. "Hey why are you running out of her like there's a fire?"

Yanking back her arm. "I know that the fight took a lot out of you. You need to eat and relax. I'll be back." I could hear her shout at the door. "Get off that leg."

About 45 minutes later she returned with a to go box filled with spicy tacos. Tia left my box in the kitchen and walked back to her room. I tried to ignore her ignoring me but if we were going to work together we had to get it all out.

I found myself knocking on her door and she gave a soft. "Come in."

"Hey, um…well when I used to train with Jerry we would eat together. So if you don't mind do you want to come out here and eat with me in the kitchen at the table? That's if you want to." Please God.

I could see her twist her hands around considering my offer. "Sure why not." She walked past me down the hall. Tia stood at the table looking at the chairs as if she didn't know what they were used for. "How's your leg?"

I rubbed at the scare for a second. "Better." Which it was. "Come sit down." I pulled a seat out for her to sit and I took the chair across from her." I opened the box and bit down into heaven. "Tia, if it's all the same to you I would really like to get to know you. I mean I don't want to be all in your business or anything just kind of want to be your friend."

Tia sat back in the chair and looked like she again was mulling over the request. "What do you want to know?" Opening her box of food.

"Like what type of music do you like what were you like as a kid. What type of men do you like?" Had to sneak that one in there.

Her eyebrow hitched. "I like all kinds of music. Remember I was a dancer. I was kind of the wild child, my sister was the smart one-"

"And you are the pretty one, right?"

Tia smiled put her head down and picked at her taco. "No way, my sister Tamara is the beautiful one." She paused for a moment. "To answer your other question. I don't know. I guess I like a guy that allows me to be my own person. I need him strong and attentive. Willing to help me but not overbearing."

"Sounds like you want a dog." Biting down on my taco.

She laughed out loud. "No, I have had plenty of those along the way, if I get any more people would think I was running a kennel." Tia looked at the sun making its reflection on the water. "It's beautiful here."

"Look I never met your sister but I know in my heart that she can't be more beautiful than the woman that is sitting across from me."

"You don't mean that." She put her hand to her mouth and looked away.

"I'm a fighter not a liar." I had to gather my words up before I screwed this up. "Tia I know that you've been hurt a lot and I can't change that, but you and I both have scars some of them fade others stick around." I rubbed my hip. "I'm sure some guy would say some crap like, let me take away your pain and heal you. I know I can't do that and if I had the power to do so, you wouldn't be the woman that you are today. I guess what I'm asking is-"

I probably ran the gambit of every cuss word in my head when I heard the knock on the door.

I scooted back from the chair, praying that it was good news and it better be. I was seconds away from cracking her shell. "What?!"

My mom didn't jump back from my loud bark like she was expecting me to loud and bull headed. She dug in her purse and handed me an envelope. "This is your money from the sale of the farm. I hope that you used the money wisely." She turned on a pair of high heels that probably equaled the amount of the contents of the envelope.

"Wait, you came all the way to Florida to give me a check? You could have left it with Randle."

She looked so tired when she turned to face me. "Devon, I thought that something like this should be given in person and not left on your doorstep." She looked back to her rental car in the driveway. "You've always been smart and I know that you will put the money to good use."

Was I really a new person? Someone that was able to forgive and forget. "Mom, do you want to come in? We got tacos."

"We?" Even in heels she was nowhere near my heights as she tried to get on her toes look pass me into the house. "Devon, if you have company I do not want to intrude." Gripping her bag and looking back at the car.

"What about you come in and I introduce you to my trainer." I released the knob on the door and by itself it opened for her.

She shook her head. "I have a flight in a few hours. Anthony saw online that you were here and again I wanted you to have it. I'm sorry."

"I fight tomorrow. I would kinda like if you know you would come. I'm sure that Anthony can get you another ticket to Georgia." As long as I've been fighting my mom has never even pretended to like the sport. She called it barbaric and dangerous. "I would love for you to be there and-"

"I can't see you get hurt again." Tightening her grip on her handbag. "For reasons that I am too tired to discuss, I know that you feel like I don't love you or I never cared for you. But I will always and forever love you and even when you think you don't need me I will be there for you Devon. I don't want you to ever forget that." She turned on your heels.

I saw a shot of blonde duck under my arm and out the front door. "Mrs. Hart, hi. I'm Tia Devon's trainer."

My mom looked at Tia then at me. "You're his trainer?" She didn't say it in a disrespectful way more surprised that her bull headed son was taking orders from a woman.

"Devon and I just sat down for a late lunch we have more than enough tacos to feed a small village." Tia looked back at me and smiled. "I would be honored to have lunch with you." Tia leaned over to my mom. "Plus, I need all the dirt on this guy." Hitching her thumb back to me.

"Well, I don't want to impose on the two of you." My mom said looking between the both of us.

Tia took my mom's hand in hers. "I insist."

The three of walked back to the kitchen and mom went on and on about the beautiful house before she sat down at the table. "Tia dear, how in God's name did you ever get hooked in with this big goof?" My mom smiled at me from her end of the table. "You are such a beautiful girl." I could read my mom's mind and one word kept vibrating throughout the house-grandchildren.

"As you know Devon was in a car accident and I was his physical therapist. He was in a bind, so he asked would I help and I accepted." Tia said shoveling tacos and black beans on my mom's plate. "Mrs. Hart I don't want you to worry. I'm also a registered nurse, so I'm able to monitor him."

"Tia, I am no longer Mrs. Hart-"She gave me an apologetic look. "You can call me Lynn. And I'm sure that you are taking good care of him." Reaching touching my hand. "You look good, Devon really good. Anthony is going to love hearing that you made a wonderful recovery."

"Well, I don't know about the rest of you but I'm starving." Tia wresting with her taco.

Nearly two and half hours later, Tia was picking up dishes and glasses. "I just text Anthony to book me another flight out tomorrow evening."

"Tomorrow evening? So you're going to stay for the fight then?" I sounded like a little kid being promised a pony.

"Yes, Devon. If this is what I have to do to get closer to you, I'll go and see you. But I can't guarantee that I wouldn't be having my hands over my eyes the whole time."

"There's something that I go to do. In the room." Tia walked fast back into her bedroom.

Once the door was shut. "Devon, that is a beautiful girl in there, please don't hurt her."

My jaw almost hit the table. "What makes you say that?"

My mom rolled her eyes. "Devon, I may be old but I'm not stupid. You thought you were so slick. Sneaking girls in the house. Me and your father knew."

Dang. I thought I had covered my tracks.

"Do you know how many pairs of panties we would find in the barn? I could have opened up my very own Victoria's Secret." We both laughed. "Seriously, Devon she likes you and she's in your corner. Be good to her."

"I like her too and-"

"A blind man can see that. You were mesmerized on how the woman can chew."

"It's more than that. I mean she's not hard to look at but she makes me…well you know like-"

"Better." I nodded. "Then that is the woman that you need to be with." My mom turned in her seat to face me. "You remember that one kid that you used to wrestle with…um the dark hair really tall." My mom was waving her hand above her head. "What's the kid's name you were probably like in the fifth or sixth grade?"

"Quincy McDowell? Yeah, what about him?"

"You remember when you started Tae Kwon Do, you were so used to boxing and you had to learn something new. You were so frustrated because you were always the best." I remembered those days, how I wanted to quit. This was way before MMA became really big and at the time I wanted to be a boxer like my old man. "And here comes this kid Quincy."

"Yeah, I hated that kid." I smiled.

"Yeah, cause he beat the crude out of you ever time you went to class." I opened my mouth she waved her hands. "Your father told me."

"He hit a growth spurt out of nowhere that dude use to punish me."

"But he made you better. When you came home after you were a whole different person. Kind of like you are right now. She's made you better. Devon, just don't be afraid of it."

I scrunched up my face. "Afraid? You don't have to worry about that."

My mother stood and put the purse strap over her shoulder. "There are people that fear failure and there are those that fear success. Both will keep you stagnant. If you like her don't be afraid of your feelings."

"I promise. I will treat her right…that's if she feels the same."

My mom hugged me tight around my neck. "That should be the least of your fears." Taking a step back. "Look, I will go to your game-"

"Match." I corrected.

"Match tomorrow."

"At one."

"I will be there. Let me get a hotel room and I will see you in the afternoon." This is probably the happiest I have ever seen my mom. The happiness looked good on her. I walked her out to her rental car and she must have given me a thousand more kisses before she drove off.

Now, back to bigger things. Tia.

I had my hand ready to knock on her door when she opened. "I like your mom she's super sweet." Tia opened her bedroom door both of us sat on the bed.

"Yeah, she can be a good lady when she wants to be. And thank you for being, well I guess you."

"You were failing miserably out there talking to her, so I thought I would help." She grinned. I could see the scar poking out of her pant leg; I wanted to trace the line with my finger.

"Well, me and my mom kinda went through what you would call a rough patch." It was more like someone dropped an Atom bomb on our relationship. "But maybe this is a new start to building something who knows." I shrugged. "But back to the conversation that we were having earlier." I exhaled. "I'm attracted to you. But I guess that you already know that, I just want to pursue something with you." I was sweating buckets over here.

"Like a relationship?" She shook her head and her golden hair fell over her shoulders. "I don't think that I'm really equipped to be someone's girlfriend, you know? You deserve like a kick ass girl. A girl that can deal with your job and all it in tells."

I pinched her elbow softly. "What does that supposed to mean? Like groupies?" She nodded. "I was winking at you, you know? You looked so adorable over there screaming my name and cheering me on. I was trying to show-off a bit." Tia turned with her mouth open. "There was no brunette behind you; I was trying to give you a hard time. And it back fired on me."

"Every time I think you are a complete asshole you switch up on me." She smiled at me bumping her shoulder into mine. "You can be an okay guy when you want to be."

"Look, if you don't want to hang out with me like that, all I can say is too bad. Because I'm going to wear you down." I held her hand.

"Really now? And how are you going to do that?" Turning to face me on her bed.

"I'm going to prove to you that I'm not just an okay guy, but a good one. A guy that you would want to be with. If that doesn't work I'll start stalking you. Popping up at your house and job. Calling you at all times of the night. I will bug you in submission and then you will have no other choice but to fall madly in love with me." I smiled letting her know my plan.

Tia cocked her head to the side and looked me over. "And you think that is really going to work…on me." Pointing back to herself.

"It's foolproof. Once you see how good life can be it's a wrap. But if that doesn't work I'll chain myself to your car."

"My goodness."

Today I felt really good. The sun was high in the sky and the salty water smell coming from the ocean didn't burn my nose like it had been. My mom was in the front role looking completely out of place. She had large designer sunglasses that made her look like a beetle, the pink suit she was wearing must of felt like a fur coat in this weather. And who in their right mind wear 3 ½ inch heels in the sand?

Remembering my mistake from yesterday, I wiped my feet not wanting to face plant again. "This guy is a monster, Devon. Watch out for his right hand, he's got some power to him." Eric Green is a mean son of cuss. He's roughly my height and weight. His shoulders are massive just ripped. If Brock Lesnar had a black big brother his name would be Eric Green.

Green came at me fist up. He and I both threw a couple jabs feeling each other out. I gave a quick glance to my mom in the stands who was biting the heck out of her nails. I told myself I will make this quick for her sake. I charged at his knees and he folded. Once he was on the ground I started to punch squatting over him. Then someone left the caged unlock and let my lion out. He blocked most of my punches I just continued to wail on him. Green made himself into a little ball and I attacked his back and ribs with hard steady punches, my intention was to have this man piss blood for the next week.

Green poked his head out of his turtle shell for a second and I introduced his chin to my knee and the next thing I knew the ref was yanking me off of Green's limp body.

I went back to my side of the cage howled and rattled the cage. The crowd was yelling my name, Tia smiled and my mom looked like her tacos from yesterday were going to make another showing on her pink suit.

Green's trainer gave me the evil eye which was suspect but I didn't care. Green was still on the mat looking around like he just woken up from a bad dream. Three were down I had one more to go.

Chapter 17

The three of us were back at the beach house. Tia had given my mom a t-shirt; she had sweated through her suit before the fight even started.

"Devon, I had no idea you were that strong, my goodness. You could have killed that young man." My mom fanned herself sitting at the kitchen table.

I shrugged. "It was either that or him beat me to a pulp."

"How are your legs doing?" Tia sat next to me.

"They're good, didn't want to use them up. Big fight is tomorrow." I faced my mom. "Are you staying for that one too?"

Shaking her head. "Sorry, honey. Anthony is going to need me home. I booked a flight for later on this evening." I wanted her to stay. I wanted her to know that all the time that I was training wasn't for nothing. "Devon, if your father could of saw you today." She smiled. "I think the Lord in Heaven and all His angels had to hold him back up from coming down to earth."

"Yeah, dad would pick me up and carried me around the cage if he were here." The old man would have had his chest poked out. Telling anybody that would listen that his son beat the snot out some kid.

"I'm proud of you Devon." Taking her purse off the table. "I didn't approve you fighting before the accident and I really don't now. But you handled yourself out there. You should feel good about it."

I stood and hugged my mom pulling her feet off the ground. "I love you mom and thank you for staying, it meant a lot for you to come." I heard her sniff and I knew that she was crying. "Don't cry mom."

"I'm not sad…it's just. Devon you are a walking miracle, you know that? I saw you. I saw pins sticking out of you. You had so many gaze pads and bandages you looked like a mummy. Now look at you. You just beat up that man without hesitation, without fear."

I put my mom back on the ground; Tia had a tear in her eye too. "You can thank Tia. She was the one that pushed me harder than Jerry. I owe her everything."

My mom took both of our hands and looked between the two of us. "Tia, dear you know Devon likes you right?"

"Mom!"

"Devon be quiet." She cleared her throat and turned to face Tia, who was turning every shade of red. "And I know that you like him too. So could the both of you please get over yourselves? The sexual tension is so thick in here you can cut it like a knife."

"Mom!"

My mom pointed a finger at me. "Devon, I am not getting any younger and you are my only child. I would love to have little Devons and Tias running around. Little blonde girls with big blue eyes. And rough and tumble boys. Some little beautiful person calling me grandma." She clapped her hands together under her chin and beamed. "Now, I think my work here is done. Call me when you win tomorrow." She got to the door and turned. "Take care of her, Devon. Love is so hard to find don't screw it up." Then she shut the door.

"So should we start on those grandchildren now or after lunch?" Tia said right behind me.

"Please, don't tempt me. I would tear you apart." I had gone months without a taste and being with Tia the poor girl wouldn't stand a chance.

"Really? You think so, huh? Bet you-you can't." She shook that perfect little bottom at me and everything else in the world really didn't matter.

"Tia." I warned.

"What you gonna do, huh?" She pushed me to the side with her hip. "I dare you." I stood there for a second and thought it out. I ran after her. Tia screamed and ran around the kitchen table. Tia could barely run from laughing. "Devon, I was joking."

"Oh no. You done started something girl and know I'm going to be the one to finish it." I chased her around and around the table. She went left then went right then down the hall to her room, squealing.

I chased her and fell to the floor. "Tia!" Gripping my hip. My eyes snapped shut; I rolled over on my back.

"Devon." She ran back to me and kneeled at my side. "Is it your hip?" The look of concern washed away when I took her by the waist and rolled her underneath me. "Liar." She shouted.

"Nope, I'm a thief I still kisses." I kissed harder than I would have liked to, so I blamed it on the build of tension between us.

Tia opened her legs inviting me in to her. Kissing me back. "Devon."

"Hmm." Still kissing that lovely mouth of hers. Tasting the pink lip gloss, was a dream that finally has come true. Now I want to taste other things. I put my hand on the button of her shorts.

"We gotta stop." But she didn't pull away. "In the trainer's rule book, all fighters have to refrain from all sexual activity. You have a fight tomorrow afternoon." Tia wiggled from up under me and put her back to the hallway wall out of breath. "As much as I want to. I don't want to be the reason that you lose. I'm sorry."

"No worries. Because I know a great way that we can celebrate the win tomorrow.

After a very long cold shower, my mind was still on that kiss and I almost missed the call. "Heard you rocking heads out there boy." Jerry's laugh vibrated through the phone.

"Doing the best that I can." I figured that Henry has told everyone in Middle Tennessee about the win. "How's Maggie doing?"

"She's better, wish your lady friend was here to help her get around some. I think she's more frustrated than anything. Maggs isn't able to go like she used to and her face isn't as slack as it was before, but all in all the old gal is hanging in there."

"That's awesome to hear. Well tomorrow is the moment of truth, that will be the test to see if I'm really good or the guys I'm fighting are really bad." Even though, the first guy was literally taken out by Washington the other two were all me.

I heard Jerry exhale into the phone. "Time will tell that story. You eat yet?" At the time I just wanted a plate full of Tia. "Not yet. Thinking about going on the strip and picking something up. Then hit mitts then get rested up for the fight tomorrow." I tightened the towel over my waist and laid across the bed.

"Not gonna hold you up. Get some food in ya and then lights out. What time you putting the gloves on?" I could tell the old man was hungry for a fight. Man, it felt like forever since the last time he saw me do damage.

"Fights at two in the afternoon. Call Ox I'm sure he will be watching the stats online."

"I just may do that, look son goodnight."

"Night."

I laid there across the bed thinking of everything that I've been through. The wreck that damn near took everything away from me, Kingsford and Washington. I stood and put some shorts on, peeking out the window the sun was going down.

The beach house was silent and I took the short walk to the end of the hall to Tia's room. I knocked no answer.

"Thank goodness you're not in a seeing contest you would lose." I hadn't realized that I walked pretty much right past her. She was leaning back on the two back legs of a chair on the balcony. The warm ocean air felt amazing on my bare legs. I took a seat next to her as we watched the ocean. "Growing up in Michigan you never get to see stuff like this." Her eyes darted to people walking on the boardwalk then back to the beach. She resembled a little girl the first time seeing the ocean.

"My dad would take me and mom down to the Alabama Gulf coast when I was a kid." I remember my dad making me run in the sand, telling me it would make me faster. While other kids my age were building sand castles and jumping waves. I ran until my legs were about to give out and I was as red as a lobster.

"Sounds like a great family vacation. All we got growing up were trips to see my grandparents in Canada."

"French Canadian, ah." I smiled at as she looked at the sunset.

"Oui. Vous etes un butt face."

"That sounded so sexy. But did you call me a butt face?"

She busted up laughing. "Who says a jock can't speak a foreign language."

"Come here."

She didn't move. "I am here."

"Tia come over here please."

She dropped the chair legs on the balcony floor and stomped all of two steps towards me. I took her hand and pulled it towards. Tia took her rightful place sitting on my knee. "Tell me if I start to hurt you."

"I have gloves that weight more than you relax." She did and straddled my knee.

If I could I would do this forever.

I was more than hyped up for the fight. The meat head that I was up against was some dude from Virginia. Pretty new to the game from what Tia told me. Never take anyone lightly is what my father would say.

My back was turned going over my combos at the far end of the tent. With my headphones jacked all the way up, I was in the zone and nearly punched a guy that tapped me on the shoulder.

He was a broad dude. Shirt had to be at least two sizes too small. Muscle bulging out trying to find release. "Ah, bro I'm sorry but the fight has been cancelled." His dark eyes looked me over.

"What? What the hell do you mean it's been cancelled?"

The meat head shrugged his shoulder, looking like he had something far more better to do than to crush my dream. "Horace Spencer's pee test came back dirty, he's out. So you are the winner."

This was b.s. I could smell it from a mile away. Our pee test results were in days ago. Washington was behind this. "Look, bro." The dream crusher said. "When something like this goes down, you are the winner. You want to go out and wave to the crowd or something."

"Hell no." I wanted to pout.

"Is the address where you're staying correct, later on today we will drop your winnings check to ya."

"Whatever."

"Do you really have to be such a big kid?" Tia said, folding her arms over her chest. "So what you didn't fight today. We can catch an earlier flight back home."

By the time we got to the beach house I had about 10 text messages from Henry. Saying how sorry he was and to call. I missed two calls from my mom and one from Jerry. I just didn't feel like talking.

Tia pulled her carry-on bag to the front door. "So you are going to be an ass for the rest of the day then."

"No. You just don't get it do you?" Honestly, I couldn't put my feelings into words.

Walking back towards me and sitting next to me on the sofa. "No, I guess I don't so why don't you explain it to me."

I took a deep breath and tried to get everything that I need to say out without sounding too stupid. "I'm pissed off on so many levels right now." I rubbed my eyes. "The first, I have something to prove-"

Tia held her hand up. "Let me stop you right there. I know you got bonked on the head, but do you remember you could barely walk a few months ago. Stop trying to fight ghost, Devon. You've done things able body men couldn't do. You proved that you can walk, run and fight. What is this need that you have? Do you want to fly next?"

"I want to be the best." I shouted and she rocked back in her seat." I closed my eyes and tried to reel it back in. "Those guys were bums that I fought. I was hoping today I was going to get a real challenge. The first guy was taken out by Washington. But the second and third." I shook my head. "In all honesty, I would have wrecked them before my car accident. What I did the last few days wasn't crap."

"I thought you did great. You hadn't fought in months and you came back, but you are going to get better. This is just a warm up to Vegas. We will train super hard and then you could prove to yourself that you are worthy of being here. Right here." She pointed to the floor.

Did she just hit the nail on the head? Was that the silent ache in me that felt out of place, like a stranger in my own home? "Maybe so. I feel like I've been cheated and a cheater all at the same time. That kid Horace was probably on some enhancement crap. He's a fake and a disgrace to the sport."

"My ex was juicing for a while. It does crazy stuff to ya." Tia rubbed the scare on her leg. "When I was laying in the hospital thinking about it all, he was raging then." She hunched her shoulders. "Things in a relationship we accept are the things that we regret."

Being in the sport that I'm in-you see it all the time. Guys pumping themselves up with that garbage. I guess every gym had their stories.

Mine was this dude, can't remember his name but he was about five inches short than me. Medium build within a month he was a monster. Flipped out one day about something small, Jerry tossed him out on his ear. The back acne and the strained voice was always a sign of a dude on steroids.

Henry told me he saw the dude a few months later looked like he was in stage four cancer, body shrunk down to almost nothing. I shook my head at the thought of a similar monster coming after Tia. I took her the hand and pulled her close to me. "Devon, it was a long time ago. My ex is probably dead or in jail or died in jail. Who cares?" She knew exactly what I was thinking and it made me smile while my face was buried in her hair."

"I'll kill him." I whispered.

"Well aren't you all sweet and stuff. Come on I managed to get us an earlier flight back home. We better get to moving our cab should be here in a second."

Tia was right, but I wanted to stay in his kick ass beach house overlooking the water. Tia standing on the balcony hair blowing in the breeze. One day.

I swear I won't try anything, I promise. Scout's honor." I put the puppy dog eyes on her, but Tia wasn't budging.

She stood on my porch looking back at her car. "Devon, you weren't even in the Scouts so don't even try it. I'm going home and getting into my own bed. Good night."

I tried to rest on the plane but I kept looking at her, just wanting more of her. I caught her looking at me when she thought I wasn't looking.

Now here we were standing here and I was practically begging for her to stay the night with me. Tia took one more step backwards to her car. "I got to get some rest and you need to lay down."

"I want to lay down with you." I poked my bottom lip out. "Please."

"Nope."

"But I said please." I folded my arms.

"So, I'm tired."

"There is a warm bed right upstairs with your name all over it." For a second I saw her consider the thought then she shook her head.

"Goodnight Devon."

"Well, can I have a goodnight kiss then?" She smiled and I knew once we kissed she wouldn't get enough. Tia blew me a kiss as she walked to her car. "Hey, what the hell?"

"There was this hot brunette behind you. Just wanted him to know that his homeboy just got handled." I laughed and waved as she accelerated down the dirt road.

I exhaled and took my bag into the empty house. It was barely five in the evening and it was getting dark. I wished that I could watch the sunset, but I knew it wouldn't be the same. Tennessee is beautiful but the way the sun hit the ocean in Florida it just didn't compare. Plus, I didn't have a hot blonde sitting in my lap when the sun was saying goodnight.

Randle left a note on the counter, saying that he was going to East Tennessee for the week but there was food in the fridge.

I thought about calling Henry but it was the weekend and I'm sure that some woman's daughter was screaming her head off in Henry's bed.

I sent a quick to my mom tell her that I was home safe. I decided to call Jerry in the morning. Throwing my dirty clothes in the washer my cell rang. "Devon, I want to thank you for all of your cooperation. If you ever need me, you know where I leave." Washington spoke as if he hadn't done about a million things illegal today.

"Sure. So we're good then, right?"

"More than good. I have received my return and Kingsford and his family are happily reunited thanks to you."

"No thanks to you. My first fight you fixed and the last one." I was anger that this bastard took my chances away from me.

I heard him chuckle. "Devon, you killed two birds with one stone. Your first opponent owed me a favor. In lying down he was able to pay me back." Yeah, by taking his family hostage, I thought. "But the last gentlemen I cannot take credit for. He was a dirty fighter, I just drew a little attention to his extra activity. All in all I wanted you to have an opportunity to win and win honesty."

I wanted to yell at him, what in the hell did he know about honesty? He probably walked crooked. "Well, our dealings are done. I pray that I never have to see you are hear from you again."

"Despite what you think of me, I hope to never see you either. Have a good night." My thumb was over the END button. "Devon." I heard him say and put the phone back to my ear. "I'm sorry that you got shot down by the blonde." Before I grabbed his throat through the phone. Washington hung up.

Chapter 18

"Henry this guy is was watching my house. He saw me and Tia, here." I was pacing my kitchen.

"He was just trying to scare you. If he wanted to do something to you, he would have done it by now." Henry exhaled. "If it makes you feel any better I got a guy checking out Tia's place right now."

I was angry on so many different levels. Washington was really starting to get under my skin. And I was the only one that should be protecting Tia. "Fine." I blurted out. "Fine. What has your friend got him?"

"Shit, nothing yet. I told you before this guy can do things and no one can see it. He has men in place to basically do all of his dirty work."

Great, the guy had his own evil minions to do his evil bidding. "So I just have to sit here and wait around."

"I swear to you nothing will happen to you or Tia. The guy is crazier than a bed bug but he is a man of his word. If he cut you lose then you are cut lose. Enjoy it and let me handle it."

Henry was Johnny on the spot. I couldn't do anything about it but worry. It was getting late and Henry had to be up and moving to get to work. I hung up the phone with a promise that I wouldn't stick my nose in somewhere it didn't belong.

You would have thought I was a king when I walked back into the gym on Monday. I received more back slaps than I could imagine. I just didn't feel like a king.

"Wow, I am getting trained by the winner of The Beast Wars." Parker mouth hung open. "I mean, I read everything online. You were killing guys. I'm sure you set some sort of record; you either knocked the guy out cold or put them in a submission move all within the first round. Wow." Yeah right wow.

"When you train hard it shows. Now show me what you been working on since I've been gone."

I couldn't believe that I shoveled this kid that crap. But it did my heart some good knowing that he was getting better. He was doing great in his walls when we were doing some mitt work.

Parker stopped and put his hands down and stuck his chin out behind me. Michael tip toed into the gym trying to keep his head down.

"Be back." I told Parker tossing him my gloves. I jogged over to Michael. "Hey, um can I talk to you for a second." Michael had a face that read he would rather hug a porcupine. He followed me into the locker room giving me a blank stare. "Look, I have no idea what the hell I did to you. But if it means anything I'm sorry."

He twisted up his face at me. "If my ribs still weren't killing me I would break your neck."

I stood there facing him, kinda wishing he would make a move. "If you would just tell me what it was I did-"

Michael dropped his bag and made large fist at his sides. "You screwed her!" He shouted. "You have to have everything don't you?"

"I have no idea what you are talking about." I really didn't.

"You're serious?" He shook his head and turned his back to me. The muscles in his back flexed and tensed underneath his Nike shirt.

"She's my sister. For Christ's sake Devon, you slept with my little sister."

Oh God. I tried to remember. Every piece of ass that I could think of ran across my mind. Blondes, brunettes, red heads my goodness I was a whore. But I couldn't think of his sister.

"So are you just going to stand there looking stupid?" I guess I was. "Dude, she's only 19 and you had to have her."

That sounded just like me. "Look, I did some very stupid things, but since my wreck-"

"What you've become a saint. I told you not to touch her, I practically begged you not to. But the first chance that you get, you bagged her."

So this is where all his animosity was coming from. "I'm sorry. I know if I had a sister I would want to kill the guy that bagged her." Michael snarled. "I mean, I'm sure your sister is a sweet girl and all and I'm sorry. That was a dick move on my part and when you see her tell her I'm sorry if I made things rough for her."

"Dude, you didn't even call her the next day." Well, I never did- now that I could remember.

"If you want me to, I'll give her a call and apologize myself. That wasn't my intent to hurt her feelings. I'm a guy and we do stupid stuff." I stood there thinking in some sort of way I was just like one of the guys that Tia probably dated.

Probably telling her that she was beautiful filling up her head with promises that I had no intentions of keeping. "Whatever bro." Michael went to the far end of the locker room and started to change into his fighting gear.

Well that's one thing that's off my chest. Man, I was an asshole.

I walked out the locker room feeling a tad bit better. At least I had a clue while Michael wanted my head on a stake.

Counting today I had seventy-five days to get ready for Vegas. When you are a kid you think 75 days might as well be 75 years, but for me it was right around the corner.

Henry and I sparred a bit and made Parker watch and I gave him tips. "Dude, did you eat your Wheaties this morning, I mean dang." Henry said out of breath. "You're killing me over here." He took his arm and lifted it above his head and stretched. That last hold you put me in." He shook his head. "If you had a little more power you would be opening jars for me for a while."

Henry wouldn't lie to me but I held back my grin. I was getting stronger and the fights over the weekend weren't all some fluke. It literally felt amazing. Just a few weeks ago I couldn't slip anything. "My power and technique are finally getting reacquainted."

"Good." Henry shouted. "Now I don't have to take it easy on you." The Ox charged at me and he and I went a few more rounds on the mats. Parker asked questions on every possible scenario in the book.

"Parker, you gotta understand this is a mental game. Your opponent goes on the offense you defense and vice versa. The challenge is finding his weakness and using it." I pointed.

Still out of breath, Henry leaned his heavy sweaty frame on me. "Kid, all you have to remember is take down, knock out or submission. And try not to get took down, knocked out or submitted and you will be fine." Henry winked.

Parker smiled. "Got it."

"Stop over thinking. Your instincts will kick it. You keep doing what you are doing now. You will accomplish your goals." Henry and I went over combos again until Parker got it.

After Henry left and Parker went to school, I kinda wandered around the gym. Trying to fill the open space that Jerry had left. Helping the younger dudes with their form and technique. Using the key that was given to me, I went into Jerry's office. It felt so strange standing in the dimly lit office without the old man being in here.

Hesitating for just a moment I sat in his office chair overlooking the gym rats. There at the file cabinets that lined the back of the wall, eight in total. I shrugged, "What the hell, might as well." I started to dig.

This guy was a saint, folks were behind on the gym dues but he made a way for them to still do what they wanted to do. I loved that guy. Don't get me wrong, I wasn't a receptionist or professional filer but I knew the alphabet. I started to get everything in order.

File cabinets over flowing with paper receipts and a mountain of crap that dated back to the mid-eighties. "Jesus, Jerry come on."

In one file drawer it was jammed packed with pictures. Pictures of Jerry and my dad from back in the day. Dad was thinner then and looked meaner than a rattlesnake with arm around Jerry's neck. The muscle tight in my father's forearm. The other tucked around my mom's waist. All three of them looked so young. My dad looked like he could fight the world and my mom and Jerry looked as if they believed it too.

For a moment I thought was that going to be me, Henry and Tia one day? Henry and I getting old, not able to run like we used to. Tia standing by my side, kids. I threw the picture back into the drawer and slammed it shut.

I blamed it on the dust bunnies seeping into my brain, marriage and kids. I couldn't-I wouldn't think that far ahead.

It took me nearly three and half hours to get the files in some sort of file. I'm sure that the old man would appreciate it.

I left instruction with one of the other trainers to lock up tonight. Out of habit, my pickup seems to go on auto pilot and I found myself in the parking lot of the hospital. I took the elevator to the third floor and started to look for a tiny Asian lady with a crazy ponytail.

"Devon?" A small voice spoke behind me. "What are you doing here?" Annie's eyes darted from right to left.

"Thought maybe you want to grab some lunch."

"You shouldn't be here. I mean it's a free country you can go where ever you want to, but why are you here really?" Her eyes narrowed.

Ok, this was weird. "There wasn't a hidden agenda just maybe a sandwich or something. Annie, is everything okay?"

"Yeah, everything is okay, why? Why would you think that everything wasn't? Did someone say something to you?" Her cheeks turned pink. "I mean you would tell me right?" Annie gnawed at the inside of her cheek.

I put both hands on her slender shoulders and she exhaled. "Why are you so crazy? You're acting like a squirrel on speed. No one's told me anything and who would?" Annie looked behind her and looked around me and put her finger in her mouth. "Annie, are you going to tell me or am I going to have to tickle you to death."

Annie took me into an unoccupied room. She pushed me against the wall which barely moved me. I looked down at her and if she didn't look so frazzled I would have laughed. "You swear that you didn't hear anything." Her hand still in the middle of my chest.

I decided to play along. I threw my hands up. "Annie, I have no idea what in the hell you are talking about. I swear."

Annie stood on her tip toes and tried to gauge my honesty. She fell back to the opposite wall. "Ok, you're not lying. Good." She put her hand over her forehead.

"Well, I know I wasn't lying about what I don't know are you going to tell me?"

Annie gave me another hard look, like she could sense any deceit. "It's Henry."

"What about him? I just saw him like a few hours ago-"Then my worst fear gripped me. "No. You let him hit?"

Back on tip toes she covered my mouth. "Could you please keep your voice down? Don't forget I'm at work." She uncovered my mouth and fell back on the wall. "And no, I didn't let him hit."

My stomach was in knots. "Then what?"

"We went out to dinner and-"

"And what?" My voice went up a few octaves.

Annie slumped. "Well, oh my goodness I can't believe this." She covered her face.

"Annie, if you didn't let him hit then what happened?"

"I kissed him Devon."

My body relaxed. "Oh. Well at least it's not the end of the world or anything."

Annie punched me in the stomach and it tickled. "You don't get it. I haven't kissed another man since my husband. It's just." She looked down.

My second greatest fear was creeping in. "You like him, don't you?" She nodded yes. I pinched the shoulder of her scrubs and pulled her into my arms. Pushing her ponytail out of my mouth. "Darlin, it's okay. Henry is a good guy he's a male whore but... Do you want me to talk to him for you?"

She jerked away. "NO! If you say something then he'll know that I kinda like him and then I will look so stupid. Devon, just promise me that you won't say anything." The pocket of her scrub pants lite up. She pulled the phone out of her pocket and looked at it. "It's him."

"Answer it."

Annie cleared her throat. "Hello." Granted I was listening to a one sided conversation, but he must be saying all the right things, she was smiling. "Yeah, well Luke has guitar practice tonight." She listened for a second and laughed. "You mean right now?" Annie looked up at me in horror. "Um, I guess if you want to go to lunch like right now we can." She bit at her lip. "Right now. You're in the parking lot right now!" She put her hand over the phone. "Devon, I'll talk to you later."

"I guess my work here is done." I kissed her on her forehead and walked out of the room. Trying to find a route that I wouldn't run into Henry. I followed the trail right to Tia's class.

I could hear her barking orders to some poor bastard before I opened the door. "I don't need your ego; I already have one thank you. Now if you don't mind could you go back over there and do some legs lifts." Tia rolled her eyes at some guy that had difficulty picking up his face with one hand.

Her face lite up when she saw me and then it faded. "What are you doing here?" She was trying to cover that bright smile with her hand.

"I'm sorry that I had to make an appointment to see my girl."

"Your *girl*? Thanks for letting me know." Tia pulled at the hem of my shirt and smiled.

Smiling back down at her, I shrugged. "You were going too slow so I decided to make it official. You're mine and no one can change that." I wanted to kiss her so bad and I guess she knew it too. Tia took a step back.

"I get off in a few hours."

"I want to get off now." Having to push my hands in my pockets to keep from grabbing her and carrying her out of here caveman style.

"Pervert."

"Thank you. You coming over tonight. I'll find something for us to eat.

"Let me handle food. Now get out of here." Playfully pushing me out the steel door. "Tonight."

"Tonight." Hopefully this will be the first of many.

I couldn't resist in texting her one more time before I got home. Telling her that I couldn't wait to see her. This girl has really taken over all of my sense. I see her when I close my eyes; I can taste her pink gloss the smell of her hair still lingers. Her warmth when she sat on my lap, I still feel.

I took a look at my reflection in the kitchen window. "Dude you got it bad." Tia texted back and said that she was going home first to change and she would be right over.

I tried to clean up the house best I could. Considering that I only really lived in two rooms of the house. My bedroom and the kitchen, but by five o'clock everything was in its place. Fresh sheets on the bed. Dishes cleaned, dried and put away.

So I waited.

And waited some more.

I heard the beating on the front door and before I could open it all the way a raging Ox ran in. "You busy?" He said stomping passed me into the kitchen.

"Well kinda, Tia is-"

Henry had his head in the refrigerator pulling out a beer. "You know when you told me not to mess with your friend Annie?" I decided to play dumb. "Well, I kinda did." Throwing his head back with the beer.

"Henry, I asked you not to. What did you do to her?"

My best friend shook his head and stared to the far corner of the kitchen. "It wasn't me I promise." He exhaled so dramatically I thought I was in a high school play. "So last week the day that you and Tia go to Florida I ran into her-"

"You expect me to believe you just ran into Annie? Where at the grocery store?" I folded my arms and leaned against the kitchen sink.

"Honestly it was the gas station. Anyway, I had to convince this girl to go out with me. I wore her down." I growled at him. "Not in a bad way."

"How in the hell do you wear someone down in a good way, Henry. Come on man she's a good person and a good friend. I told you to leave her alone."

"No, no just listen. Dude, I'm not going to lie to you. I wanted to hit it sooooo bad. I mean she's cute as all get out-and that little body."

"Henry!"

"Ok, but then we go out to dinner. She's so smart and cool you know? I mean, I could like to talk to her and stuff. She's not like the other chicks that I have dealt with."

"I know, the Annie doesn't have to take her clothes off to make a living."

"True, so that whole weekend we're hanging out. Talking on the phone. I like her."

"So what's the problem then?"

"We went to lunch today and I take her to the sandwich shop and then I run into Cara."

Running into one of your conquest is bad, but running into a crazy one with another woman on your arm is nuclear. "Is Annie alright? I mean did Cara say something or do something to her?" I would have to get Cara committed if she'd done something to my buddy.

"Just gave her the evil eye. Then walks up to the both of us and asked if she could come over tonight and get her panties back." Henry sighed and put his head in his hands. "Annie is a classy lady, just tried to ignore it all. I apologized like a thousand times, man. She just got out the car and went back in without a word. I screwed this up big time."

A part of me was glad that this came to an end before it even really starts, but I'd never since the Ox so broke up before. I heard knocks at the front door. "Come in." I shouted.

Tiny footsteps rounded the corner. "Devon, how in the world could you be friends with such and assho-"Annie stopped short and saw Henry standing there. "I'll go." She turned on her heels.

"Annie." I picked her up by her waist and her little feet were still moving like they were still walking. "Look, both of you two are my friends and I don't want any drama. So please could you two figure this thing out….tonight."

"I would have brought more food if I thought that you were having a party." Tia said carrying two large take out boxes.

Annie faced Tia. "Tia, I'm sorry to come in on you and Devon's date. I'll see you tomorrow at work."

Before she could take another step. "Annie, look I'm sorry. I truly mean that." Henry pleaded. "I never meant for you to see that."

"No, you just didn't want me to find out. But it's cool." She shrugged. Turning to look at me. "Can I go now?"

"Nope not until the two of you come to terms with this."

"Nothing to talk about. He's a whore and I don't want to be a notch on his bed post, I promise that I will stay out of his way if he stays out of mine."

"Can't promise you that sweetie." Henry walked closer to her and she looked like she was going to climb the wall to get away from him. "Annie, I like you and I think you kinda dig me too. I just want to see where this goes."

"Not interested. Can I go?"

"You are such a hypocrite." Tia said and everyone in the room mouths dropped. "When I was in Florida you feed me all this crap about just let it go. Don't be afraid to love and all that other mess. Now you got this guy here that likes you and you want to throw it all away." Tia looked her friend in the eyes and sighed. "It's hard I know but man, you got to start somewhere."

I could see the wheels turning in Annie's head. She looked up at all of us. "Can I go now?"

Tia, myself and Henry all said at the same time. "No." Her shoulders slumped.

"There is only one way that we can solve this disagreement. Annie you have to fight him." I said to the disbelief of everyone in the room.

"Are you crazy?" She shouted.

Tia's eyes widened then she smiled. "Don't worry girl just one swift knee to his crotch and he will be down."

Henry covered himself with both hands. "Come on, D." He pointed at Annie. "Really?"

"My money is on Annie. She may be small but she's quick." I said.

"This is ridiculous." Annie whined.

"And so is this argument. Henry is a whore, we all know that." I said.

"Devon, really thank you." Henry snarled.

"And you're welcome. Cara is one crazy chick. Henry had to change his phone number twice because of her."

"Well you shouldn't have slept with her." Annie shoot at him.

"It was an accident."

Annie huffed and made her way to the door. I took her back to the kitchen. "Look, I've never seen my Henry act this way. So there is something there. Just talk it out."

The two of them just looked at each other. "So there won't be a fight? Dang." Tia said.

"It wouldn't really be one." Henry said low.

"Just because you're bigger than me doesn't mean that I would just let you take me down." Annie stomped closer to Henry.

"Devon." Henry looked at me for help and I started a random conversation with Tia about the weather. "Whatever." He turned to walk out.

"Hey, you just don't get to walk out." Already feeling defeated Henry kept walking.

And just like the little spider monkey that I came to know and love, Annie pounced on his back. Henry was trying to grab at her, but the girl was too quick.

These are the moments that I wish I had my phone on me to record this. Henry was grunting and Annie was pulling the whole episode had me and Tia in tears.

So not to hurt her, Henry gave up and started to jump and down to shake her. Annie held on as long as she could, slipping from his back Henry caught her before her feet hit the ground. "Are you done you little tree monkey?" Henry said trying not to laugh.

"Only if you are you big dumb heifer. And another thing-"Annie was silenced by Henry's kiss.

"Well, I'll be. Never thought a close encounter with a domestic violence charge could turn out to be so beautiful, did you?" Tia leaned next me and I smelled her hair.

"It was either this." I pointed at the two making out in my kitchen. "Or Henry would be in the hospital and Annie being his nurse."

Chapter 19

"Dude are you sure? I mean thank you but…"

"You can use the cabin until you go to Vegas. You stay up there for a couple of weeks. Work on your cardio, get use to the altitude and maybe get some from Tia."

I groaned. Everything else I could do but getting into my girlfriend's pants was another story. Henry planned to let us use his family's cabin in West Virginia to train. But it was going to be like Florida all over again. With Tia down the hall and I couldn't touch her with the King of the Cage on the line. "Just because you and Annie go at it like rabbits doesn't mean that everyone else should try and multiply the earth. Thanks again man."

"Hey don't talk about my lady like that. And don't mention it. I just want you to win this thing, bring the title back to the South."

I stretched my long legs on Jerry's desk. The King of the Cage match put a mild worry in my belly that I was trying my damnedest to ignore. A lot of people were on me to win, I felt that I could. Matter of fact, I was more than 95% sure that I could tie this thing in a bow, but that looming 5% was a knife twisting in me.

"I'll be at the gym tomorrow morning to drop of the keys."

"Thanks."

Whenever thing started to go right in my life, then I would start to worry. I was close to the same position that I am in now years ago, about to go from amateur to pro. Then my dad died then everything went smooth to hell for me.

Now I get a weekly call from my mom. Tia is more than perfect and she started to work with Maggie on her off days. The gym was packed. Guys were getting better and stronger and I was able to help.

I felt like a big shoe was hovering over my head about to drop at any second on me. Like I needed another knock to the dome.

I texted Tia and told her about West Virginia. She got back with me to say that Mackenzie was more than willing to take over her classes for her in her absence and it wouldn't be a problem. That's one thing I didn't have to worry about.

Since Florida, Tia and I have been inseparable. It was funny, I remember the first time I saw her and wanted to have her. Then that swiftly turned to a deep rooted hate for her. Then caring then back to hate-indifference and finally back to me not wanting to make a move without her by my side.

It was getting close to closing time and I for one wanted to get the heck out of there. I was mentally tired of going over every possible scenario in my head of losing. And not just losing the fights in Vegas but everything.

After the last gym rat was out, I checked the backdoor and started switching off lights. I set the alarm and locked the front door and there was Michael and his crew. "Devon, I hope you didn't think it was over." Before I could really take his head off like I wanted to, I heard the ping of an aluminum bat bounce off my back.

The pain from hitting my knees on the pavement to the crack of the bat, my mind didn't know which pain was worse. "Home run." One of his friends laughed.

I had to get up, had to stand but I was kicked down to the ground kissing the curb. My body was jerked left and right from the four men kicking the living crap out of me. At one point I was able to get back up on my hands and knees and had my arm kicked from under me. "Now how does it feel to be kicked to the curb Devon?" Michael said over me. Taking his foot and rolling me over to face him.

"It feels like the same way I banged your sister. Painful and boring."

Michael's leg bent up to his chest and I closed my eyes and waited for him to kick in my chest, leg or hip.

Then nothing.

I opened my eyes. And I saw two angels beat the snot out of Michael and his gang.

As everything around me start to turn black, I heard Michael scream of pain and the loud thud of that shoe dropping.

"Mom, I really think this times he's dead."

"Luke!"

My eyes sprang open. I didn't have to guess where I was or how I got here. Dang, was this my same room?

"You made it through surgery just fine Devon. You should be discharged in a few days." Annie said.

Henry, Tia and Annie all looked down at me trying to smile. Luke who looked like he was looking at a dead man. I guess I've been close. I turned to Henry. "So am I going to get the keys to the cabin now?"

Henry and I were the only two that found humor in my attempt at humor. "Dammit Devon you could have been killed." Tia looked like she had been crying. "They used you like a soccer ball last night. They broke a screw in your hip." Wiping tears with the back of her hand. "We aren't going to Vegas."

"You'll make a strong recovery. The muscle that you've built saved you from a lot of damage that could have happened. But you won't be completely healed until at least a month after the fights, I'm sorry." Annie put her head down and Henry put his arm around her and held her tight.

I sat and thought for a second before I spoke. "I've had some really stupid things happen to me. Horrible things, earth shattering things. And everyone in this room has helped me out. Annie, just your spirit has made me want to be a better human. Henry, your friendship has been unmatched. Tia…girl. You make me want to be the best guy for you." I paused. "I'm going to Vegas. I'm going to fight and I'm going to win. Now Henry give me the key."

I put my hand out, he gave an apologetic look to the ladies dug into his pocket and put the key in my hand.

Tia was the first to speak. "This is insane."

"Well, you didn't fall for me for my good looks, did ya? Where's your sense of adventure? Annie, how long I got in here?"

"Besides having major surgery and if everything goes the way it should, no blood clots or bleeding I would say two days."

"Cool, I have two full days to sit on my butt after that it's time to train like I've never done before."

I heard thunder at the door and we all turned. My angels, instead of white robes and harps they were in t-shirts and jeans. "Get out the bed ya pussy."

"Yeah, stop ya crying."

I saw pure rage cross Tia's, my lady was ready to peel their foreheads back.

"Ducks, what's up?" Henry hugged both of them. Huey and Louie Duck were the definition of hardcore MMA fighters. Twins, identical to the way they cut their hair and brushed their teeth.

Both had that olive colored skin, deep Sicilian roots with black hair and jet black eyes. Whenever they were in town we would joke that we should take hypodermic needles full of their sweat and inject ourselves. Then maybe just maybe we would be has big and bad as they are.

Huey spoke first. "The kid that jumped you he and his friends are down the hall. Do you want us to end them for ya?" Annie clutched the neck of her scrub in horror.

I shook my head. "They're not worth it. When did you guys get back, how did you know I was at the gym."

"Heard about the damage you laid down in Florida, wanted to come down and congratulate you. So we swung by the gym-"Louie said.

"Then we saw the meat heads. So we got a twofer. Got to see you and knock some heads." The brothers looked at each other and smiled.

"I appreciate it. You guys didn't come soon it would have been a wrap for your boy over here." I said and I could feel my medication slowly fading and the itching pain in my leg started.

"Us two." Louie said. "You still gonna fight in Vegas?"

"Be there if I have to walk." I smiled.

Tia threw her arms out, "Is everybody crazy? Devon are you serious about still trying to fight. You couldn't get up right now to use the bathroom if you wanted."

The Duck brothers looked at each then at me. "Spunky one aren't ya? I like her." Huey said eyeing Tia

"Back off Huey before we all eat fried duck tonight." Huey smirked down at me and put his hands up in surrender. "Tia, I'm gonna need you more than ever right now. I wouldn't have gotten this far without you. Don't step out on me."

"I wasn't planning on leaving but I don't want to watch as you kill yourself."

"Darlin, you let this man stay in a box-" Huey stared.

"That would kill him." Louie ended.

The trip to Spruce Knob, West Virginia was silent. Tia insisted on driving making the excuse of saving my legs. Whatever. Don't get me wrong it felt awesome that someone cared enough about me to drive nine and half hours for me, but her worry was making me worry.

This time of year, it had already rain a river and it was dark going up over four thousand feet. By the time we made to Henry's cabin, I was more than tired, stiff and sore.

Annie let me know that the screw in my hip simply broke. There were no fragments and they just reopened the incision that I had before. It itched like a bitch.

"I'll make a fire, go and have a seat on the couch." I knew that she was trying to help me and I knew that she cared.

"Tia, could you please let me be a guy. How about you go and take a seat on the couch and relax. You drove none stop all day." The tension in her arms began to relax and she closed her eyes. I put my hands on her neck and began to dig into the strained shoulders.

She began to melt under my fingertips. "Devon, you need to eat."

"Well, there is just one certain meal I have in mind." I kissed her neck.

Tia was either too tired or blocked out my sexual innuendo. Her head fell forward and she let me go to work on her neck, back and shoulders. "Babe, you are in knots."

"I'm just a tad bit stressed is all."

"A brick could probably bounce off you right now. Go in the room lay down for a few hours." She didn't move and I didn't stop. I picked her up and cradled her in my arms. Pushing the bedroom door open I put her on the bed. I think she was already sleeping by the time her head hit the pillow.

I texted everybody to let them know that we made it safe and training would start first thing in the morning. Henry let me know that we had enough food to last us if we wanted to hide away for the remainder of the spring.

Stretching my legs, I looked around the cabin. Henry and I made a pit stop here once when he and I went to New York for a bachelor party for a buddy of ours a few years back. It was nice, hardwood floors covered the one level cabin. Large stone fireplace that Henry's father and grandfather built almost twenty years ago.

From what he told me, this was their family's summer get away. There was a ton of trails to follow and a great lookout point that his brother's kids loved.

Unfortunately, I wouldn't be enjoying any of the sights. Only sight in view was Vegas and winning it all. I took off my boots and pulled off my shirt. There are three other bedrooms in the cabin, but there was only one that I wanted to be in.

Tia was curled up on her right side; arm under the pillow the other hand was in between her knees. Besides the drizzle outside and her slow breathing was the only sound in the cabin.

Crawling slowly up the center of the bed, trying my best not to disturb her I got under the covers and closed my eyes.

"Devon." She whispered.

"Yeah."

"In my heart I know that you can win. I really want you to believe that." Rolling over towards me, scooting to rest her head on my shoulder. "I just don't want you to get hurt." Putting her hand on my chest.

"Tia, I've had more broken bones than the law should allow. It's a sport, a sport that I love and I want to never stop doing." I bent down and kissed the top of her head. "Don't worry sweetie, I'll be okay."

"I know that you will, it's just why you can't get a regular job like Henry. The guys a cop."

I slowly sat up pulling her into my lap. "So let me get this straight. You would rather for me to get shoot at every day then fight in a sanctioned arena." I gave her a blank look.

"Then do what the Duck brothers do. Whatever they do." Tia putting head under my chin.

"No one knows what the Ducks do. They never talk about it. Like one day they're here then the next they are in the wind."

"Come on."

"I swear, from what I've heard they both work in some sort of black ops thing. Real, hush hush stuff." I rubbed Tia's knee. "What I want you to do it train me and hard too. Give me no mercy."

Sliding off my lap she got under the covers. "You asked for it."

I thought my lungs were going to explode. "Come on Devon you got fifty more. Let's go." Tia was on my back as I ran up a slope.

"I'm not a mule." I huffed.

"Could have fooled me." Kicking me on my thigh for me to giddy up. "You got this. Now attack the mountain. Let's go." She barked and the added 110lbs of beautiful woman bounced as I trudged upward.

Fifty must be her favorite number. I did fifty of this and fifty of that. I ran, I punched and I kicked until I thought not only my leg but my arms were going to fall off.

Finally the rumble of the heavens stopped her. We saw an ugly storm approach. "Let's pack it in before we drown." Tia and I barely beat the down pour before we got in the cabin.

"I'll get some wood out of the shed." I told her hoping that she would go inside of the weather but when I got back to the porch she stood there waiting for me, smiling. "Woman." I just shook my head.

"Come on get out those clothes before you catch death in them." She pulled my half sweaty half rained on shirt over my head.

"Are you coming on to me?" The look she gave me was one of amusement. "I mean, you rip my shirt off. Leaving me here shaking like a leaf. If you wanted me naked all you had to do was just ask."

Tia tossed my shirt by the fireplace and walked slowly to me. Her walk caught me off guard. It was slow and deliberate. Pressing herself against my bare chest. "I want you naked and in the shower now. I can't have my champ sick now can I?" She put her finger to my lips. "Now be a good boy." She cooed to me and like a good boy, I was under the shower head wondering how I got here.

The hot water felt good on my achy body. My stiches were healing up nicely and not like the other day were they were seeping a bit.

"Hey save some hot water for me." She shouted.

"Save water share a shower." I shouted back. I waited praying that she would come in the shower with me. Nothing. So I lathered up for the second time and rinsed. With one leg out the shower was the most beautiful woman in the world.

"Want this?" Tia had the towel pinched between her fingers, arm extended out to me.

"That would be helpful." I grabbed at it and she pulled back. "What are you going to give me for the towel?" She had the towel clenched in her hand.

I stepped fully out of the shower and let her get a good look. Her eyes went left then right then finally on the ground. "I will give you all of this." Standing there butt naked like the day I was born.

Her eyes still on the ground, her cheeks had turned crimson. "You're naughty." Putting the towel on by the sink, she walked out of the bathroom."

"You asked for it."

I slept like a rock. I gave Tia the pleasure of being my little spoon, with my arm securely around her waist. She couldn't move if she tired.

Tia was being a good trainer for letting me have one day off in the middle of the week. She was already up and making breakfast. I was trying to remember when I started to change. It was sometime after the accident. Memories of things came back like dreams that I didn't wish to remember. How I just dropped Henry off and gave mitt work to Ronnie. I slept with Michael's baby sister, which nearly got me killed. And as recent to when I first met Tia, how I wanted to use her up and not look back.

What type of person was I? To do these things with no regard for other people? I rolled over to my back and stared at the wood ceiling of the cabin. The way that I spoke to my mom and her husband. I had to be the biggest idiot in the world, or a fool to treat people around me that really cared about me that way.

I had a lot of things to atone for; I scratched at the new/old scare on my hip and drew a nail with crusted blood. Great.

"If you think I'm serving you breakfast in bed you have another thing coming." Tia's voice echoed through the cabin.

"Coming dear." My girl had a spread laid out for me. Bacon and eggs. Hash browns, milk and orange juice.

"I pushed you to the limit yesterday so eat and we will do some mitt work indoors today." I nodded with a mouth full of food. She watched me eat and I could only wonder what she was thinking. Could she look at my ugly mug every day or was she counting the seconds until she could escape? Whatever it was I was glad she was here with me.

"I hope you know that I'm going to win." I gulped down some juice.

"Well, if you fight anywhere close to the way that you eat you will demolish the competition." She said smiling with her hand under her chin, looking at me. "Get your grub on, wash up and get some clothes on. We have work to do."

For the next two hours, Tia and I ran through every combo known to man. "Come on Devon, I'm not a piece of glass. Come on a kick." She stood her ground as I kicked the hell out her padded arms. I almost felt bad but she kept encouraging me and pushing. For not only my benefit but for hers I gave her everything that I had.

Her blonde bangs were plastered to her forehead with sweat and she looked so sexy. I guess I got wrapped up in looking at her and she tagged me right on the side of my head. "Focus."

"I can't, looking at you is like looking at my very own wet tee shirt contest." Damn, she looked so amazing; this is how she probably looked going a round with me.

She looked down and in fact she had sweated through her shirt. "Ok, since you've had your fun. I'm going to have mine. Put on your boots." She ordered.

Before I could say anything she was outside waiting for me. By the time, I got my boots and my jacket she was up the trail. She kept walking ahead of me, and with a sore leg sprinting to catch her was murder.

"Glad you made the party." She said without looking at me.

"Where are we going?"

"You tell me. Do you want to joke around or do you want to win?" I had to look at her square in the face and she was serious as a heart attack. I had to smirk, my girl meant business. "Wait." I stopped and she stepped behind me and jumped on my back. "Now run."

We were coming up on an incline, and I paused. "Hold on." I ran up the incline praying that I wouldn't lose my footing and hurt her or myself. Tia held on by my shoulders.

Leaning in my ear every few yards she'd whisper. "You can do this. I believe in you." It was hard to run, smile and be horny all at the same time. So I ran and focused. We finally got to a clearing in the woods and she hopped off my back. Tia looked around and to our left was a tree with a low hanging branch. "I need a hundred pulls up." I had my hands on my knees out of breath. "Today Devon, I need them now."

I did what I was told. The bark digging into my palms. I could feel my hands beginning to slip. "If you let go of that branch we'll start all over again, now come with it." I readjusted myself and started pulling.

One hundred felt like a few thousand when I finally dropped back to the ground. "What next?"

"Thought you would never ask." That smile that made me fall in love with her had turned sinister. "Now climb it."

"The tree?" I pointed.

"No the air, yes the tree. Climb it and when you come down you give me 100 pull ups. Then you climb it again and give me seventy-five. Then you climb it, come down and give me fifty." She stopped and gave me a look as if I insulted her. "When I speak you give me high knees. Now go." I did what I was told. "Once you get to twenty-five, you will go in increments of five. Get it?"

"Got it."

"Good. Now move."

The tree wasn't particular high but it had been years since I climbed a freaking tree. By the time I was able to do 10 pulls. Tia was gone. She was no longer sitting on a rock. "Tia!" I shouted. "Tia!" I don't know where the energy came from but I busted out of the clearing into some surrounding trees. I was panicked. "Tia!"

"You are going to scare the trees you keep hollering like that." She walked up behind me. I wanted to pull her into my dirty shirt.

"High knees, Devon." I inhaled and got to it.

"I found a lake back there. When you finish this you're taking a swim."

"Skinny dipping?"

"In your dreams." Tia pointed to my tree.

When I did my final pull up she threw me a bottled water. "Giddy up." She climbed on my back and she gave direction to the lake.

The spot was beautiful. The water was still and sun that poked around a cloud just right illuminated it, making the tiny ripples in the water shine. "Get in."

I caught her eye when I pulled off my shirt and jeans. "Like what you see?" I smiled standing there in my boxers.

"Do you want to throw away all your training on a piece of ass? Even though that piece of ass is mine?" She folded her arms and looked at the lake. "I'm not worth it."

I wanted to push the issue, but stepped out into the cold water. "What now coach?" My teeth chattered.

"Swim to the far part of the lake. Get out give me 100 jumping jacks. Swim to me and give me jumping jacks. Then swim to the West corner and repeat, then the East and repeat."

I had swum to the middle of the lake and shouted. "Then what?"

"Then you repeat it until I'm tired of looking at you."

My legs were pretty much useless when I jogged back to the cabin with Tia on my back. "Go wash up. I'll fix dinner."

I wanted to ask her if she would carry me, but decided to hold the request in fear that she may make me do it all over again.

I took a shower and put on some fresh clothes on and meet my beautiful lady in the kitchen. "Hey good looking, what you got cooking."

"Chicken breast, mixed vegetables and brown rice." She smiled over her shoulder. I was starved for her and what was on the stove. I closed my eyes and for a moment I thought I was going to doze off. "Hey, you need something in you before you go to sleep."

"I want to be in you before I go to sleep." My words slurred with fatigue. She ignored me and I was glad because I was too tired to even look to see her reaction.

We ate and I could barely get up to go to the bedroom. I fell into the bed face first; Tia smiled and hollered "Timber." Any other night I would have pulled her close to me, but my arms which still smelled like tree bark didn't want to cooperate. I was dead to the world.

"Devon, Devon wake up!" Tia was shaking the hell out of me.

"I'm up. What?" I was drenched in sweat and I was standing up on the side of the bed. I looked down at myself. My short nails were digging into my palms and I was shaking. Tia had the covers up to her neck. It was still dark outside.

Speaking slowly to me. "You were having a nightmare." She looked terrified.

I got back into bed. "What did I say?"

"Nothing. You were just pushing down. Really, like kicking your right leg." She kissed me on the cheek. "You were pressing the brake down in your dream. You may have acute PTSD."

"I'll deal with it." I hugged her tight. "We'll deal with it." She kissed me on the cheek again and got up out of my embrace. "Since we are both up, let's get it." She started to go through her clothes in her bag. "Put some clothes on, were going on a night hike."

I tried my best not to look at the nightstand clock when I put on some sweats. Leaning down to tie my tennis shoes the clock mocked me at 4:15am.

The sun was sleeping on the other side of the earth when I came out to the living room. Tia was on the area rug on her belly. Slowly, she pushed up on her hands and stretched, her pony tail almost reaching her little behind. "You need to stretch." Still facing forward.

I'd rather do high knees. I got down on all fours and looked how she was laying. "Yoga?"

"You will thank me later. You need to get those big ol muscles loose." Tia got back on her belly, and lifted her legs and arms off the ground and held the pose. "Do what I do. This is going to help your back."

"Tia, um I'm a dude and dude just don't get there yoga on." Tia gave me a look that made me wants to run back to the bedroom and put the covers over my head.

"If you tell anyone I will deny, deny, deny." She and I centered our chai for about thirty minutes. And I would be lying if I said that the stretching did me a world of good.

It must of rain last night there were puddles everywhere. Tia got on my back and pointed back to the incline. "Charge."

"Tia it's pretty slick out here, I don't want to fall and hurt you."

"I trust you. No giddy up. There's a carrot in it for you when we get on top of the hill." I was too tired to come up with something sexual to say so; I trotted up the hill with my lady bouncing on my back.

When we got to the clearing. I looked up at my tree and she smiled. Bark still digging in my hands I attacked my pull ups. "I'm getting better."

"No you're not. You're too slow." Standing next to me as I pulled up and down. "I timed you last time I need you to work harder. This is fourth quarter, this is the last round. Whatever the analogy you want to use. I need more from you." She took a step back. "When you get to a hundred climb that bad boy."

I had no idea that she was timing my performance. Was I that bad? I pushed myself harder; I zipped up the tree and came back down. I jumped up for the branch and she stopped me and gave me a look. So I gave her high knees and she smiled.

"Next time I need you to give me fifty jumping jacks."

"Yes coach."

"After that, I want fifty burpees."

"Yes coach."

"After that I need for you to run through some of your combos with me."

"Yes coach." She nodded and I did my pull ups, scurried up the tree, gave her the jumping jacks and everything except the kitchen sink.

The sun was up and I desired to take her in my arms so we could enjoy the sun rise, but I thought she would bite me head off. It seemed like the earth started to wake up around us. Birds chirped, and other woodland animals started to stir around us.

"You did well, let's pack it in. You need to eat."

I was in much better shape than before my wreck, I could feel it. My arms looked amazing in the bright sun. She got on my back and we headed back down the hill. My breakfast was lighter than it was from the yesterday morning, but I was good with it. I sank the last bit of orange juice. "Can I shower?"

Tia gave me that beautiful smile and I let the hot water beat the crap out of me. With a clean pair of shorts, I came back into the living room shirtless and barefoot. I stood in front of her waiting for her to acknowledge me. She kept looking at her fashion magazine. "Hey." I said.

"Hey." She licked her thumb and turned the page. I felt like I was in sixth grade naked standing in front of my class. "Are you going to grow roots there?" Tia said.

"What is your problem? I mean I know that you have to train me, but dang. You are being really-"

"Mean?"

"Yeah, kind of."

She tossed her stupid magazine to the other side of the sofa. "I don't think you are taking this serious."

My mouth dropped. "What the hell do you mean? I'm working my ass off over here."

She shook her head. "Devon, I really need for you to dig in. We have two weeks before we go to Vegas. Two." She shoots up two fingers in my face. "You are nowhere where you need to be."

"Well, I'm sorry ya see I got into this wreck a few months back and I'm trying to get my sea legs back." I shouted down at her.

She pushed me by my shoulders and not from her shove but I took a step back. "Yeah, you want to win who the hell doesn't? But I want you hungry for it. I don't give a damn if you fight your hardest and lose, I want you to give it everything and you aren't showing me that. I'm wasting my time."

"So you want to walk out? Now?" I started to worry, what was I going to do if she wanted to leave?

"Don't walk out on yourself, Devon."

I turned and started for the door. I stepped out on the porch, the sky was clear and not a cloud to be seen. I started to run up the incline, full speed and ran back; Tia stood on the porch and watched. There was a log that was used as a stopper in front of Tia's car. I picked it up and put it on my shoulders. And ran like I was being chased by wild animals.

Tia never left but watched me. By the tenth time, I threw the log to the ground. My lungs burned and I knew my shoulders were scratched to hell. I turned to her and started to jog in place. Pushing my knees to the blue sky, "What else do you need from me coach?

Chapter 20

"Where are we going?" Tia said holding on to my back.

"You'll see."

"Devon, I can't see a thing with this thing over my eyes." I felt her hand leave me shoulder to go to touch her face.

"You better not touch that blind fold." I pinched her thigh that was in my hand. "Patience is a virtue."

I put her down and took off the blind fold off. "Devon." She looked back up to me and all I could do was smile. This was our last night here at the cabin and I really wanted to make it special. "You like it?"

"I love it." Candles lead the way from where we were standing to the tied down boat. I picked her up and carried her to the waiting boat. I put her in and began to row to the middle of this darn lake. If the wreck didn't give me nightmares, this lake would. I spent most of my time in here swimming like I was Michael Phelps or something.

"I made you some sandwiches and juice. Sorry there's nothing romantic in here." I pulled the oars into the boat.

"It's perfect." She put her hands in the water.

"Here." I gave her a blanket. "Don't want you to freeze out here while I'm trying to be romantic."

"No one's done this for me before. When did you have the time to do all of this?" Wrapping the blanket around her shoulders.

"It wasn't easy. I had to wait till you took a nap and get you out here fast before a little critter took our dinner."

She looked up to the dark sky. "It so quiet here. I love it, Devon I truly appreciate this."

"You remember when you said that you weren't worth it? You are more to me than anything. I want you to understand that I would give it up for you."

Tia shut her eyes and dropped her head. "I would never want you to do that."

"I know that you wouldn't want me to, but I would." I leaned back into the little boat. "My mom was right; you make me so much better. Without you…I just don't know what I would do. I remember asking my doctor to give me the best physical therapist and he gave me you. You push me, you get on my nerves but I wouldn't want it any other way."

"Devon." Looking at her, the stars in the sky had to be envious at her sparkle.

"Tia, I'd smell sea salt forever in Florida. Kick dirt in Nashville and get unmovable splinters in Spruce Knob all for you."

"Devon, I'm pregnant."

"What?" I almost stood and rocked both into the water.

Tia busted out laughing so hard, I thought she was going to flip the boat. "I'm joking. You were being so serious thought I would kill it." She paused and started to giggle still looking at my shell shocked face.

"There is no other man that has driven me crazy like you have." She rolled her eyes. "In the best of ways and in the worst but I feel the same way about you."

You couldn't wipe my smile off with soap and water. "I'm glad." I held her hand.

"Devon."

"Yeah."

"Still not gonna sleep with you….yet."

Damn.

I hadn't worn a suit since I buried my father. How in the heck do people live these things? Parker stood right next to me in the elevator. This had to work and if it didn't I was more than screwed. I had only four days till Vegas and if this meeting was a bust, there was no Vegas, no King of The Cage and everything that I've done to get here was all in vain.

"Devon, don't stress. My dad is a cool guy."

Of course he's cool to you the man puts food on your table and clothes on your back.

"Hello, Parker what are you doing here?" A slender red head came around the receptionist desk to greet us. Man, she was hot but not better than what I had waiting for me.

"Well me and my friend Devon are here to see my dad. Is he busy?"

"Parker, your dad doesn't know that we were coming?" I covered half my face with my hand. This kid was going to be the death of me. I glanced at the only watch that I ever wore, which was my father's it was 8:45am.

He put his lanky arm around me. "Dude, I'm his kid he'll see us."

"About, that. Parker, your father will be in and out of meetings all day."

If I knew without a shadow of a doubt that I wouldn't be convicted and sent to prison for the rest of my life, I would have killed Parker right there with witnesses.

Parker and I sat down in the plush high rise office building. I had no idea that Parker's father was a boss like this. I knew that they had a bit of money but my goodness. "Devon, try to relax my dad is just like everybody else's dad."

I'm sure your father worked at a mill for the better part of his life. Have hands rough with caked dirt under the nail. Face prematurely wrinkled from the harsh sun of working on the farm. I'm sure if Parker's father owned a farm, he would have people do all the heavy lifting for him.

I loosened my tie and did my best to relax. A guy my size had to be careful not to knock over or break something that would take several lifetimes to replace or repair.

Parker smiled over at me and picked up a magazine of the glass and steel coffee table. "This is going to be awesome."

Awesome had lost all of its awesomeness but 1:17 p.m. I watched people go in and out of Parker's father's office all morning and part of the afternoon. My dream was slipping away from me like the hands ticking away on the very loud and very expensive wall clock. I closed my eyes and laid my head back on the leather seat. What would Tia do? If she was in one of her moods she would kick the door in and make him apologize to her for making her wait. That wasn't going to work.

Henry would have pulled his service revolver out and took the red head for hostage. I smiled at the thought. Annie. My dear little Annie, she would sit here patient and polite. And she would probably pray. I wrinkled my nose at the thought. The last time I talked to the guy upstairs my father still died, I was almost barred from the sport and I refused to speak to my mom.

I watched another round of business suits walk into his office. What the heck, by the time the guy comes out to see me, I've already meet God anyway. I closed my eyes, peeking to take a look at Parker who was immersed with ogling the receptionist at the copy machine. Here goes: *God, this is Devon. Well I guess you already knew that. God you know I need this more than anything in this world. I'm not going to fill you up with empty promises, like church every Sunday or no premarital sex. Just my friend Annie would tell me to call on you when I needed you. And right now I need you.*

My hands were clasped in front of my, and with one eye open I was relieved that no one was paying me any attention. So I continued. *God, I know that I'm not the best person, but I guess I'm not the worst either. Just help. Help me be a better fighter. A better friend and a good boyfriend for Tia. Since we are here, God look out for her. I think there are things that she hasn't told me about her past. Just help me heal her heart or you can do it. You are probably better at it than I am. While you are at it. Make sure that Henry and Annie go the distance. I know that they are different but if you find it in your will keep them together.*

I didn't have anything left to say, so I just whispered. "Amen."

"Parker, your father is ready to see you both." The receptionist smiled.

"We got this bro." Parker smiled and led the way to his father's office. Stepping in to the office, my jaw hit the floor. The whole back wall wasn't a wall at all but glass. I could see all of downtown Nashville from this room. The desk was of heavy mahogany. Everything was black and grey. "Devon. I've heard so much about you. Come on in and take a seat." His father who I've only met a few times. Usually him running to pick the kid up and take off in his luxury car.

"Thank you, sir for meeting with me on such a short notice." I gave Parker the side eye. "I'm aware that you are a busy man so I will keep this very short." I cleared my throat and everything that I had rehearsed to say was lost somewhere in my head.

Parker's father, Parker Campbell, Sr. which I read on the steel door before I came in. Sat back in his executive chair. He didn't look bored or excite to hear my pitch, I was pretty certain that he had probably heard like a thousand of them today.

"Sir-"

"Just call me Parker, please Devon. All the things that you have done for my son here. You can call me whatever you want to but sir." The older Parker smiled.

"It was really nothing. Parker is a good kid, he listens to instruction. When you tell him something he is Johnny on the spot with it."

His father stood and leaned against his desk. "Please." He waved his hand at me to take a seat. "After Parker's mother passed away last year. He lost all interest in everything. School, friends-"He looked at his son who was twisting around in his pressed dress shirt. "You were able to reach him when I couldn't. Devon, you have no idea what a God send you have been to my family." Parker, Sr. grinned at the both of us. "Parker showed me an article about you."

"Me?" I looked at the kid whose cheeks I would have guessed were bright red, but his head was down.

"Son you never told him?" All we could see was the top of his head shake back and forth. "Just like my old man. Embarrassing the heck out of your son, right?" He put a hand on his son's shoulder. "Parker saw that you got into a bad accident, a very bad one to my understanding." That was the understatement of the year, but I nodded. "After he read it, he wanted to be just like you. He trained at home for a while, but it wasn't working out. So I agreed to drive across town to send him to the gym that you trained at, just to get a chance to meet you. He's one of your biggest fans."

I was totally in shock. The kid kept his cool around me. "Wow, Parker you never told me."

Like I thought the kid was red as a beet. "Didn't want you to think I was some sort of stalker or something."

I was speechless; I really didn't have any words. "My son's confidence has grown by leaps and bounds. He is back into his advanced placement courses in school. And he told me how you and your friends helped him talk to the girl he likes." His father was beaming at him for a second. "I'm sorry; I know that you are a busy man with training for your match that's taking place in what?" He looked at Parker.

"In four days." I said. "Parker, these last few months have been a world wind for me and time seem to go so fast when you are in a rush." I swallowed. "I was hoping that you and or your company can sponsor my trip to Vegas. Again, I know its short notice and all but it would be greatly appreciated."

The older Parker looked at me then at his son…and he laughed. Not just a giggle when someone asks you something so wild and crazy, but Will Ferrell hilarious. Fall out on the floor funny. If it wasn't Parker's father I would out choked the hell out of him. After he finally calmed down from his laughing fit, he held on to his gut and wiped tears. Looking at my stunned face. "Devon you will have to excuse me. I swear great minds think alike. Parker what do you think those late night meetings were for?" He took his son by the back of his neck and spoke in his face, just like my father used to do to me. "Son, I love you so much whatever you are into as your father I have to get into." Turning to face me. "I will not bore you with legal jargon but my company and I have secured ownership of Wicked Beast Apparel."

If Parker's father wouldn't take it the wrong way I would have kissed him. Wicked Beast was one of the few apparel shops just for MMA. Equaling Tap-Out and Affliction. "Parker, I want to thank you so much for this. Wow Wicked Beast?"

"I know that this isn't your first rodeo so to speak. So there is the legal aspect of it. You can only wear Wicked Beast clothing in and out of the cage and if-"He paused and smiled. "When you win there will be endorsement deals and the like for you. This will be a win-win."

I hugged him and his son. Feeling like I had already won. I got into the elevator alone, Parker and his father wanted me to go to a late lunch with them but I declined. I hit the button to the Garage Level, and I whispered. "Thank you Lord."

I knocked on the old wooden door and I could barely contain myself. I knocked again and waited. Jerry's face lite up when he saw me. "Maggie was wondering where you had run off to. The old girl was missing you."

I hugged the old man and pushed passed him. Maggie was sitting at her favorite spot in the kitchen. The smile wasn't like it used to be, it sagged a bit on the right. She spoke my name, which sound like a deaf child trying to talk. I gave her the flowers that I had hidden behind my back. "To the most beautiful woman in the world. These flowers are the only thing that I could find that has a hint of you beauty." She struggled to stand and hugged me around my neck. "Thank you for letting me borrow your husband all these years. I thank you for being the mother that I needed. Thank you for everything, Maggie." I felt tears on my shirt and I pulled back to look at the woman that stepped in when I needed a mom. "Pretty people don't cry." I wiped her face with my shirt.

"What you got my lady crying about Devon. " Jerry mocked a frown. "You may be big but I will put your big butt down." Jerry threw a few jabs at me; I had to admit the old man was still quick.

I sat them both down and told them about Spruce Knob the meeting with Parker's father. By the time I got the end. Maggie was crying and Jerry was smiling from ear to ear. "You know son you could have been wiped clean off the planet. You are here for a reason for what I have no idea. Take this moment and cherish it for the rest of your life, you understand me?" I nodded.

"I'll be leaving in the next few days so I just wanted you to know." I stood to walk to the door. Maggie took my hands and closed her eyes. I couldn't understand what she was saying but I had the feeling she was praying for me and I needed all I could get.

Chapter 21

Tia and I landed in McCarran International Airport Friday morning. Heaven knew that I should have got some rest on the plane, but my nerves kept creeping into my sleep. My knee bounced up and down from our lay over in Memphis all the way to Las Vegas. Tia kept looking at my leg but she didn't have to say anything. She just put her hand over mine.

The hotel was on the strip and if my whole livelihood didn't depend on these next few nights, I would have loved to show off my girl around the town. Maybe next time, I thought. She sat on the edge of bed and took off her strappy sandals. "Devon, come sit next to me please." I still had my overnight bag in my hand, standing there on the side of the queen sized bed. "You are the strongest competitor here. What you've been through most men would have thrown in the towel. Settled for some desk job, but look at you. You're in Vegas living out your dream. Never lose sight of that."

"I'm trying. Just got the pre-fight jitters is all. I'll be fine." I kissed the top of her blonde head. I toed off my shoes and leaned back on the bed. Tia straddled her legs over me and the nerves and fatigue all went away. "Tia. The way things are going right now. I would break you in half, so could you please get off me."

I heard her snicker. "Take a nap pumpkin. We have to be in the lobby at five to register and do weight in, k?" She kissed me on the lips and the removal of her heat leaving me I rolled over and punched the heck out of the pillow

I don't know how long I had been asleep but when my eyes fluttered open I was in the dark. I sat up slowly and tried to focus. I heard voices coming from the other end of our suite. Opening the door I was blinded by the hallway light and familiar laughs coming out of the front room reminded me of home.

"Bout time sleepy head thought you were going to miss registration." Henry stood and got me in a bear hug. "You know I'll still put you down."

"Dude, I was the one sleeping so how is it that you are the one dreaming." I punched him in the ribs.

A floppy ponytail came from around the couch. "Hey now, you better watch you're hitting. That's my man." Annie got under Henry's arm and made a mean face that wouldn't intimidate anyone.

"You guys are here. Thought you both had to work." I said wiping sleep out of my eye.

Henry hugged me hard. "Bro, I wouldn't miss this day for anything in the world."

"Besides, Luke would have walked here if we didn't take the day off to get here." Annie said. I looked at my two good friends and thought how they looked so good together. I guess my accident has drawn two people together.

Tia came up behind me and bumped me with her hip. "Watch it mister." She said as she walked by me and winked. "Go and wash up, registration in in less than an hour."

"Well, we are will be down the hall if you need anything. Luke is in there practicing guitar for a bit and then we are going to dinner. The two of you are more than welcome to come with us." Annie said looking so comfortable in the arms of my best friend.

"Baby, I told you. D, has to get some rest and the food will probably be too heavy for him." Henry pinched her cheek and twisted her lips. "First fight is at eight tomorrow night. We'll let you rest, see ya." Tia and I walked them to the door.

I took a quick shower and cut the already short sleeves off my black and white Wicked Beast shirt. It was meat head central in the lobby. There were a ton of guys that I knew from being in the sport but there was some up and comers there too.

Tia tried to lag behind me like a trainer and not my girlfriend, with parts of me respected but the other wanted me to beat the crap out of the guys getting an eye full. The lobby was huge like any Vegas lobby would be; it took us fifteen minutes to get to the section reserved for heavy weight class. I stood in line and gave my name, took off my shoes and was weighted in.

"Simple as pie." I said to my trainer/girlfriend. At this point I really didn't care who saw us, I took her hand and lead her back to our suite.

Tia and I ran through some combos and did some mitt work. "Push up time." I got on the ground and began to push up off the ground. Tia made her home on my back Indian style going over, the things that she saw in the lobby. "From what I saw there will only be few guys that can handle you. The rest not so much."

"Ya think?"

"I know. I just don't see how you guys do it. I saw so many injuries downstairs you would of thought it was an ER." She rubbed my shoulders. "We hit it first thing in the morning. Lite breakfasts, then we run. Get some rest and then you win." I couldn't see her on my back but I knew she was smiling.

"Remind me to thank Henry for letting us use his cabin." I told Tia. It seemed like every meat head had the same idea that we had. At seven that morning it was closing in at 90 degrees and they were all loosing wind.

"Your stamina is way better and the altitude helped, huh?" Tia kept up with me as we jogged down the strip.

I smiled, not winded at all.

Where in the heck would I be without my friends? All of them playing their own part in my recovery and my victories. I just didn't want to let any of them down. I wanted them all proud of me, because I was so proud of each of them.

By seven that evening I was in the locker room. Tia and Annie stood by the door of the locker room whispering like girls do, I guess. Henry was here and it felt good for him to be there. I was finally able to give my all when doing mitt work, without breaking Tia's nails. "You've gotten faster." Henry couldn't help but look impressed. Luke's eyes darted back and forth watching me punish Henry's mitts

"You got five." One of the event personal informed us.

"You got this babe." Tia smile.

"Go out there and kill 'em." Annie snarled.

"Do what you do best." Henry smirked.

"Hey who has my walk out music?"

Everyone stopped and looked at me. Henry was the first to speak. "Tia, um do you have it?"

Pure panic washed over her face. "What is that?"

"This isn't good." Henry said as he looked at me.

I tried to keep calm, Tia already felt bad enough. "Walk out music puts your opponent on notice. It's music to get you in the mood to fight."

"Like when you listen to Tupac?" She spoke up in between gnawing at the inside of her jaw.

"It's the personality of the fighter." I ran my mitted hands through my short hair.

"Mom, take me to the car." Luke squeaked over the adults trying to come up with a quick plan.

"Luke left a ton of CDs in the car." She took her son's hand and darted out of the locker room.

I exhaled. "One problem solved now you have another one in the cage." Henry rubbed at my shoulder. The event guy poked his head back in and told us they were ready. I wore a sleeveless Wicked Beast hoody over my head and bounced to the other side of the arena. Henry was digging into my shoulders loosing me up.

I whispered a thanks to God that the other guy was going first. His walk out music came on; it was some rap music with the bass cranked up to 12. It shook the arena. The crowd went crazy. "See what I mean." I said to Tia who was probably feeling like left out food. I kissed her sweet mouth. "No worries baby."

I couldn't really see the guy. He looked like a dot from where I was standing, and then my stomach began to rattle when I heard. "Now Devon Hart." The crowd was on their feet but nothing came out of the speakers. I heard Tia sigh behind. "Babe, its fine."

"We don't need no stinking music." Henry giving us his best Latino accent. I made my descent down the ramp. And I heard the familiar lick coming from an electric guitar. As I started to jog to the cage. There stood little Luke in the middle of the cage, the microphone stand as low as it would go and still the microphone had to be pointed downward so he could be heard.

The kid closed his eyes and what came out of his mouth left the crowd and myself included stuck with our mouths open. "*Well, I stand up next to a mountain. And I chop it down with the edge of my hand. Well, I stand up next to a mountain and I chop it down with the edge of my hand. Well, I pick up all the pieces an make an island. Might even raise a little sand. Cause I'm a voodoo child.*" The kid just ripped Jimi Hendrix-Voodoo Child. Looking at him you wouldn't believe it was an elementary school kid singing like that.

Luke only hit the first verse and you would have thought by the crowd's reaction they were there for a concert, not a fight. Annie ushered Luke out of the cage and gave me quick peek on my cheek. "Just win Devon."

The crowd fall out of the trance that Luke put them in and I was ready to go. My opponent is a stocky white guy. His dark blue spikey Mohawk looked just as ridiculous the tribal tattoos that ran the length of his arm. I was probably just a bit short of being a whole foot taller than him. But he looked powerful. He resembled a bowling ball with feet.

The referee let us know the rules and we touched gloves. I swung on the dude but he slipped me and caught me in ribs, I backed up pushed the sting of his punch out of my head. He came at me again; this guy was going to try to knock in my rib cage if I let him. I landed a perfect right to his jaw and he staggered backward. "Now, D. Take him now!" Henry hollered.

I wasn't going to give him a chance to recover; I seized the moment and hit him with everything I had. The dude had heart, he tried to block but I had stamina on my side. Landed punch after punch to the dude's head.

I finally had him pinned to the cage rotating from head shots to body punches. With his dwindling strength he was able to shove me. I could hear Henry yelling behind me. "Give it to him!"

I took another step back and a flash of what happened weeks ago ran and settled in my mind. It was now or never. I pivoted on my left leg and brought my right up. Knowing I was going to pay for it later but I twisted and caught the guy on his temple by the heel of my foot.

The fat lady had sung.

There was a small amount of blood from my scab, but I would live. Henry, Annie and my new hero Luke decided to stay and watch the rest of the fight. But all I really wanted to do was get off my leg and sleep until it was time for me to fight tomorrow night.

I could see Tia in the bathroom brushing her teeth. She had on a pair of yoga pants and tank top. "Babe, you did wonderful tonight, I'm so proud of you." She said over the running water in the sink.

"Come to bed." I groaned. She skipped to the room and lay beside me. "Thank you for all you do."

"Well, I'm glad that Henry is here. He is better equipped to help you. He knew exactly what to do and when to do it. Hell, I had no idea what walk out music was." Putting her head on my chest.

"I told you not to worry about that." I pinched her shoulder. "Everything seemed to be going so fast. I take the blame for all of that. There is no way you would have known. Now come over here and give me some sugar and go to sleep." Tia leaned up and planted one on me and molded her body next to mine.

All was right in the world.

The next morning, I knew that spinning kick was going to haunt me. I could barely get out of bed. I reached to my right and came back with a hand full of warm sheets. I could hear Tia rummaging around in the front room. Through all my pain I still smiled. Just the thought of her sticking it out with me made me long for her.

I was dragging my leg when I heard another voice in the room with Tia. Turning the corner, I saw Washington sitting on the couch with her and my insides froze. "Finally, you're up." Tia said smiling. "This is a reporter from The Vegas Tribune; he wanted to do a story about you." Tia came to my side, she had only heard about Washington in Florida but never saw his face.

"Tia, honey do you mind if I talk to him alone." If I would have blinked I would have missed the sudden look of disappointment on her face. Tia mustered up a fake smile and retreated to the bedroom. I watched her leave and once the doors were closed. I limped to Washington pulling up from the coach by his collar and slamming him into the wall.

"I'm happy to see you too, Devon." The madman laughed.

"What the hell are you doing here? If I even think you are close to her I will kill you." My knuckles were turning white and my hands shook.

Washington put long slender fingers over my hands. "Now Devon, you know as well as I do that if I don't walk out of this room in the next few minutes I have people in place to go into the room down the hall and put a bullet in each one of your friends." He closed his eyes and thought. "But not before one of my men has a taste of the Asian girl and I'll make Henry, the cop watch and her son." Patting my clenched fist. "You can let go now."

I held on for a moment longer. "What do you want?"

"Why is it that when I come around people always think that I want something? I mean, could it be that I wanted to congratulate you on your win last night? Or I just simple missed you." Washington gave me a smile that made my stomach turn.

"I'll ask you again, why are you here?" I was losing patience rapidly. "And the only thing that I'll be throwing is a punch and your sorry tail out of here."

Washington put his hands up in surrender. "It's just a token of my appreciation from our last transaction." He reached into his inside suit jacket pocket and for a second I thought was this the way my life was going to end. With him pulling out a gun and putting me down for good. "A woman that beautiful should be more than just a girlfriend

Devon." He put a light blue colored box on the coffee table. "Now!" He clapped his hands loudly. "Now go and win."

"I'll do my best." Eyeing the box.

"I hope you do, I have money riding on this fight." He didn't wait for me to walk him to the door, Washington left on his own.

I called Henry to let him know that Washington was in my hotel room and alone with Tia. Henry reassured me that he would have eyes on him and not to worry. I hung up my cell and had the strong urge to hurl the box across the room.

I peeked in on Tia who was barefoot curled in the bed watching something on television. "How was the interview?" Not looking at me.

There were so many things that I could tell her right now and none of them would be true. "You remember the guys that broke into our beach house in Florida. Yeah, that was there boss."

After I held down a very hysterical Tia and told her that I would never let anyone hurt her, ever she finally calmed down and took a nap.

My leg was still biting at me when I made the trip down the hall. Henry answered the door on the first knock. He stepped passed me in the hall. "Is Tia okay?"

"How did you know I told her?"

"Because you not angry anymore but upset. When your girl hurts so do you."

"You tell Annie?"

He looked at me as if I went crazy right before his very eyes. "Hell, no. Like she isn't neurotic all by herself. I'm not going to say a word to her."

We stood there in silence or a second. Both of us thinking of the same thing, how are we going to get Washington out of our lives…for good.

I dug into my pocket and pulled out the jewelry box. "This is what Washington gave me to give to Tia."

"Bro, this is a Tiffany box." Henry opened the box and it seemed the whole hallway was illuminated with sparkles. "This ring cost more than us." He handed it back to me. "So what you gonna do with it?"

"I mean, I think… I love Tia and I could see us one day getting married but not because Washington says so. And definitely not with this ring." I shoved it back into my pocket. "Henry we got to do something to catch this fool."

"Don't you think I know that?"

"He has money riding on the match tonight. There's got to be away that we catch him, like illegal gambling or something."

"Dude, this is Vegas and this is the biggest fight of the year. Everybody and they momma is gambling right now. Look, you should get back to Tia and get mentally prepared for tonight." Henry was right; I turned to console my girl before he stopped me. "By the way, you'll be fighting a dude by the name of Brian Brewster tonight. Kids, good coming straight out of Flint I think. He's quick and strong."

I hunched my shoulders. "I'm faster and tougher."

Tia put on a brave face for me when we got to the locker room. Luke was asked by the commissioner to play Voodoo Child again. It was going to be great for the kid. Because tonight's fight was going to be televised.

"No matter what happens tonight. I want you to know that you can I love you." Tia whispered in my ear. I've never been one of those guys afraid of the L word, just never felt the need to say it.

I kissed my girl. "If it were possible I think that I would love you more."

Henry and I hit mitts. Annie was with Luke near the cage waiting for the other match to end. Event staff came in and told us he was ready. This has been the moment that I'd been waiting for. The day that my dream of going pro in the sport that I have dedicated my life to.

The three of us stood on the ramp and Luke hit the guitar strings and just like the night before the crowd went bananas. "Alright, Devon you can beat this guy. He has nothing on you."

The announcer had the mic in his hand, "Tonight's challenger will be Brian 'The Bruiser' Brewster."

Tia turned instantly pale and as she whipped her head to look in the direction of Brewster. "Tia. Tia, honey are you okay?" I had to shout over the noise of the crowd.

"Devon, I'm sorry I can't...I can't do this." She dropped the towel and I saw her run back up the ramp.

Someone had took a scalpel and gutted me right there in the cage. I turned to Henry who matched my puzzled look. "Devon, I don't know. But right now you got to find your focus and now. This Brian kid is no joke."

I felt naked and exposed. Like I was caught with my pants down in front of the crowd. Brewster, looked strong, the mystery of him must be in his technique. The referee went over rules and I couldn't concentrate on what was going on. The crowd was too loud. The referee spoke to slow. My heart was out of my chest and this guy had every intention of beating my skull in.

The bell rang. I put my hands up and for a split second I didn't know what to do with them. Brewster gave me a combo to my face and chest and I fell back against the cage. My forearms were getting a beating. Henry was an exaggerator but never a liar, I kicked Brewster off me and he hit me with a quick right to the temple. Yeah the kid was quick.

My head snapped back and he was on me again. The shot to my temple left me dazed and all I could see were his gloves coming straight to my face.

"Don't go to the ground Devon. You hear me? Don't go down?" Henry was directly behind me.

At this point in the fight I was being his punching bag. I was losing and horribly from the way that Henry was losing his crap behind me. "Don't give up on me, now Devon." He shouted.

I sprang off the cage and tackled him and got a few licks in before the bell rung. "You got to get Tia out of your head right now Devon. Or else you are going to lose this thing. You've worked too hard for this. Don't throw it away now you are too close." Henry pressed cold metal under my eyes, I could feel them both begin to swell. Annie came up to the entrance to the cage and shouted something to Henry. My head was still ringing.

"Ox." I said. There was too much I wanted to say at the moment but not enough time to say it. I wanted to thank him for being a good friend to a loser like me.

Henry turned to me and he had a face that said play time is over. "What I'm about to tell you could help you lose this fight or help you win it." He said it so fast that I tried to grasp every word. "Annie just spoke to Tia. Brian Brewster is her ex. I don't know what that means, but she told us to tell you. He has a bad ankle. Bad football injury in high school. So you know what to do. Lock him up."

The bell rung to indicate the beginning of the second round. The new information swirled around in my head like water being flushed down a toilet.

Brian looked like he hadn't even thought about sweating; he came out me with the same power as before. Punch now at my body, feeling like he was crushing my ribs with every landed blow.

Then it dawned on me or literally it hit me. The guy that ruined Tia's hopes and dreams of being a professional dancer were crushed by the same hands that are currently drilling a hole in my side. I remember the vanilla shampoo that she uses in her hair that seems to stay on the pillow. And how I put my face in it and told her that I would kill him for her.

Yeah, my leg was crap and this may be my last fight. And sure I have loan sharks visiting me on a regular basis, but I keep my promises.

I gave Brewster a kick to his waist and just like I thought he went to his side in pain, I charged him lifting him up off the mat and dropping him to the ground. Put every bit of weight on him. I heard the air go out of him.

I was on top of him and gave him a few punches to his face. I cradled his leg in my arm. His left leg was sandwiched between my right leg and my knee. I prayed that my leg would hold out longer than him. My arm was tucked under his shin and I pushed off with everything with my left palm

I faced the mat and pushed off with my foot to his chest sliding my hand to his Achilles tendon. "Pinch him down." Henry yelled. I knew I was doing a good job by the excitement in his voice.

Brewster was tapping the hell out of my shoulder screaming in pain. "Did she scream when you were beating her?" The referee broke us up and announced me as the winner.

Henry hugged me. "Go to her." I pushed passed the crowd of fans to the locker room. Tia was sitting on the floor, knees drawn up to her chest.

"Baby." I crumbled to the floor to her and pulled her close. "I would have given you his leg but the damn referee stopped me."

"Your face." Her eyes were blood shot, tears ran down her face.

"I was born like this, no worries." I kissed her over and over again.

"Devon, I just couldn't look at him I-"

"Shhh. I got him in an Achilles lock his left leg is hamburger." My face hurt but I smiled anyway.

"Devon it was his right ankle that was injured not his left."

"Oh well now he has two bad ankles." I kissed her again. "Could you stand up for me please." Tia stood bracing herself against the concrete wall. "Would you please give me the honor of being your wife?"

Tia tried to conceal her laugh. "Devon, I think you have a concussion."

"No, I don't want coconuts. I'm allergic. Tia, will you marry me?"

"It would be my pleasure to be your husband, Devon."

Chapter 22

I'd be lying to you if I said that I didn't miss it. The screams from fans and the traveling. But I have a wife now and things had to settle down.

Jerry retired and handed the gym over to me and Henry to run. I love it. Being able to help others reach their goals. Parker is competing in his first fight in a few months so I'll be training him. I knew that I wasn't going to make promises that I couldn't keep but Annie's got me going to church. Don't get me wrong, I'm not your every Sunday guy but I know that God saved me. Saved me from a life that was leading nowhere and fast. And most of all saved me from myself.

My nightmares aren't as frequent as they once were. My wife and I talk it out; there was really no sense of trying to hide it from anyone. She has allowed me to be more open about myself and with my feelings. So to use one of Annie's terms I'm indeed blessed.

Speaking of Annie, her and Henry are still dating and still arguing over everything under the sun

It's a shame that I had to be knocked around and put flat on my back and have everything stripped from me to get everything that I needed out of life.

Standing there look at Tia in the kitchen fixing dinner. I had to be the luckiest guy that walked the planet. "Hey sweet thang, how bout you come over here and give me some sugar."

"Stop that you sound so hillbilly." Throwing her dish rag at me.

"You love it when I talk redneck to you." I tried to pinch that little bottom of hers but she was too quick for me. The kitchen phone rang and she left to get the mail. "Don't think you got away from me woman. I know where you live.

"Yeah, yeah, yeah. Get the phone." She said over her shoulder.

"Hart residence."

"Devon. So glad to hear your voice. I have a favor to ask of you and I'm sure that you can help an old friend." Barry Washington said.

ACKNOWLEGMENTS

This book wouldn't have been possible without the quick wit, smarts and talent of my dear friend N.L. Everhart. Without you sharing your story the rest of us would be deprived of your inward and outward strength-I give you a thousand thanks.

May you and your family stay eternally blessed.

Your 'twin' sister

E. Hale

Made in the USA
Charleston, SC
28 March 2015